Watership Down

ANIMATION: KEY FILMS/FILMMAKERS

Series Editor: Chris Pallant

Titles in the Series:

Toy Story: How Pixar Reinvented the Animated Feature
edited by Susan Smith, Noel Brown and Sam Summers

Princess Mononoke: Understanding Studio Ghibli's Monster Princess
edited by Rayna Denison

Norman McLaren: Between the Frames by Nichola Dobson

Hayao Miyazaki: Exploring the Early Work of Japan's Greatest Animator
by Raz Greenberg

Snow White and the Seven Dwarfs: New Perspectives on Production, Reception, Legacy edited by Chris Pallant and Christopher Holliday

Allegro non Troppo: Bruno Bozetto's Animated Music by Marco Bellano

Grendel Grendel Grendel: Animating Beowulf
by Dan Torre and Leinors Torre

Coraline: A Closer Look at Studio LAIKA's Stop-Motion Witchcraft edited
by Mihaela Mihailova

Genndy Tartakovsky: Sincerity in Animation
by Kwasu David Tembo

Watership Down

Perspectives On and Beyond Animated Violence

EDITED BY
CATHERINE LESTER

BLOOMSBURY ACADEMIC
NEW YORK • LONDON • OXFORD • NEW DELHI • SYDNEY

BLOOMSBURY ACADEMIC
Bloomsbury Publishing Inc
1385 Broadway, New York, NY 10018, USA
50 Bedford Square, London, WC1B 3DP, UK
29 Earlsfort Terrace, Dublin 2, Ireland

BLOOMSBURY, BLOOMSBURY ACADEMIC and the Diana logo are trademarks of
Bloomsbury Publishing Plc

First published in the United States of America 2023
Paperback edition published 2024

Copyright © Catherine Lester, 2023, 2024

For legal purposes the Acknowledgements on p. xiv constitute an extension of this copyright page.

Cover design: Louise Dugdale
Cover image © Alamy

This work is published open access subject to a Creative Commons Attribution-NonCommercial-NoDerivatives 4.0 International licence (CC BY-NC-ND 4.0, https://creativecommons.org/licenses/by-nc-nd/4.0/). You may re-use, distribute, and reproduce this work in any medium for non-commercial purposes, provided you give attribution to the copyright holder and the publisher and provide a link to the Creative Commons licence.

Bloomsbury Publishing Inc does not have any control over, or responsibility for, any third-party websites referred to or in this book. All internet addresses given in this book were correct at the time of going to press. The author and publisher regret any inconvenience caused if addresses have changed or sites have ceased to exist, but can accept no responsibility for any such changes.

Library of Congress Cataloging-in-Publication Data

Names: Lester, Catherine, editor.
Title: Watership Down : perspectives on and beyond animated violence / edited by Catherine Lester.
Description: New York : Bloomsbury Academic, 2023. | Series: Animation : key films/filmmakers | Includes bibliographical references and index. |
Summary: "The first exclusive academic study of the aesthetic, cultural and historical significance of a landmark British animated film, Watership Down"– Provided by publisher.
Identifiers: LCCN 2022028595 (print) | LCCN 2022028596 (ebook) | ISBN 9781501376993 (hardback) | ISBN 9781501376962 (paperback) | ISBN 9781501376986 (epub) | ISBN 9781501376979 (pdf) | ISBN 9781501376955 (ebook other)
Subjects: LCSH: Adams, Richard, 1920-2016. Watership Down--Film adaptations. | Watership Down (Motion picture) | Violence in motion pictures. | Animated films--Great Britain--History and criticism.
Classification: LCC PN1997.W343 W38 2023 (print) | LCC PN1997.W343 (ebook) | DDC 791.43/72--dc23/eng/20220901
LC record available at https://lccn.loc.gov/2022028595
LC ebook record available at https://lccn.loc.gov/2022028596

ISBN: HB: 978-1-5013-7699-3
PB: 978-1-5013-7696-2
ePDF: 978-1-5013-7697-9
eBook: 978-1-5013-7698-6

Series: Animation: Key Films/Filmmakers

Typeset by Deanta Global Publishing Services, Chennai, India

To find out more about our authors and books visit www.bloomsbury.com and sign up for our newsletters.

CONTENTS

List of illustrations viii
Contributors x
Acknowledgements xiv

Introduction: *Watership Down* in context 1
   Catherine Lester

PART I   Bringing the warren to life 23

1. 'We consider the conduct of this film highly unsatisfactory and unprofessional': Film Finances and *Watership Down* 25
Llewella Chapman and James Chapman

2. Revisiting the production of *Watership Down* through the Arthur Humberstone Animation Archive 41
Klive Humberstone, Nigel Humberstone and Chris Pallant

3. 'Trying to eat grass that isn't there': Unearthing a Lapine Corpus in Richard Adams's *Watership Down* and its film adaptation 60
R. Grider

PART II   Animal stories 73

4. Animating utopia: Aesthetic instability and the revolutionary gaze in the film adaptation of *Watership Down* 75
Lisa Mullen

5 'Whenever they catch you, they will kill you': Human–animal conflict in 1970s British children's cinema 89
Noel Brown

6 They watered ship down: Eco-doom and ecopedagogy in adaptations of *Watership Down* and *The Animals of Farthing Wood* 103
Hollie Adams

7 *Watership Down* Under: When rabbits came to Australia 118
Dan Torre and Lienors Torre

PART III   Aesthetics of sound and image 133

8 'English pastoral melodies': The traditions and connotations of Angela Morley's musical score for *Watership Down* 135
Paul Mazey

9 'I know now. A terrible thing is coming': *Watership Down*, music and/as horror 149
Leanne Weston

10 Pastel dreams and crimson nightmares: Colour, aesthetics and *Watership Down* 163
Carolyn Rickards

11 Prince with a thousand faces: Shifting art styles and the depiction of violence in *Watership Down* 176
Sam Summers

PART IV   Affective and ethical encounters with the rabbit 191

12 Drawing blood: The forms and ethics of animated violence in *Watership Down* 193
Joshua Schulze

13 'Won't somebody *please* think of the bunnies?': *Watership Down*, rabbit horror and 'suitability' for children 206
Catherine Lester

14 Mourning Hazel-rah 222
Catherine Sadler

Guide to further research 237
Index 240

ILLUSTRATIONS

Figures

1.1	John Hubley's animation for *Rooty Toot Toot*	35
1.2	John Hubley's alleged surviving animation in *Watership Down*	35
2.1	Memo from Rosen to *Watership Down*'s animation staff, 13 December 1976	50
2.2–2.3	Model sheets showing the development of *Watership Down*'s characters	51
2.4	The breakdown of a dog in motion, by Arthur Humberstone	53
2.5	A fake production memo addressed to Humberstone from the production office, requesting that he 'refrain from singing on the company's time'	56
2.6	A playful caricature of Humberstone	57
2.7	A fake model sheet depicting a cartoon Humberstone	58
2.8	Humberstone at work during the production of *Watership Down* at Nepenthe, London	58
3.1	The car's appearance	71
8.1	A 'rabbit's-eye-view' framed by foreground elements	140
8.2	Grasses act as a 'repoussoir' element	144
8.3	Long shot of Watership Down	145
8.4	The scale of the landscape is emphasized	146
11.1	An illustration of Furniss's continuum of animation styles	178
11.2–11.3	Successive shots of Bigwig's face build in proximity and gory detail	183
11.4–11.5	The two parallel fight scenes differ markedly in terms of graphic detail	186
11.6	*Watership Down*'s styles plotted on Furniss's continuum	188
12.1	*Watership Down* storyboard illustrating the prologue's rabbit massacre	200

13.1	User-generated memes that affirm *Watership Down*'s popular status as a 'traumatizing' children's film	207
14.1	Hazel's death scene	226
14.2	*Claire: Last Kiss (after Beuys) 7 May 2011.* (From the series 'Claire: Last Days', 2011.) Julia Schlosser.	231

Tables

1.1	Development of the *Watership Down* Voice Casting from the Desired Cast to Final Film	30
3.1	Lapine Language Data from the Novel *Watership Down* (1972) by Chapter and Data Tag, Chapters 1–10	66
3.2	Lapine Language Data from the Film *Watership Down* (1978) by Section and Data Tag	66

CONTRIBUTORS

Hollie Adams is a secondary school English teacher based in Devon, who previously taught sociology in the University of Limerick, Ireland, where she received her MA in comparative literature. In her studies and teaching career, Hollie found that her students had plenty to say about *Watership Down*, the environment and humanity's impact upon the earth. This led to her interest in ecopedagogy and analysing texts and their environmental messages. In her spare time, Hollie can be found reading, playing rugby or struggling up Devon's many hills. She plans to continue writing about the environment and the way it is presented in texts while being inspired by her students.

Noel Brown is Senior Lecturer in Film at Liverpool Hope University. He has written several books on aspects of children's film, family entertainment and animation, including *Contemporary Hollywood Animation* (2021), *The Children's Film: Genre, Nation and Narrative* (2017), *British Children's Cinema: From The Thief of Bagdad to Wallace and Gromit* (2016) and *The Hollywood Family Film: A History, from Shirley Temple to Harry Potter* (2012). He is also co-editor of *Toy Story: How Pixar Reinvented the Animated Feature* (2018) and *Family Films in Global Cinema: The World Beyond Disney* (2015), and editor of *The Oxford Handbook of Children's Film* (2022).

James Chapman is Professor of Film Studies at the University of Leicester and editor of the *Historical Journal of Film, Radio and Television*. He specializes in British cinema and television history, and his most recent publications are *Hitchcock and the Spy Film* (2018), *Contemporary British Television Drama* (2000) and *The Money Behind the Screen: A History of British Film Finance, 1945-1985* (2022).

Llewella Chapman is a film historian and a visiting scholar at the University of East Anglia. Her research interests include British cinema, costume, gender and the UK heritage industry. Her monograph, *Fashioning James Bond: Costume, Gender and Identity in the World of 007*, was published in October 2021. Llewella has just completed a BFI Film Classic on *From Russia with Love* and is working on a research monograph, *Costume and British Cinema*.

R. Grider is an independent scholar who holds a master's degree from North Dakota State University, with a focus primarily on animal rhetorics, animal narratives and invented languages. Most of their work, though spanning across genre and medium, explores the intersection between animal agency and linguistic invention by looking at language and rhetorical schema as cultural material. To date, much of this work has been centred on Richard Adams's *Watership Down*.

Klive Humberstone and **Nigel Humberstone** are film music composers and founding members of In The Nursery, the Sheffield-based band formed in 1981. In The Nursery's music has been used on countless film soundtracks and trailers including *Game of Thrones*, *Gran Torino*, *Beowulf*, *The Aviator*, *Interview with the Vampire*, *Along Came a Spider* and *The Rainmaker*, as well as the *La Femme Nikita TV* series. Parallel to their studio works, In The Nursery have developed their Optical Music Series, an ongoing repertoire of new soundtracks for silent films. They also manage the Arthur Humberstone Animation Archive which covers materials from Arthur Humberstone's forty-five year career in animation from training at Gaumont British Animation, Moor Hall through work on Halas and Batchelor's *Animal Farm* and subsequent classic animated features and TV shows including *Yellow Submarine*, *Watership Down*, *The Plague Dogs* and *The BFG*.

Catherine Lester is Lecturer in Film and Television at the University of Birmingham. Her research centres on the intersections of the horror genre and children's cinema, the subject of her monograph *Horror Films for Children: Fear and Pleasure in American Cinema* (2021). She has also published on children's media in *Global TV Horror* (2021), *Discussing Disney* (2019) and the Fantasy/Animation Research Network. Her rabbits Hazel and Gizmo are a significant source of inspiration, in life and in scholarship.

Paul Mazey is the author of *British Film Music: Musical Traditions in British Cinema, 1930s-1950s* (2020). He has published articles on aspects of British film music in the *Journal of British Cinema & Television* and *Revenant* journal, and co-authored with Sarah Street the chapter 'Pianos, Affect, and Memory' for the edited collection *Musicals at the Margins* (2021). He has taught film and television at the University of Bristol.

Lisa Mullen is a teaching associate in modern and contemporary literature and film at the University of Cambridge. Her work spans questions of embodiment, ecopoesis and the ethics and hermeneutics of form. She is the author of *Mid-Century Gothic: The Uncanny Objects of Modernity in British Literature and Culture after the Second World War* (2019), and her next book will be *Orwell Unwell: Interruptions of Embodiment in the Fiction and Journalism of George Orwell*.

Chris Pallant is the author of *Demystifying Disney: A History of Disney Feature Animation* (2011), *Animated Landscapes: History, Form and Function* (2015), *Beyond Bagpuss: A History of Smallfilms Animation Studio* (2022), editor of *Animation: Critical and Primary Sources* (2021), and co-author of *Storyboarding: A Critical History* (2015) and *Snow White and the Seven Dwarfs: New Perspectives on Production, Reception, Legacy* (2021). He is the founding editor of Bloomsbury's *Animation: Key Films/Filmmakers* book series (2017–present). He currently serves as president for the Society for Animation Studies.

Carolyn Rickards is an independent researcher. She collaborated on *Colour Films in Britain: The Eastmancolor Revolution* (2021) and has featured in the *Journal of British Cinema and Television*, *Screen*, *Fantasy/Animation: Connections Between Media, Mediums and Genres* (2018) and *Sixties British Cinema Reconsidered* (2020). She is currently writing a monograph on *British Fantasy Cinema*.

Catherine Sadler is based in the UK. She was awarded a PhD in Creative Writing from the University of Hull in 2020 and works in contemporary visual art and literature programming, most recently directing the literature festival in Hull. Her doctoral thesis investigated loss and mourning in relation to women's creative practice and the archive.

Joshua Schulze is a doctoral student in the Department of Film, Television and Media at the University of Michigan. His research revolves around materiality in film and film culture, environmental media, and horror, and his work has appeared in *CineAction*, *Quarterly Review of Film and Video*, *Journal of Popular Film and Television* and *Horror Studies*.

Sam Summers is an associate lecturer in animation at Middlesex University. He is the author of *DreamWorks Animation: Intertextuality and Aesthetics in Shrek and Beyond* (2020) and the co-editor of *Toy Story: How Pixar Reinvented the Animated Feature* (2018), as well as writing a number of book chapters and articles looking at adaptation, aesthetics and intertextuality in animation history.

Dan Torre is a senior lecturer in the School of Design at RMIT University in Melbourne Australia. He is author of a number of books, including *Animation – Process, Cognition and Actuality* (2017), *Cactus* (2017), *Carnivorous Plants* (2019); co-author of *Australian Animation: An International History* (2018) and *Grendel Grendel Grendel: Animating*

Beowulf (2021), and author of other forthcoming volumes on animation. Previously he has worked in the animation industry.

Lienors Torre is a senior lecturer in the School of Communication and Creative Arts at Deakin University in Melbourne, Australia. She is co-author of the books *Australian Animation: An International History* (2018) and *Grendel Grendel Grendel: Animating Beowulf* (2021). She is also a practising artist and animator.

Leanne Weston is an Institute of Advanced Study Early Career fellow at the University of Warwick. She has written on televised music histories for *The Velvet Light Trap* and is a contributor to collections on *Watership Down*, and the films of Jane Campion, examining the function and meaning of film scoring.

ACKNOWLEDGEMENTS

My favourite *Watership Down* rabbit has always been Bigwig – brave, stubborn, chunky Bigwig – but reflecting on the origin and journey of this book, I feel rather like Fiver. As soon as the Animation: Key Films/Filmmakers series was announced, I knew I wanted to pitch an entry on *Watership Down* but was unsure whether anyone else would share my vision. To my delight, series editor Chris Pallant responded to the idea with Hazel-like conviction. Chris went on to be the Keynote speaker for the 2018 conference at the University of Warwick that formed the basis of this book, for which he went above and beyond by recruiting Nigel and Klive Humberstone, who have been so generous with their time and effort in granting access to their late father Arthur's archive of animation treasures. My deepest gratitude goes to Chris, Nigel and Klive for their collaboration, which I hope will not end with the publication of this book. Equally, this book would not exist without the rest of the 'Watership rabbits', that is, the authors within this book and the other speakers and participants of that 2018 conference. It has been a pleasure to go on this journey with you all, and a relief that it has been far less perilous than that of our lapine counterparts.

There are many more people to acknowledge whose support was indispensable. Rob Stone and James Walters were also firm believers in my conviction that *Watership Down* was worth writing about (even in the face of a disbelieving 'Chief Rabbit'). Rachel Moseley, the Humanities Research Centre at the University of Warwick and the Society for Animation Studies contributed the funds that allowed the 2018 conference to take place. The British Film Institute provided access to integral archival resources, and Lucy Bolton, fellow bunny-obsessive, helped with a small but wonderful Iris Murdoch reference. Julie Lobalzo Wright, Filipa Antunes, Isabel Galleymore and Rob Stone all provided feedback on proposals, chapters and works-in-progress, and Esther Santamaría Iglesias provided fantastic indexing services. My wonderful friends have helped simply by existing, but my thanks go especially to Matt Denny for always being a willing audience to my *Watership Down*-related rants, hare-brained ideas and general excitement.

None of this would have happened without the people who introduced me to *Watership Down* in the first place: my family, especially my dad Mike, for introducing me to the film as a teen and for generally fostering my love of stories; and Valerie Sanders, for whose MA children's literature module at the University of Hull I first read the novel and wrote an essay that would spiral into the obsession that fuelled this book. Thank you, of course, to Richard Adams, Martin Rosen and the dozens of animators and crew members who made this remarkable film.

Finally, thank you, as always, to Craig, who has endured so much of my rabbiting on over the years – I love you – and to my own rabbits Hazel and Gizmo, who are a dependable source of comfort and inspiration.

Catherine Lester, September 2022

Introduction

Watership Down in context

Catherine Lester

> All of it is just, uh, a miracle. A miracle that I must say does not occur again . . . there has not been, or will ever be, I think, another movie quite like *Watership Down*.
>
> – GUILLERMO DEL TORO[1]

Watership Down, the 1978 British cel-animated feature produced, directed and written by Martin Rosen, and the bestselling 1972 novel by Richard Adams on which it is based are indeed relatively anomalous. The novel is often considered uncategorizable: an adventure story about rabbits that might be a comfortable bedfellow with the works of Beatrix Potter and other children's animal stories were it not for its epic scope, complex language and allegorical potential that have prompted comparisons with adult literature from Homer to Margaret Atwood.[2] The film, though pared down in order to compress the 500-page novel into a 92-minute runtime, successfully translates the narrative and emotional core of Adams's tale to the screen.

---

[1] 'A Movie Miracle: Guillermo del Toro on *Watership Down*', in *Watership Down*, Blu-ray (USA: The Criterion Collection, 2015).
[2] Robert Miltner, '"Watership Down": A Genre Study', *Journal of the Fantastic in the Arts* 6, no. 1 (1993): 63–70; Adam Scovell, 'More Handmaid's Tale Than Peter Rabbit – Why Watership Down Remains a Terrifying Vision of the Land', *British Film Institute*, 12 March 2018. https://www2.bfi.org.uk/news-opinion/news-bfi/features/watership-down-martin-rosen-richard-adams (accessed 3 November 2021).

The story begins with a young rabbit Fiver experiencing a premonition of the imminent destruction of his home, Sandleford Warren, in order to make way for a housing development. Fiver and his brother Hazel are joined by a small group of other rabbits to flee the warren in search of a new home, which they eventually find on the titular Watership Down, but not after encountering several dangers along the way in the form of other animals and from indifferent humans. On arrival at Watership Down, however, an existential threat emerges when the rabbits realize they have no female rabbits – does – among them to breed with. With the help of an injured seagull, Kehaar, the rabbits plan to break some imprisoned does out of a nearby rival warren, Efrafa, that is run like a concentration camp by the totalitarian rabbit General Woundwort. The film climaxes in a bloody battle in which multiple rabbits are graphically maimed on screen before victory and peace are secured for the Watership Down Warren.

This brief summary should indicate that *Watership Down*'s subject matter is unusual for what is typically expected of mainstream, English-language feature animation. When we take this into account alongside the film's difficult road to the screen it is, as del Toro describes, something of a miracle that *Watership Down* was made at all. Rosen, an American film producer who had never directed a film before, let alone an animated one, purchased the rights to the novel after it had received widespread acclaim and worldwide, crossover success with adults and children. According to his recollection, Rosen read the novel in 1975 while developing another production in the Himalayas and phoned Adams to purchase the film rights as soon as he returned to London.[3] However, Rosen had little idea of how he would bring the story to the screen, either visually or financially. Help with the latter came from upstart Canadian producer Jake Eberts, for whom *Watership Down* would be his first project. According to Eberts it was a risky venture from the start due to the UK film industry being in a time of crisis, with falling cinema attendance and the closures of production arms of several major Hollywood studios.[4] Even so, a budget was secured of nearly £2 million, making it 'one of the most ambitious animated films to be produced outside the Walt Disney studios' at the time, according to Rosen.[5] With this funding Rosen established the animation studio Nepenthe Productions, which set up its operation in a run-down warehouse on, of all places, Warren Street in the centre of London. Even then, production challenges were numerous. Rosen was not the film's original director – this

---

[3]Calum Waddell, *Taboo Breakers: 18 Independent Films That Courted Controversy and Created a Legend from BLOOD FEAST to HOSTEL* (Tolworth: Telos Publishing, 2008), 212.
[4]Jake Eberts and Terry Ilott, *My Indecision is Final: The Rise and Fall of Goldcrest Films* (London: Faber and Faber, 1990), 13–14.
[5]Martin Rosen quoted in Iain F. McAsh, 'How Rabbits Took over a Studio in Warren Street', *Film Review*, November 1978: 54.

was experimental animator John Hubley, who was controversially sacked from the project in 1976, with Rosen stepping in to take his place. The production was even threatened by an unexpected rise in the prices of film stock and crucial animation tools like pencils and rubbers.[6] After the film's completion seeking distribution was also a struggle, but *Watership Down* eventually premiered in the UK in October 1978 to become a commercial hit. The final film is best remembered today for its intense emotional effects arising from its stark portrayals of death, violence and its increasingly relevant criticism of human impact on the natural environment. Yet this very brief overview only skims the surface of *Watership Down*'s fascinating development, aesthetic and cultural significance, and historical and industrial contexts. This book is dedicated to considering how and why *Watership Down* is so striking, how it came to be and why it continues to endure as a seminal work of animation that is as beloved as it is controversial.

However, to suggest that *Watership Down* is truly unique would be disingenuous. As remarkable as it is, it forms part of a transnational wave of animated films produced in the 1970s and 1980s that were anticipated by some as holding the potential to provide a 'mature' alternative to Walt Disney Animation, which was then suffering an identity crisis in the wake of Walt Disney's death in 1966 and the shifting industrial and cultural climate of New Hollywood.[7] *Watership Down* was released in close proximity to Ralph Bakshi's *The Lord of the Rings* (1978), with which it was repeatedly compared in British and North American press coverage: ahead of their release, the *Daily Mail* asked if the pair would 'herald the rebirth of an art form that has enthralled millions?', a question that was suggestively placed beneath an image of Mickey Mouse, who was then celebrating his fiftieth anniversary.[8] *Watership Down* has also been grouped with animated oddities like *Fantastic Planet* (Laloux, 1973), *The Last Unicorn* (Rankin and Bass, 1982), the films made by Don Bluth after his famous defection from Disney in 1979, and *The Plague Dogs* (Rosen, 1982) and *When the Wind Blows* (Murakami, 1986) in what Calum Waddell terms an unofficial trilogy of 'serious, adult-oriented animation' produced in the UK.[9] *The Plague Dogs* is notable as Rosen's

---

[6]McAsh, 'How Rabbits Took over a Studio in Warren Street', 52.

[7]For information on the Disney studio at this time, see Douglas Gomery, 'Disney's Business History: A Reinterpretation', in *Disney Discourse: Producing the Magic Kingdom*, ed. Eric Smoodin (London: Routledge, 1994), 78–9.

[8]Paul Donovan and Douglas Thompson, 'Booming Bunnies', *Daily Mail*, 17 October 1978: 24; Michael Barrier, 'Going by the Book', *Michael Barrier*, 8 March 2011. http://www.michaelbarrier.com/Funnyworld/LOTR/LOTR.html (accessed 25 October 2021), reprinted from the original in *Funnyworld* 20 (1979); David Ansen, 'Hobbits and Rabbits', *Newsweek*, 20 November 1978: 79.

[9]Tasha Robinson, '*Watership Down*', *The Dissolve*, 23 February 2015. http://thedissolve.com/reviews/1398-watership-down/ (accessed 25 October 2021); Jim Seale, 'Disney Disciples', *Sight and Sound* 52, no. 2 (1982): 77; Waddell, *Taboo Breakers*, 211.

follow-up to *Watership Down*, also based on source material by Adams, and for being even more emotionally harrowing than *Watership Down* due to its bleak representation of the issue of animal vivisection. In this context, *Watership Down* is not quite as anomalous as it first appears, and many of these films could be equally deserving of entries in the Animation: Key Films/Filmmakers series, all for entirely different reasons. *Watership Down*'s particular significance thus comes from both the specifics of its peculiarity – its strange alchemy of animation, talking rabbits, realist violence, surrealist folk horror and fantastical myth that very nearly did not make it to the screen – and that it is emblematic of a flashpoint in the history of animation. As described by Walter Chaw in a retrospective review, *Watership Down* 'arose in that extended lull between Disney's heyday and its late-Eighties resurrection' and 'point[ed] to the dwindled potential for American animation to evolve into . . . a mature medium for artistic expression of serious issues'.[10] Given the ongoing dominance of the Disney studio over the landscape of Western animation, it is an apt starting point to burrow into this relationship between *Watership Down* and Disney to examine what it reveals about the industrial landscape of animation in the 1970s, how this affected the reception of *Watership Down* and the way this film is remembered today.

Rabbits in the shadow of a mouse

Many within the growing field of Disney studies would no doubt take issue with Chaw's ungenerous characterization of the studio's animated output, which can be just as serious, mature and emotionally devastating as *Watership Down*; indeed, Disney films from *Pinocchio* (Luske and Sharpsteen, 1940) to *The Lion King* (Allers and Minkoff, 1994) can usually be found mentioned alongside *Watership Down* in discussions of emotionally scarring animated films. Even so, the relationship between *Watership Down* and Disney is one of contradictions and tension. On the one hand, *Watership Down* itself invites such comparisons: it is an animated film about talking animals, a section of the film industry that Disney has long had cornered, and former Disney animator Phillip Duncan, who animated the rabbit Thumper from *Bambi* (Hand et al., 1942), was lured out of retirement to work on *Watership Down*. This decision made sense, as *Bambi* is known for its hyper-realistic approach to representing animals and nature, a style known as 'Disney-Formalism'.[11] This style is enabled

---

[10] Walter Chaw, 'Watership Down (1978) – DVD', *Film Freak Central*, 8 May 2002. https://www.filmfreakcentral.net/ffc/2015/02/watership-down-1978-the-criterion-collection-blu-ray-disc.html (accessed 30 May 2022).
[11] Coined by Chris Pallant, Disney-Formalism is defined as a style that 'prioritised artistic sophistication, "realism" in characters and contexts, and, above all, believability'. Chris Pallant,

in part by the multi-plane camera, a Disney invention that creates a realistic sense of depth in animation, and which was employed on *Watership Down*. The influence of Disney-Formalism, and *Bambi* in particular, can also be seen in *Watership Down*'s uncompromising representation of human disregard for wildlife, its anatomically correct representations of rabbits – achieved, like *Bambi*, through the careful study of live animals – and painstakingly realized watercolour backgrounds and landscape vistas, which were accurate to the real Watership Down in Hampshire.

On the other hand, Paul Wells claims that 'it might properly be argued that all cartoon animation that follows the Disney output is a *reaction* to Disney, aesthetically, technically, and ideologically'.[12] This is true of *Watership Down*, as Rosen and Hubley, the film's original director, went to great pains to avoid the Disney style – or at least, the widespread cultural *perception* of this style as associated with sanitized fairy tales, anthropomorphization and childishness. Despite Hubley having got his start in animation by working as a layout artist at Disney, he and his wife and collaborator Faith gained a reputation for 'frequently turn[ing] their backs on the animation tradition rooted in Walt Disney's cartoons', and it was precisely this eschewing of the Disney stereotype that got John Hubley hired for *Watership Down*.[13] Even after Hubley's ousting from the production and replacement by Rosen (a conflict addressed in greater detail in Part I of this book), Rosen was intent on distancing *Watership Down*'s rabbits from any associations with Disney. As part of this, he considered filming *Watership Down* in a variety of media including stop-motion animation, puppetry, live rabbits and even humans dressed as rabbits, in order to avoid what he called the 'cute and cuddly' connotations of hand-drawn cel animation.[14] While Walt Disney considered his films to be for 'the child in all of us, whether we be six or sixty',[15] Rosen has always been adamant that *Watership Down* was intended as an animated film for adults, as indicated by his refusal to compromise on bringing the novel's violence and persistent sense of threat to life.[16] He also made significant effort

---

'Disney-Formalism: Rethinking "Classic Disney"', *Animation: An Interdisciplinary Journal* 5, no. 3 (2010): 342.
[12] Paul Wells, *Animation and America* (Edinburgh: Edinburgh University Press, 2002), 45; italics in original.
[13] Mike Barrier, 'John and Faith Hubley, Traditional Animation Transformed', *Millimeter*, February 1977: 42; BFI press clippings file: 'Turning a Fine Buck', *The Sunday Times*, 9 November 1975.
[14] Martin Rosen quoted in McAsh, 'How Rabbits Took over a Studio in Warren Street', 53.
[15] Walt Disney quoted in Rudy Behlmer, *America's Favorite Movies: Behind the Scenes* (New York: Frederick Ungar Publishing Co., 1982), 60.
[16] Adams, too, bristled at the idea of his novel being a children's novel, despite it having originated from stories he told his pre-teen daughters. Richard Adams, 'Some Ingredients of *Watership Down*', in *The Thorny Paradise: Writers on Writing for Children*, ed. Edward Blishen (Harmondsworth: Kestrel Books, 1975), 163–73.

to communicate the film's tone and content through its promotional materials, such as the trailer and poster. On the latter, Rosen claimed,

> I insisted that the one-sheet indicate how strong a picture it was by having Bigwig the rabbit in a snare. I reckoned a mother with a sensitive child would see that – a rabbit in a snare with blood coming out its mouth – and reckon, 'well maybe this isn't for Charlie – it's a little too tough'.[17]

In actual fact, the poster does not show any blood, nor does the image feature in the film itself. While the poster does reference a bloody scene in which Bigwig almost dies from being caught in a wire snare trap, the poster shows a dramatic silhouette of Bigwig with the snare around his neck and his head pointed up towards the sky in a cry of pain, against a backdrop of the countryside landscape at sunset. Still, Rosen's intent to communicate the film's tone and intended audience comes through – even if this was not powerful enough to offset the child-friendly expectations set by its rabbit characters, animated form and that it was awarded a U certificate, indicating suitability for all ages, by the British Board of Film Classification (BBFC). The latter was a decision that Rosen personally opposed, to no avail.[18]

The unfortunate irony is that while *Watership Down* tried to resist associations with Disney and held the potential to provide a viable, more 'adult' alternative to Disney's domination of Western animation, it was partly the legacy of the Disney studio that resulted in the film receiving a mixed critical response upon its release. The consensus in its native Britain was especially harsh. The *Daily Mail*, for example, opined that 'Watership Down is by no stretch of the imagination a Disney-type animation feature film. Sadly, I have to say, if it had been I might have enjoyed it more.'[19] Similarly, the *Observer* called it 'sub-Disney', finding the rabbits to be 'blandly drawn' and concluding that '"Watership Down" is not to be sneezed at, but it is difficult to enthuse over'.[20] However, the Disney legacy was evoked positively by critics on both sides of the Atlantic, with Gene Siskel praising *Watership Down* as 'more mature than what we usually expect or get from an animated feature film' (though his co-host Roger Ebert disliked it).[21] The

---

[17]Martin Rosen quoted in Ed Power, 'A Piercing Screen: How Watership Down Terrified an Entire Generation', *Independent*, 20 October 2018. https://www.independent.co.uk/arts-entertainment/films/features/watership-down-film-bright-eyes-rabbits-disease-martin-rosen-richard-adams-disney-a8590226.html (accessed 5 October 2021).
[18]Glenys Roberts, 'The Rabbits of Warren Street', *The Times*, 19 October 1978: 11.
[19]Margaret Hinxman, 'What a Beastly Affair!', *Daily Mail*, 20 October 1978: 32–3.
[20]Philip French, 'Bunnies in the Molehill', *The Observer*, 22 October 1978: 32.
[21]'Watership Down (1978) Movie Review - Sneak Previews with Roger Ebert and Gene Siskel', *YouTube*, 17 May 2019. https://www.youtube.com/watch?v=ou_Ulc-Z184 (accessed 21 October 2021).

Guardian's negative review singled out the seagull Kehaar as a highlight for his 'most Disney-like' animation.[22] *Newsweek* and *Films and Filming* were more effusive, with the latter awarding it the status of 'far and away the most exciting and totally involving animated feature since Disney's peak years'.[23] Consistent across many of the reviews was the identification of the prologue sequence, which stands out thanks to its abstract style that is unlike anything in the remainder of the film. Widely credited as the only part of Hubley's work that remains in the final film, it is interesting that this most un-Disney-esque sequence was singled out for admiration. This includes a cutting review from animation historian Michael Barrier, who found everything aside from the prologue to be 'very stupid' and showed 'no sign that any intelligence was at work in making [it]'.[24] Most damning of all was Barrier's view that the film was so unremarkable that 'it is almost as if *Watership Down* . . . had never been released at all'.[25]

Evidently, Barrier was off the mark. Despite the mixed critical response, *Watership Down* was a financial success at home and worldwide.[26] 'Bright Eyes', written for the film by Mike Batt and performed by Art Garfunkel, became the bestselling single of 1979 in the UK.[27] Most importantly, *Watership Down*'s initial popularity did not fade, and if anything has only grown over the past four decades, especially in British cultural memory. This is in large part down to television, where the film has been regularly broadcast from the 1980s onwards, especially on or around Christmas, Easter and other national holidays. No doubt enabled by this televisual afterlife, *Watership Down* has a reputation as one of the most distressing children's films ever made. Barely a week goes by without it being named on a seemingly endless supply of online articles that rank the 'most traumatizing children's films' or a related topic.[28] This is despite – or more likely *because* – of the fact that it was never intended to be a 'Disney-esque' film for children, which

---

[22] Derek Malcolm, 'The Buck Stops Here', *The Guardian*, 19 October 1978: 12.
[23] Ansen, 'Hobbits and Rabbits', 79; Julian Fox, 'Watership Down', *Films and Filming*, December 1978: 34.
[24] Barrier, 'Going by the Book'.
[25] Barrier, 'Going by the Book'.
[26] John Lui, 'Director of Seminal Animated Film Watership Down to Come to Singapore for Masterclass', *The Straits Times*, 14 October 2015. https://www.straitstimes.com/lifestyle/entertainment/director-of-seminal-animated-film-watership-down-to-come-to-singapore-for (accessed 25 October 2021).
[27] Liam Allen, 'Was it a Kind of Bad Dream?', *BBC News*, 3 March 2009. http://news.bbc.co.uk/1/hi/entertainment/7919049.stm (accessed 25 October 2021).
[28] At the time of writing, the most recent example is Joel Hunningham, '35 Movies That Scarred Us for Life as Kids, According to Lifehacker Readers', *Lifehacker*, 29 October 2021. https://lifehacker.com/35-movies-that-scarred-us-for-life-as-kids-according-t-1847964047 (accessed 5 November 2021).

then conflicted with its positioning as one by film regulators, distributors, broadcasters and critics.

A 'Universal' film? *Watership Down*, film classification and the child audience

Unlike its source novel, the *Watership Down* film has received surprisingly scant academic attention.[29] Within public discourses, however, a great deal of ink has been spilled – like the blood that seeps over the field in Fiver's vision – over the film's contentious relationship with film classification and child audiences. Part of the intention of this book, as alluded to by its subtitle, is to look beyond the traumatic reputation that has so far eclipsed the numerous other things to say about it. Equally, however, this book intends to study the film's legendary representations of animated violence and death in detail, and from a variety of theoretical approaches, to further aid understanding of this film and of animated violence generally. In order for the rest of the book to do this, this chapter places *Watership Down*'s reputation as an emotionally distressing and devastating children's text in historical and industrial context that has hitherto been absent from discussions of the film. Doing so reveals that *Watership Down* has not always been received as a 'traumatizing' children's film at all and illuminates the many factors that contributed to the development of this reputation over time.

Adams's novel, simply by virtue of being about rabbits, had an ambiguous relationship with children despite its intimidating length and language that bespeaks a teen or adult audience of address. The film, by virtue of its translation to the screen in a form strongly associated with children's entertainment, automatically made the story more accessible to a wider and younger audience. As mentioned earlier, Rosen attempted to mitigate against misconceptions of the film being for children through marketing, but it was nevertheless received as a children's film by critics and audiences. In the UK, this seems to have been compounded by the film premiering in mid-October, coinciding with the half-term school holiday. Barry Norman drew attention to this timing and framed it as a family film on his programme *Film '78*.[30] *Watership Down* would not go into wide release in the UK until mid-December, but even this connotes family viewing through proximity to the Christmas holiday. Other publications also positioned the film as a children's text, with the *Spectator* calling it 'a straightforward children's adventure', although *Monthly Film Bulletin* considered it to be *too* childish:

---

[29]There are some notable exceptions; see the Guide to Further Research.
[30]*Film '78* (1978), [TV programme] BBC One, 15 October.

'it is hard to imagine that there is much here for the adult admirers.'³¹ Most critics acknowledged the film's potentially disturbing aspects, with some issuing caution that the film might not be suitable for '*very* young' children, but none seemed to think that it should be off limits to children as a whole.³² *The Guardian* dismissed any concerns about the film's potential negative effects on children by declaring that 'It is not true . . . that the film is too violent and disturbing for children. What, pray, about some of Grimms' fairy tales?'³³

One of the key factors that causes confusion about the film's intended audience is its age rating. Rosen's view that the film is meant for adults is reflected in its age classification from countries like Indonesia (17+) and Hong Kong (II, meaning not suitable for children). This is offset by the more inclusive categories it received in other territories, including North America (PG), Malaysia (U) and of course the UK, where the film was contentiously rated U for 'Universal', indicating suitability for viewers of all ages. In their 1978 classification report, the BBFC reasoned that

> Animation removes the realistic gory horror in the occasional scenes of violence and bloodshed, and we felt that, while the film may move children emotionally during the film's duration, it could not seriously trouble them once the spell of the story is broken, and that a 'U' certificate was therefore quite appropriate.³⁴

This has received a great deal of derision in the years since, because commentators disagree with either the rating decision itself or the logic underpinning it. Gerard Jones falls into the latter camp in his essay for the Criterion Collection. Finding value in the way that *Watership Down* has a frank but profound approach to death, Jones takes issue with the BBFC's 'implication that a family movie should aspire to tell a story that children will promptly forget'.³⁵ For better or worse, *Watership Down* is anything but forgettable, as attested by the fact that the BBFC continues to receive

---

³¹Ted Whitehead, 'Sententious', *The Spectator*, 21 October 1978: 30; John Pym, 'Watership Down', *Monthly Film Bulletin*, 1 January 1978: 208.
³²Fox, 'Watership Down', 34; emphasis in original; David Robinson, 'Down the Rabbit Hole and into Disneyland', *The Times*, 20 October 1978: 15; Jay Scott, 'British Bunnies Triumphant in Warren Piece', *The Globe and Mail*, 20 January 1979.
³³Malcolm, 'The Buck Stops Here'.
³⁴'Watership Down', *British Board of Film Classification*, 15 February 1978. https://darkroom.bbfc.co.uk/original/1b0cb7188e02ac62c6cdcce5f2d1b928:2199e5760ab7c37b5b037fdee3a35735/watership-down-report.pdf (accessed 25 October 2021).
³⁵Gerard Jones, '*Watership Down*: "Take Me with You, Stream, on Your Dark Journey"', *The Criterion Collection*, 26 February 2015. https://www.criterion.com/current/posts/3475-watership-down-take-me-with-you-stream-on-your-dark-journey (accessed 25 October 2021).

regular complaints from parents and guardians about its permissive rating.[36] The organization is also occasionally called upon to address its rating of *Watership Down* in public, such as when the film has been broadcast on television in timeslots when children are likely to be in the audience. In 2016, for example, Channel 5 was criticized for broadcasting the film on the afternoon of Easter Sunday, putting the film, and its age rating, back in the spotlight. Head of the BBFC Dave Austin was interviewed on national radio about the film's rating just three days later.[37]

Incidents like this cast the BBFC's classification decision as a terrible mistake that continues to haunt them, but this characterization does not take into account the context in which the film was originally classified. When the BBFC assessed *Watership Down* in 1978, the age categories looked very different from today. Aside from U the available ratings were: A for 'Adult', an advisory rating that warned that a film's content might be unsuitable for 'young children' and required children to be in the presence of an adult; AA, which only permitted access to anyone aged fourteen and above; and X, which was completely off limits to anyone under eighteen.[38] The BBFC therefore effectively had the choice to classify *Watership Down* U or A. The latter would not have legally restricted children of any age from seeing the film, only that it would have provided the cautionary effect that Rosen intended the poster to communicate. The BBFC examiners evidently did not consider such a warning necessary. Far from being a blunder on the part of the BBFC, we can instead interpret this as a very deliberate decision that favoured inclusivity and gave child audiences the credit of being able to handle challenging content and themes. This is arguably a refreshing move that contrasts with the prevailing scholarly view that restrictive film classification makes 'children of all ages . . . the real victims of obsessive BBFC censorship decisions taken ostensibly in their interests'.[39] Moreover, although the U rating is now widely considered as practically synonymous with children's entertainment, it does not necessarily mean that a film is *for* children, only that it is safe for them to view – and even then, only children above the age of four. Nor does it mean that a film will be entirely without distressing elements, merely that for a film to attain a U rating it must 'offer reassuring counterbalances to any violence, threat or horror', which *Watership Down* does through moments of humour and triumph.[40]

---

[36] 'Watership Down', *British Board of Film Classification*, https://www.bbfc.co.uk/education/case-studies/watership-down (accessed 25 October 2021).
[37] 'BBFC Head: Watership Down Should be PG', *BBC Radio 5 Live*, 30 March 2016. https://www.bbc.co.uk/programmes/p03phyqs (accessed 25 October 2021).
[38] 'History of the BBFC', *British Board of Film Classification*. https://www.bbfc.co.uk/education/timeline (accessed 25 October 2021).
[39] Geoffrey Robertson and Andrew Nicol, *Media Law*, 5th edn (London: Penguin, 2008), 150.
[40] 'BBFC Podcast Episode 95 – U', *British Board of Film Classification*. https://www.bbfc.co.uk/about-us/podcasts/bbfc-podcast-episode-95-u (accessed 25 October 2021).

According to archival documents presented by BBFC Education Officer Emily Fussell in 2018, the classification of *Watership Down* attracted little public pushback from parents and guardians at the time of its original release, which aligns with the lack of concern from critics.[41] In a contemporaneous response from the BBFC to an aggrieved parent of a child who had been distressed by the film, the organization claimed to have only received 'one other' similar letter. In defence of the classification, the BBFC's reply compared the film with similarly scary but beloved children's classics *Snow White and Seven Dwarfs* (Hand et al, 1937) and *The Wizard of Oz* (Fleming, 1939) and claimed that the children aged between five and eight of two BBFC examiners had seen the film 'and all of them enjoyed it very much without appearing to be seriously distressed by it'. One more letter of complaint took issue not with the film itself but with two trailers shown beforehand that did not seem fit to run in front of a film that children might see: they were for the X-rated sex comedies *Confessions of a Window Cleaner* (Guest, 1974) and *Confessions of a Driving Instructor* (Cohen, 1976).

Even if these documents indicate that *Watership Down*'s classification was not especially controversial in 1978, its status as a distressing children's film has only intensified with time; in part, this is likely due to people who saw the film as children growing up and being able to articulate their own memories and experiences, which are crucially lacking from the contemporaneous critical responses and classification documents penned by adults. As suggested earlier, television broadcasting strategies have also played an instrumental role in contributing to the incongruity between *Watership Down*'s 'child-friendly' perception and its content, as the time of day at which a film is broadcast can be a strong indicator of target audience. Home media distribution strategies also figure, and in the case of *Watership Down* this seems a key contributing factor as the VHS and DVD covers have shifted over the decades towards dominant trends in the marketing and distribution of children's films. The promotional image of Bigwig that Rosen intended to ward off young children and their guardians appears on UK editions of the VHS released in 1982 and 1992.[42] The blurbs on both covers foreground the dangers that the rabbits encounter on their journey,

---

[41] Emily Fussell, 'The Classification History of *Watership Down*', unpublished conference paper, 'The Legacy of *Watership Down*: Animals, Adaptation, Animation', 10 November 2018, University of Warwick. In the researching of this book I requested access to the BBFC's archive files for *Watership Down*, but this was not possible on account of the ongoing coronavirus pandemic. For this reason, the documents referenced throughout this paragraph are transcribed from Fussell's 2018 presentation, and they may not present a complete account of *Watership Down*'s classification history.

[42] 'Watership Down', *VHS Collector*, 26 May 2013. https://vhscollector.com/movie/watership-down (accessed 25 October 2021); 'Watership Down on Guild Home Video', *Video Collector*. http://www.videocollector.co.uk/watership-down/18227 (accessed 25 October 2021).

including mention of a 'rabbit holocaust' in the 1982 blurb, which is typeset against a pale grey background. There is little about this cover that bespeaks an intended audience of children, although the blurb does conclude that 'All ages will delight' in the film. By 1999 another VHS cover adopted a more colourful design. Gone is Bigwig's silhouette, replaced instead with images of Hazel and Fiver against a bright-orange background.[43] The 2002 Deluxe Edition DVD that is still in circulation leans further towards a Disney-esque aesthetic: the characters are set against a countryside landscape and a bright blue and yellow sky, and they look more rounded and polished than they do in the film itself. Looking at this shift in paratexts, it is unsurprising that the combination of talking animated rabbits, U certificate, 'child-friendly' broadcasting strategies and home media releases reinforced the perception of *Watership Down* as a children's film and therefore would not adequately prepare anyone, adult or child, for the markedly more mature – or 'traumatic' – contents, style and tone of the film. The poster image that Rosen carefully selected and intended to provide caution is now used almost exclusively for Blu-ray editions, including a Criterion Collection release, that are targeted towards adult collectors and cinephiles more than children and general audiences.

When handling the 2018 miniseries adaptation of *Watership Down*, the BBC (who co-produced the series with Netflix and broadcast it in the UK) were clearly aware of the importance of broadcasting and marketing strategies to communicate intended audience. Speculation about whether the series would be as violent as the film was in the air as soon as the series was announced in 2016, and closer to its release there was an obvious desire on the part of the BBC – a trusted public service broadcaster – to avoid controversy.[44] The first episode was strategically scheduled on BBC One at 7.00 pm on Saturday, 22 December: a timeslot that indicated family-oriented Christmas viewing, but when children at the younger end of the spectrum were likely to be in bed. Prior to the broadcast, the BBC and the miniseries' producers also attempted to manage public perceptions much in the way that Rosen had done with the 1978 film. The most surprising publicity strategy came from the official CBeebies Facebook page, which posted a trailer with the caption:

'While we won't shy away from the darkness in the book, visually it won't be as brutal and scarring,' assures executive producer Rory Aitken.

---

[43]'Watership Down [1978]', *Amazon UK*. https://www.amazon.co.uk/Watership-Down-VHS-John-Hurt/dp/B00004R6CJ (accessed 25 October 2021).
[44]Julia Raeside, 'Watership Down without the Claws? You Shouldn't Have Bothered', *The Guardian*, 29 April 2016. https://www.theguardian.com/commentisfree/2016/apr/29/watership-down-remake-without-claws (accessed 26 October 2021).

OK BBC One, we'll trust you.
(NOTE: still not for kids, this isn't the 70s!)[45]

CBeebies is a BBC television channel aimed at pre-school children, that is, *not* the intended audience of *Watership Down*. However, by posting this trailer to the channel's social media account, which is followed largely by the parents of pre-school children, the BBC advertised the series to part of its intended audience (adults) while also warding against anticipated concerns about its suitability for children arising from the legacy of the 1978 film, which many of those same adults probably watched as children. This strategy appeared to have worked, as there was no discernible backlash against the series in terms of its effects on children.

The miniseries' intended audience is echoed by its BBFC rating of 12 for 'references to crime, threat, violence'.[46] This seems less of an indication of its levels of violence, which are tame compared with the film, than how much the standards of the BBFC and public attitudes about children's media have changed since 1978.[47] Indeed, in 2016 Austin responded to criticism of the film's U certificate by asserting that if it were submitted for re-classification under his tenure at the BBFC (which would only happen if a new format of the film were to be released), it would be classified at least PG. In addition to the violence, Austin cited the use of a swear word by Kehaar: 'Piss off!'[48] This would satisfy repeated requests from the distributor over the decades that the film be rated PG, but submissions for re-classification in 1985 and 1989 both upheld the U, with the BBFC considering it to be it to be 'a children's experience despite certain scenes' in 1985.[49] Similarly, in 2013 the U rating was deemed 'reasonable and defensible' by the BBFC examiners.[50] Austin's promise was finally fulfilled in August 2022, when a 4K re-master of the film triggered another submission to the BBFC. *Watership Down* is now classified PG in the UK for 'mild violence, threat, brief bloody images, language'.[51]

---

[45]'Watership Down: Official Trailer BBC', *Facebook*, 4 December 2018. https://www.facebook.com/cbeebies/videos/372533660182938 (accessed 26 October 2021).
[46]'Watership Down', *British Board of Film Classification*. https://www.bbfc.co.uk/release/watership-down-q29sbgvjdglvbjpwwc01mtizndk (accessed 26 October 2021).
[47]A comparison of the aesthetic depiction of violence between the 1978 and 2018 versions of *Watership Down* appears in Chapter 11. See also Catherine Lester, 'Watership Down: Family-friendly BBC Version Risks Losing the Power of Epic Original', *The Conversation*, 13 December 2018. https://theconversation.com/watership-down-family-friendly-bbc-version-risks-losing-the-power-of-epic-original-108699 (accessed 5 October 2021).
[48]'BBFC Head: Watership Down Should be PG', *BBC Radio 5 Live*.
[49]Quoted in Fussell, 'The Classification History of *Watership Down*'.
[50]Quoted in Fussell, 'The Classification History of *Watership Down*'.
[51]'Watership Down', *British Board of Film Classification*. https://www.bbfc.co.uk/release/watership-down-q29sbgvjdglvbjpwwc0yotyxnjm (accessed 24 August 2022).

The point of outlining this classification timeline is not to try to pin blame on the BBFC, or anyone else, for *Watership Down*'s 'traumatic' legacy. In part this is because to ascribe blame would imply that the film's emotional effects on children are inherently negative and that children should be shielded from them – an assumption that several of the chapters in this book take issue with. Rather, my intention here is to reveal the complex web of factors at play in how the film's reputation came to be. Moreover, *Watership Down*'s (now historic) U certificate and legacy as a 'traumatizing' film are vital facets of its cultural identity, and it seems likely that it would not have remained in the public consciousness for as long as it has were it not for these factors. Arguably, it is precisely the *lack* of violence and other controversial elements in the two subsequent television adaptations of the novel – the aforementioned 2018 miniseries and a British-Canadian cel-animated series (1999–2001) – that meant they have not had the lasting impact of the film. Despite the careful publicity strategy described earlier, the 2018 miniseries appeared to over-correct in its caution not to offend despite its marketing towards teenagers and adults, and it ended up being widely criticized for its lack of violence, as well as its subpar, 'ugly' 3D computer-animation.[52] The 1999 series, a British-Canadian co-production, was by contrast targeted explicitly at child audiences through its broadcast on children's channels: CITV in the UK and YTV in Canada. Unlike the film, the series had a merchandise roll-out of plush rabbit toys and figurines. As such, its sanitized approach to the story does not appear to have attracted significant attention on account of it meeting the expectations that its broadcasting and promotion set up.

Interestingly, Rosen (who executive produced both television adaptations) framed the 1999 series as a way to atone for the transgressions of his film. Ahead of the series' broadcast he discussed his intention to make it more accessible to children than the film, from it being aired on children's channels to making the rabbit characters more visually distinct from each other and more inclusive in terms of gender.[53] The series changed the gender of some of the core rabbits from male to female and added original female characters, including a mouse voiced by Jane Horrocks. The 2018 miniseries further diversified the cast in terms of race, class and regional dialect, including the voices of British stars such as Daniel Kaluuya, John Boyega, Olivia Coleman, Rosamund Pike, Peter Calapdi and Mackenzie Crook. These changes respond to one of the most common criticisms of Adams's novel relating to its conservative politics. The core group of characters are all male, resulting in a fundamental flaw in the utopia of their new home: the inability to breed and ensure the longevity of the warren. They resolve this by breaking some oppressed does, and bucks along

---

[52] Ben Travers, 'Watership Down' Review: Netflix Makes a Stunning, Scarring Story a Hare Too Ugly', *IndieWire*, 20 December 2018. https://www.indiewire.com/2018/12/netflix-watership-down-review-2018-miniseries-1202029873/ (accessed 27 October 2021).
[53] Clare Mount, 'Character Reference', *Creation*, January 1999: 10–11.

with them, out of enemy warren Efrafa. One of the most searing criticisms of the novel's treatment of gender comes from fantasy novelist Ursula Le Guin, who wrote that female rabbits are represented as 'mindless breeding slaves'.[54] She concludes that it is 'not, to my mind, a book to give to any child, or any adult either', which raises questions about the 'suitability' of the text for children beyond its violent and horrific elements.[55]

The 1978 film does little to correct the novel's failings: a lone female rabbit, Violet, is added to the Sandleford escapees, but she is quickly killed by a hawk in service of the narrative that relies on a lack of does in order to progress. The film also makes some troubling representational moves with regard to sexuality and race. Cowslip is queer-coded through his effeminate voice, mannerisms and the unnatural purple and orange hues of his warren, all of which underscore his status as strange and untrustworthy.[56] Elsewhere, Blackavar – a dark-furred prisoner rabbit of Efrafa – suffers the most gruesome death in the film (despite surviving in the novel) and is voiced by Clifton Jones, one of only two Black members of the cast. The other is Derek Griffiths, who voices two Efrafan soldiers. If nothing else, the 1978, 1999 and 2018 adaptations of *Watership Down* function as an effective demonstration of the ways that attitudes to representation in children's media and animation – whether that is representation of violence or identity – have shifted over the intervening forty years.

There is clearly more to be said on the matter of *Watership Down*'s representational politics and 'suitability' for children, and these topics are addressed at greater length throughout this book, along with examinations of issues that have been overshadowed by the overwhelming focus on its 'traumatic' legacy. Like the film itself, this book presents a journey to, through and beyond *Watership Down* to examine it in a range of contexts and from multiple approaches and vantage points. And just like any journey, this one is aided by a map.

'That's it, Hazel. That's where we have to be!' Charting the course

Just as *Watership Down* opens with a story of creation – 'Long ago, the great Frith made the world' – this book begins with not one but *two* narratives of

---

[54]Ursula K. Le Guin, *Cheek by Jowl: Talks & Essays on How & Why Fantasy Matters* (Seattle: Aqueduct Press, 2009), 80.
[55]Le Guin, *Cheek by Jowl*, 82.
[56]For further ideological criticism of the novel, including its representation of Cowslip's Warren, see Christopher Pawling, ed. '*Watership Down*: Rolling Back the 1960s', in *Popular Fiction and Social Change* (London: The Macmillan Press, 1984), 212–35.

how *Watership Down* came to be (and how it almost did not), each drawing from very different archival sources. Opening 'Part I: Bringing the Warren to Life' is Llewella Chapman and James Chapman's chapter containing their findings from the archive of Film Finances, a British company that provided 'guarantees of completion' to hundreds of films between 1950 and 1980, including *Watership Down*. The archive contains detailed first-hand accounts of the infamous change of director from Hubley to Rosen. As the authors explain, these 'demonstrate the conflicting creative agencies and economic determinants that shaped *Watership Down*' and reveal just how close the film came to never being completed at all.[57]

Chapter 2 draws on a more personal source: the Arthur Humberstone Animation Archive, which is privately held by his two sons Klive and Nigel who co-author the chapter with Chris Pallant. The late Humberstone was Senior Animator on *Watership Down*, a position that granted him a great deal of influence over the film's aesthetic and a front-row seat to the change in director. Drawing on Humberstone's carefully preserved archival documents, their own autobiographical memories, those of people who worked with Humberstone and his unpublished memoirs, the authors shine a light on this key figure of the British animation industry but whose influence is hitherto relatively unknown. While the sources consulted in Chapter 1 provide an economic perspective of the *Watership Down* production as being persistently on the brink of disaster, the Arthur Humberstone Animation Archive provides insight into the jovial and supportive working atmosphere at Nepenthe, as well as the directorial style of Rosen. As an inexperienced animator, Rosen claimed to have approached the production as if it were 'a "live" feature film', in his words.[58] This is evident from the use of an imitation 360-degree shot in Cowslip's Warren, a rarely attempted feat in cel animation that the film's director of animation Tony Guy reportedly thought impossible.[59] This is just one example of how Rosen's outsider experience brought a unique approach to the production of *Watership Down*, which Humberstone, Humberstone and Pallant characterize as one of 'creative freedom rather than directorial disorder'.

A further challenge in bringing *Watership Down* to the screen was the issue of how the fictional rabbit language of Lapine, which Adams invented for the novel, would be depicted. R. Grider addresses this difficulty in

---

[57]The behind-the-scenes troubles with *Watership Down* did not end with the film's completion. In 2020 the Richard Adams estate won back the adaptation rights to the novel, which Rosen had incorrectly claimed to have owned. Ruth Comerford, 'Richard Adams' estate wins back Watership Down rights', *The Bookseller*, 2 June 2020. https://www.thebookseller.com/news/richard-adams-estate-wins-back-watership-down-rights-1205075 (accessed 1 November 2021).
[58]McAsh, 'How Rabbits Took over a Studio in Warren Street', 53.
[59]Ray Conlongue, 'Rabbits a Lively Challenge', *The Globe and Mail*, 19 January 1979.

Chapter 3 by taking a linguistic approach to comparing the use of Lapine in the novel and the film. As Grider points out, the film faced the problem of having to translate Lapine without the benefit of the glossary and footnotes in the novel, the use of subtitles that might have alienated younger viewers, or the Lapine dialogue being cut altogether. In fact, the film's pressbook contained a 'Glossary of Rabbit Terminology', but this would not have been available to the general public.[60] As Grider demonstrates, this was not an issue as the film seamlessly integrates Lapine into the audio-visual medium and represents its rabbits with the same degree of realism and immersion that Adams strove for in his novel.

The representation of *Watership Down*'s anthropomorphic subjects continues in 'Part II: Animal Stories'. Both the novel and film have been interpreted as countless political and religious allegories, all of which Adams rejected by maintaining that 'it's just a story about rabbits'.[61] Nevertheless, the chapters in this section demonstrate the value in considering what we can learn from *Watership Down*'s representations of filmic animals by situating the film within specific cultural, industrial and political contexts. In Chapter 4 Lisa Mullen provides a rebuttal to Adams by arguing that the use of animation in the film adaptation of his novel prompts a reconsideration of the rabbits' allegorical function. Considering animated animals to be 'the perfect vehicle for utopian what-ifs', Mullen argues that the film's animated medium is characterized by an inherent instability that 'teeters on the brink of destruction' and thus reveals the 'insufficiency of utopia' in the film.

In Chapter 5 Noel Brown considers *Watership Down* as part of a cycle of British animal films for children in the late-1960s and 1970s that includes the live-action films *Ring of Bright Water* (Couffer, 1969), *The Belstone Fox* (Hill, 1973) and *Tarka the Otter* (Cobham, 1979). For Brown, these films are notable for their unsentimental depictions of human–animal relations that buck the trends of anthropomorphization familiar to a majority of children's animal stories. However, only *Watership Down* is well-remembered today. As such, Brown argues that the other films in the cycle are 'long overdue for rediscovery' on account of their 'critiques of human aggression and self-absorption, and their implicit demand for a greener politics [that] remain pertinent today'.

Indeed, in Chapter 6 Hollie Adams traces the continued relevance of *Watership Down*'s ecological concerns from 1970s Britain to the present day

---

[60] *Watership Down* Pressbook (1978), British Film Institute Special Collections, PBS – 50833.
[61] Richard Adams quoted in Mark Brown, '"True meaning" of Watership Down Revealed Ahead of TV Revival', *The Guardian*, 10 December 2018. https://www.theguardian.com/culture/2018/dec/10/true-meaning-watership-down-revealed-ahead-of-revival-its-rabbits (accessed 26 October 2021).

through comparison with a spiritual successor, the animated television series *The Animals of Farthing Wood* (1992–5), and the 2018 *Watership Down* miniseries. Framing her chapter with her experience using 'ecopedagogy' as a school teacher, Adams contextualizes her case studies against the worsening climate emergency. She shows that these and similar texts may hold immense value for a generation of children growing up as eco-citizens and as starting points for teachers and guardians wanting to facilitate 'ecopedagogical' conversations.

In Chapter 7, Dan Torre and Lienors Torre conclude this section by thinking about the relevance of *Watership Down*'s animals beyond its British context. The novel and film both have international appeal and influence: from Swedish progressive rock artist Bo Hannson, who released the album *Music Inspired by Watership Down* in 1977, to Mexican filmmaker Guillermo del Toro quoted at the opening of this chapter. A particularly illuminating cultural context from which to consider *Watership Down* is that of Australia. The film explicitly invites this through its opening prologue, which was designed by Australian production designer Luciana Arrighi and influenced by Indigenous-Australian art. The rabbit massacre depicted here has the potential to take on different resonance in Australia, where rabbits are even more likely to be considered pests than pets. Torre and Torre take this as a starting point to compare *Watership Down* with representations of rabbits in Australian and British animation, from *Rabbit Stew* (Porter, 1952) to *Peter Rabbit* (Gluck, 2018). In so doing, they reveal a productive dialogue between the Australian animation industry, rabbits and this otherwise very British film.

We return to *Watership Down*'s British – or rather, English – roots in 'Part III: Aesthetics of Sound and Image'. When it comes to the music of *Watership Down*, one's thoughts are likely to go straight to the tearjerker 'Bright Eyes', but the score by Angela Morley and Malcom Williamson arguably has a far more significant role in shaping the film's emotional soundscape. Indeed, the score, sound effects and voice cast were highlighted for praise by several critics in 1978, even when they were not enamoured with the film as a whole.[62] In Chapter 8, Paul Mazey situates the score within the tradition of 'English pastoral melodies', which emphasizes the film's accurately recreated representation of the real Watership Down. Mazey argues that by 'evok[ing] an atmosphere of Englishness' and nostalgia, the score aids in the faithful translation of Adams's novel to the screen. This chapter also draws long overdue scholarly attention to Morley, a key British figure of the music and film worlds, and one of the few women with an above-the-line role in *Watership Down*'s production.

---

[62]Phillip French, for example, found the film's visual style to lack 'vitality', but he favourably compared the quality of sound to that of a radio play ('Bunnies in the molehill').

Of course, fear and terror are not the only emotions that are evoked by *Watership Down*, as acknowledged in Catherine Sadler's Chapter 14, which provides a fitting conclusion to this collection by attending to the film's extraordinarily poignant (and non-violent) depiction of Hazel's death. Sadler draws from her memories of seeing the film aged nine which she realizes now, as an adult, was a profound and radicalizing experience. Combining this reflection with theories of mourning, animal studies and feminist practices of grieving, Sadler shows that the grief evoked by Hazel's death 'allows us and impels us to think differently about rabbits, and . . . to (re)consider the importance of our relationships to and with other species'. Given her own childhood experience with the film, Sadler argues that mourning Hazel at the film's close may be particularly valuable for child audiences, and that it is therefore not such a terrible thing that the film was for so long rated U after all.

Hazel's death marks the end of the film, but it is not the end of his story or of the other rabbits on Watership Down. Although Hazel's physical body turns still, from it emerges his spirit, its ephemerality rendered in pencil rather than the corporeal solidity of ink and paint, and follows the Black Rabbit of Inlé over the Down and into the sky. The voice-over that accompanies this repeats the god Frith's message to El-ahrairah, the prince of rabbits, that we heard at the beginning of the film: 'All the world will be your enemy, Prince with a Thousand Enemies. And whenever they catch you, they will kill you. But first they must catch you, digger, listener, runner, prince with the swift warning. Be cunning and your people will never be destroyed.' This seems a fitting summation of the film itself and the way that the indelible mark it has left – on animation history, on popular culture and on the memories of generations of children – refuses to fade away.

In keeping with this sentiment, this book does not claim to have the last word on *Watership Down* or to leave no stones unturned. One particular gap that should be addressed here is that of adaptation. Although adaptation is touched upon in some of the chapters, the primary aim of this collection is to focus on the film as a work of animation and of cinema. This takes permission from Adams himself, who said that 'a film is not a book' as they require 'different tools [for] a different job';[65] similarly, nor is a film a television programme, a stage play, a role-playing game, a radio play, a punk album or any of the other media into which the *Watership Down* story has been translated. These interpretations and their relationship with the novel and film are deserving of more dedicated attention than is possible here, just as the film itself is arguably rich enough to merit much further

---

[65] Richard Adams, 'Preface', in *The Watership Down Film Picture Book* (Harmondsworth: Penguin Books, 1978), n.p.

exploration beyond these pages. Indeed, an academic conference held at the University of Glasgow in 2022, to mark the 50th anniversary of Adams's novel, confirms that this book is just one part of a much larger conversation about *Watership Down* in its various forms. With this in mind, the 'Guide to Further Research' at the end of the book points readers towards existing resources on the film and its contexts.

PART I
Bringing the warren to life

CHAPTER 1

'We consider the conduct of this film highly unsatisfactory and unprofessional':

Film Finances and *Watership Down*

Llewella Chapman and James Chapman

Watership Down (Rosen, 1978) was an undoubted commercial success upon its release in Britain in October 1978. According to the figures released by the British Film Fund Agency, the body set up to oversee payments from the Eady levy which returned an additional sum to the producers and distributors of British films calculated as a percentage of their box-office receipts, *Watership Down* had received Eady payments totalling £490,528 after its first full year on release.[1] This indicated a total distributor's gross of £1,290,863 and made *Watership Down* the third most successful British film of 1978–9 behind the superhero blockbuster *Superman* (Donner, 1978) and the James Bond picture *Moonraker* (Gilbert, 1979) and ahead of such films as *Midnight Express* (Parker, 1978), *Death on the Nile* (Guillermin, 1978), *The Wild Geese* (McLaglen, 1978), *Force 10 From Navarone*

---

[1] '"Superman" tops Eady '79', *Screen International*, 19 January 1980: 16–17.

(Hamilton, 1978) and *Porridge* (Clement, 1979). There is much anecdotal evidence to suggest that the film made significant profits for its backers. The Canadian merchant banker Jake Eberts, who helped to raise the £50,000 for producer Martin Rosen to purchase the film rights to Richard Adams's novel, reported that the investors of development money 'got their money back with interest, plus an additional £450,000, making a total of ten times their investment'.[2] And in the third volume of his triptych on the British film industry, Alexander Walker makes the (admittedly barely credible) claim that *Watership Down* 'eventually returned to investors 5,000 times their stake'.[3]

However, *Watership Down* very nearly did not reach the screen at all. The travails of the film's production, notably the firing of its original director John Hubley, were reported in the press at the time, but the published accounts do not reveal anything like the full extent of the difficulties that came close to derailing the film.[4] *Watership Down* had a tortuous journey to the screen: it went heavily over budget and schedule, nearly ran out of money and was the subject of a lawsuit that was aborted only by the death of the plaintiff. This chapter documents the troubled production history of *Watership Down* based on the records held by the Film Finances Archive: the budgets, cost reports and correspondence in the archive not only shed new light on the circumstances surrounding the firing of Hubley – a controversial decision that had a significant bearing on the style of the finished film – but also demonstrate the conflicting creative agencies and economic determinants that shaped *Watership Down*.

Film Finances had been incorporated in London in 1950 by a former independent producer, Robert Garrett, who had made films in collaboration with American producer Otto Klement in the 1930s and with Anthony Havelock-Allan in the late 1940s.[5] Its business was not making films or even investing in film production but rather the provision of guarantees of completion: a guarantee to the investors in a film that it would be completed on time and according to an agreed specification without any further call upon the investors in the event of the film exceeding its budget. The role of the guarantor was to ensure the successful completion and delivery of the film. Film Finances would scrutinize the script, budget and production schedule provided by the producer and for a fixed fee (usually 4 to 5 per

---

[2] Jake Eberts and Terry Ilott, *My Indecision is Final: The Rise and Fall of Goldcrest Films* (London: Faber and Faber, 1990), 16–17.
[3] Alexander Walker, *Icons in the Fire: The Rise and Fall of Practically Everyone in the British Film Industry 1984–2000* (London: Orion, 2004), 6.
[4] British Film Institute (BFI) press clippings file: William Hickey, 'Oscar-winner Sacked from £2m Film', *Daily Express*, 14 September 1976.
[5] Charles Drazin, 'Film Finances: The Early Years', *Historical Journal of Film, Radio and Television* 34, no. 1 (2014): 2–22.

cent of the budget) would enter into an agreement to advance any additional funds necessary for completion if the film went over budget. The guarantor would monitor the progress of the film and would intervene if it felt the production was running out of control: as a last resort a condition of the guarantee agreement was that Film Finances had the right to take over the production.

Film Finances soon became an important but largely invisible player in the British film industry. Between 1950 and 1980 – the period covered by its extensive archive that has been made available to researchers – it guaranteed approximately 800 feature films: these included a good number of well-known British pictures, including *The African Queen* (Huston, 1951), *Moulin Rouge* (Huston, 1952), *Richard III* (Olivier, 1955), *Reach for the Sky* (Gilbert, 1956), *Room at the Top* (Clayton, 1959), *Saturday Night and Sunday Morning* (Reisz, 1960), *Dr No* (Young, 1962), *Tom Jones* (Richardson, 1963), *Zulu* (Endfield, 1964), *Straw Dogs* (Peckinpah, 1971) and *The Wicker Man* (Hardy, 1973), as well as many lesser-known films. Its client base included both independent British producers and at one time or another most of the major Hollywood studios who were producing films in Britain. Its history mirrored the wider history of the British film production industry, especially the increasing prominence of American interests in the financing of films and the transition from producers raising their finance through loans from clearing banks against the security of a distribution guarantee from one of the majors to consortium funding involving multiple partners and distribution pre-sales which had become the norm by the 1970s.

There are two important points to understand about Film Finances. It was not an equity investor in the film: it would recoup any advances (plus interest) from the box-office receipts ranking behind the primary investors and ahead of the producer for recovery, but it did not take a percentage of any profit. And its guarantee did not provide a blank cheque to producers: additional expenditure had to be agreed and did not extend to so-called improvements to the film that had not been budgeted in the papers submitted to Film Finances. The production of *Watership Down* would highlight two particular issues: the extent to which the film changed during the course of production from the original proposition agreed by the guarantor, and that the producer lost control of the film as it ran over schedule and over budget.

Film Finances' involvement in a film usually began shortly before the commencement of principal photography: a completion guarantee could not be offered until the script, finance and budget for the film were in place. Martin Rosen applied to Film Finances for a completion guarantee for *Watership Down* in May 1975. At this point the film was budgeted at an estimated £950,562 and was scheduled for release in 1977. The American animator John Hubley was to direct the film, with his wife Faith Hubley in the role of 'creative consultant'. John Hubley's career extended back to the

1930s: he had started out as a background and layout artist for Walt Disney in the 1930s, working on *Snow White and the Seven Dwarfs* (Hand et al., 1937), *Fantasia* (Algar et al., 1940) and *Bambi* (Hand et al., 1942), and later creating the character of 'Mr Magoo' for United Productions of America (UPA). Rosen told the *Sunday Times* that he chose Hubley 'after scanning the field' of possible directors because he 'had the greatest sense of story'. 'What's more', Rosen added, 'he'll make a film about rabbits. Not Disney rabbits. Not Beatrix Potter rabbits. But rabbits who can do everything a rabbit can do, but don't because they lack the intelligence.'[6] Rosen's finance was provided by a consortium of investors including Goldcrest Films (founded by Jake Eberts to provide 'seed money' and partly owned by the publishing group Pearson Longman) and several London merchant banks and investment trusts.[7]

The task of assessing *Watership Down* for a completion guarantee fell to Film Finances' consultant John Croydon, a former production accountant and studio manager whose career in the British film industry extended back to the 1930s and took in experience of the British Lion Film Corporation, Ealing Studios and managing director of Merton Park Studios. Croydon's role was to scrutinize the budget and schedule to ascertain whether they were appropriate for the length and complexity of the script. His report to Film Finances' chairman Robert Garrett indicated that the papers for *Watership Down* were not yet complete:

> As yet we do not have a script, story board or plan of production (the latter in lieu of schedule) and therefore it is difficult to comment. It seems that preparation, animation, post-production and delivery will take approximately 15 months. The story board is to take 10 weeks, design and animations between them about 6 months, 3 months for photography and the total period of employment of the editor, his staff and equipment is 15 weeks on an 'all in' deal.[8]

Croydon, despite his years of experience, had not previously been confronted with an animated feature ('Presumably these people are expert at animation, but I know nothing about them'), and he admitted that he was out of his depth in trying to determine whether the budget and schedule were appropriate. In fact *Watership Down* was the first animated film that Film Finances had guaranteed: all their previous guarantees had been for live-action studio or location pictures. Nevertheless, Film Finances accepted the proposition

---

[6] BFI press clippings file: 'Turning a Fine Buck', *The Sunday Times*, 9 November 1975.
[7] 'UK Books Giant to Fund Films', *Screen International*, 30 April 1977: 1.
[8] Film Finances Archive (FFA) (London) Realised Film Box 589: *Watership Down*: John Croydon to Robert Garrett, 16 May 1975.

and issued Rosen's Nepenthe Productions with a letter of intent on 21 May 1975: this was an agreement in principle to guarantee the film subject to certain conditions including oversight of contracts and an undertaking from the director that in his view the budget and allocation of film stock were sufficient. The agreed budget in the letter of intent was £928,276, slightly less than the budget originally submitted by Rosen, and Film Finances's fee for providing the guarantee was £48,465.[9] Hubley's confirmation duly followed, and *Watership Down* started production in October 1975.

From the outset, Rosen provided Film Finances with monthly production reports. In the first, Rosen explained that Hubley's 'recent trip' to London had been 'most successful', and a reconnaissance trip had been made to the actual Watership Down in the Hampshire Downs to assist with the design concept of the film.[10] Rosen also noted that Nepenthe Productions had managed to secure the services of Phil Duncan, a former Disney animator, as an animation supervisor, writing that 'although [Duncan] retired from active animation some years ago, this project has induced him to become active once again. It is our opinion that an animation supervisor of Mr Duncan's ability will provide a solid base of experience for the entire animation staff here in London'.[11] Rosen outlined the ways that 'considerable progress' had been made in his second report, particularly in regard to the film's storyboard, and that the 'rough dialogue will be completed by 15 November, and should be ready for submission to the investors' representatives shortly before the Christmas holidays. . . . Character and model design is underway, although definitive characterizations . . . will not emerge until the entire design concept of the film has been established.'[12] Furthermore, Rosen assured Film Finances that the UK-based animators would be ready to commence work on the film's preliminary animation layout from the 'first week of January'. Over the following months, Rosen's reports continued in a similarly positive vein, confirming to Film Finances that the production was on schedule, such as in the reports dated 8 December 1975 and 4 January 1976. In the former, Rosen explained the storyboard would be completed by 18 December for the investors' representatives to view, and in the latter he confirmed: 'Overall, I think it safe to say the production is on schedule – some areas such as the selection of a composer and voices are still to be determined, while other key areas are considerably advanced. Production design and layout have progressed extremely well, and directorial preparation is at a stage where key scenes can be submitted to our animators.'[13]

---

[9]FFA Box 589: Robert Garrett to Nepenthe Productions, 21 May 1975.
[10]FFA Box 589: Production report, Martin Rosen, 1 October 1975.
[11]FFA Box 589: Rosen, 1 October 1975.
[12]FFA Box 589: Rosen, 10 November 1975.
[13]FFA Box 589: Rosen, 4 January 1976.

Table 1.1 Development of the *Watership Down* Voice Casting from the Desired Cast to Final Film

Character	Draft Cast as of 10 February 1976	Proposed Cast as of 22 April 1976	Final Cast in Realized Film (1978)
Hazel	Michael Caine	Victor Spinetti	John Hurt
Fiver	Tom Courtenay	Dudley Moore	Richard Briers
Blackberry	Victor Spinetti	Job Stewart	Simon Cadell
Holly	Leonard Rossiter	Ron Moody	John Bennett
Cowslip	Denholm Elliott	Denholm Elliott	Denholm Elliott
General Woundwort	Harry Andrews	Harry Andrews	Harry Andrews
Bigwig	Michael Graham Cox	Michael Graham Cox	Michael Graham Cox
Kehaar and Rowsby Woof	Zero Mostel	Zero Mostel	Zero Mostel
Hyzenthlay	Helen Mirren		Hannah Gordon
The Chief Rabbit	Ralph Richardson	Ralph Richardson	Ralph Richardson
Pipkin		Roy Kinnear	Roy Kinnear
Dandelion		Richard O'Callaghan	Richard O'Callaghan
Silver		Derek Griffiths	Terence Rigby
Campion		Nigel Hawthorne	Nigel Hawthorne
Clover		Mary Maddox	Mary Maddox
Cat		Lyn Farleigh	Lyn Farleigh

In the production reports that followed in early 1976, questions of who to cast in the lead roles were addressed. On 10 February, Rosen made it clear to the artists that the production team was meeting 'with a view to committing them' to *Watership Down* (Table 1.1). These casting choices are revealing as the original suggestions were very different from the actors who provided the voices in the realized film and were indicative of wanting to cast 'stars' of the British new wave cinema of the early 1960s. Rosen did, however, offer the caveat that 'Scheduling problems, availability and price may very well alter this list. Consequentially, there are alternative choices to fall back on should it be necessary.'[14] Indeed, the *Evening Standard* reported on the alleged issues with employing the cast in March: 'With animation already underway for two months, producer Martin Rosen has no firm idea exactly how Fiver, Bigwig, Dandelion and the other rabbits will look.'[15] By April, however, these issues appear to have been resolved, with Rosen reporting on an updated cast list employed in the realized film. By comparing the two early suggested cast lists with the final cast in the realized film in the table, only Harry Andrews (General Woundwort), Michael Graham Cox (Bigwig), Denholm Elliott (Cowslip), Zero Mostel (Kehaar) and Ralph Richardson (the Chief Rabbit) remained part of the main cast as originally proposed in the production reports. For Hazel and Fiver, the two lead roles, Michael Caine and Victor Spinetti were considered for Hazel before John Hurt assumed the role, and Tom Courtenay and Dudley Moore were the first and second choices to play Fiver before Richard Briers.

By 22 April, Rosen reported to Film Finances that 'the production of *Watership Down* is on schedule and the recent cost statement reflects an estimated saving of £6,600'.[16] Furthermore: 'Principal voice recording has been completed, although considerable pick-up work will be necessary throughout the production. Music recording will take place during the week beginning 10 May, and concentrates on those story areas which require music for animation.'[17] This suggests that the cast listed in the third column of the table, 'Proposed Cast as of 22 April 1976', had actually been employed at this point during the film's production: as a consequence of the major issues that were to arise, certain members of this cast had to be replaced due to the subsequent delays caused in the production and the different approach to animation that *Watership Down* would eventually take.

On reviewing the correspondence available in the Film Finances Archive, it becomes evident over the course of the production that although previous production reports sent from Rosen up until June 1976 were highly positive, tensions were emerging between Hubley and Rosen in relation to their individual visions and intentions for *Watership Down*, with Rosen referring to the issues as 'soft areas'.[18] Blaming Hubley, Rosen believed that 'Directorial decisions, from which all animation flows, have not been made in key areas including layout and background approval and confirming the colour techniques to be employed on the

---

[14]FFA Box 589: Rosen, 10 February 1976.
[15]BFI press clippings file: 'Wanted: New Heroes to Rival Bugs and Thumper', *Evening Standard*, 18 March 1976.
[16]FFA Box 589: Rosen, 22 April 1976.
[17]FFA Box 589: Rosen, 22 April 1976.
[18]FFA Box 589: Rosen, 28 June 1976.

film'.[19] Tellingly, Rosen offered his own views in this report as to his own interpretation and approach towards the adaptation: 'I have asked that "FIVER BEYOND" (Chapter 26) [Rosen's emphasis], not included in the storyboard, be reinstated in the film. The macabre realization of the fate of Sandleford can be highlighted much more effectively through this scene, than reliance upon exposition. It will also confirm Fiver's visionary characteristics.'[20] Rosen wrote to Hubley Studios to iterate his concerns with the director's approach, namely his 'lack of availability' which was causing the production to go over schedule, and that 'Periods of inactivity, particularly in the animation, layout and editing departments during his extended absences have alternated with intense activity when many staff have had to work long periods of overtime'.[21] By 6 August, according to Rosen's production report, the issues between the director and producer had gone some way towards being resolved: 'I am pleased to confirm that the steps taken as indicated in the Report of 28 June have effectively remedied the problem areas. Whereas the animators had 228 feet in work on 28 June, there are now 802 feet in production, with approximately 1,000 feet ready to be handed out.'[22]

However, the truce between Hubley and Rosen was not to last, and by the end of August, Nepenthe Productions wrote formally to Hubley Studios to inform the company that it was to terminate Hubley's employment due to breaches of contract. The reasons outlined in the letter mainly focussed on Hubley not keeping 'to the promises made' in relation to the film's new schedule, and that 'other breaches have been committed and in particular the film appears to depart materially from the storyboard and from the novel. . . . The situation is now intolerable and therefore to avoid irreparable damage being done to the film we have no alternative but to terminate the Agreement.'[23] In response to these accusations, Hubley Studios replied to Nepenthe Productions on 3 September arguing that the company's letter did not demonstrate that the director made any breaches of contract and that 'There are admittedly rather vague references to matters which you claim constitute a breach'.[24] Specifically, they blamed Rosen's 'refusal to adopt the animation techniques recommended by Mr Hubley', and

> Mr Rosen's complaints about Mr Hubley's absence from the studios indicated a lack of understanding on his part that there were times when it was more important for Mr Hubley to be working in collaboration

---

[19]FFA Box 589: Rosen, 28 June 1976.
[20]FFA Box 589: Rosen, 28 June 1976.
[21]FFA Box 589: Rosen to Hubley Studios, 9 July 1976.
[22]FFA Box 589: Rosen, 6 August 1976.
[23]FFA Box 589: Nepenthe Productions to Hubley Studios, 27 August 1976.
[24]FFA Box 589: Hubley Studios to Nepenthe Productions, 3 September 1976.

with the animators in Los Angeles than attending the studios. . . . You also complain of departures from the storyboard and novel. Sub-clause 2(c) [of the contract between Nepenthe Productions and Hubley Studios regarding Hubley's services as director] recognises that it would not be in the interest of the film to insist on rigid adherence to a previously prepared storyboard and departures are permitted with the approval of the producer.[25]

In the letter's conclusion, Hubley Studios informed Nepenthe Productions that they believed Hubley's termination to be 'unjustified', and they would attempt to claim the following damages: the balance of the director's fees and expenses, including travel and hotels, 12.5 per cent of the profits 'as defined by the First Schedule to the Agreement', and damages caused to Hubley's reputation.[26] Nevertheless, Rosen made the executive decision to terminate Hubley's services on *Watership Down*, deciding to direct and produce the film himself.

On being interviewed by Michael Barrier for *Funnyworld* magazine on 26 November, Hubley reflected on the reasons he believed his contract had been terminated, mainly caused by differences in his and Rosen's approaches towards *Watership Down*:

Well, I guess essentially what was involved was a conflict – interpretation of the contract. I always assumed that I had total creative control, and we started running into conflicts over what to do and how to do it, schedules, money, all kinds of things. It just got impossible. So the producer, having had most of the cards, I guess, in terms of the contract, or in terms of what he thought was the contract, said, 'Okay. I'll finish the picture.'[27]

Certainly, it is evident from later reports in *Screen International* that Rosen's issues with Hubley were mainly those of creative difference:

One of the problems was that the characters weren't emerging as characters. I'm not an animator. I'm a film-maker and to me everything serves the story. I find most animators are very myopic. They look at the beauty of the design to the exclusion of the story. . . . I'm interested in how you tell the story. And as I wrote the screenplay, it was logical for me to direct it as well.[28]

---

[25] FFA Box 589: Hubley Studios to Nepenthe Productions, 3 September 1976.
[26] FFA Box 589: Hubley Studios to Nepenthe Productions, 3 September 1976.
[27] Michael Barrier, 'Interview with John Hubley', *Funnyworld*, 26 November 1976. http://www.michaelbarrier.com/Interviews/Hubley/Hubley.html (accessed 21 May 2020).
[28] 'The rigours of Rosen', *Screen International*, 19 March 1977: 9.

By October, it was being reported that Hubley Studios had issued a High Court writ claiming damages and £41,000 on behalf of Hubley, with the *Daily Telegraph* reporting, 'Mr Hubley claims it was agreed that his services be provided for the film, and that his company was paid £103,000. But later, he alleges, the agreement was wrongly ended.'[29] The *Daily Express* further reported that 'There had been fears that work on the film was taking too long to complete and that its topicality would go "off the boil"', and that Hubley was 'left feeling very empty' over the situation.[30] Hubley explained his perspective to Barrier:

> I filed a suit for breach of contract; he's [Rosen] probably going to file a countersuit. And beyond that, I'm really not supposed to talk about it. I've probably talked too much about it already. It's one of those unfortunate things. Doing a feature, there's an awful lot of money involved, and the people who control the money have a lot of power no matter what the hell the contract says. You just have to have a working relationship that's symbiotic. You can write five thousand pages of legal document and it doesn't mean anything if the damned working relation (inaudible).[31]

In the event, the lawsuit was dropped due to Hubley's death following a heart bypass operation on 26 February 1977. This allowed Rosen to later, and disingenuously, claim that Hubley had been sacked for 'working on the side on a *Doonesbury* adaptation for the ABC [television network]', and that Hubley's death made 'reconciliation impossible', leading to Rosen taking over as director of *Watership Down*. Other press reports support the unsubstantiated claim that Hubley's untimely death caused Rosen to take over the production.[32] However, it was actually following Hubley's sacking that he worked with Garry Trudeau on the short film *A Doonesbury Special* (Faith Hubley et al., 1977), and Hubley died during the storyboarding process for this film.

After taking over direction of the film, Rosen decided to take the animation style in a different artistic direction to Hubley, although sources claim that Hubley's early work on the film survives in the opening scenes depicting the myth of Frith and El-ahrairah. There is some weight to this argument, especially when comparing this animation with Hubley's earlier work for the animated short film *Rooty Toot Toot* (1951), which Hubley

---

[29]'Watership Film Firm Sued', *The Daily Telegraph*, 18 October 1976: 9.
[30]Hickey, 'Oscar-winner Sacked from £2m Film'.
[31]Barrier, 'Interview with John Hubley'.
[32]Ed Power, 'A Piercing Screen: How *Watership Down* Terrified an Entire Generation', *Independent*, 19 October 2008. https://www.independent.co.uk/arts-entertainment/films/features/watership-down-film-bright-eyes-rabbits-disease-martin-rosen-richard-adams-disney-a8590226.html (accessed 5 October 2021).

himself directed (Figures 1.1–1.2). Regardless, Rosen elected to omit Hubley from the credits in the realized film.

The sacking of Hubley from *Watership Down* caused Film Finances to follow the production reports for the film more closely. Managing director Richard Soames wrote to Rosen on 7 September 1976 asking:

FIGURE 1.1 *John Hubley's animation for* Rooty Toot Toot.

FIGURE 1.2 *John Hubley's alleged surviving animation in* Watership Down.

[We] have at today's date not received either the revised schedule or any details of the new circumstances [Hubley's termination] to which you refer. We are particularly anxious to have a new cost statement forecast reflecting any changes that you are considering making and confirmation from your financiers that they have been kept fully informed and are agreeable to your proposals.[33]

Following this, Film Finances were duly sent the latest cost statement on the film, indicating an estimated budget overage of £33,764 and an estimated delivery date of 3 September 1977. Rosen explained that 'our contractual date for delivery of the film to Watership Productions Ltd., is at present 31st July, 1977', and that 'a further sum of £83,000 from Distribution sales is available to meet the first overcosts that may be incurred as a result of the extended period'.[34] Film Finances explained that they required confirmation from the film's financiers, Watership Productions Limited of Jersey, that they were 'agreeable' to this new arrangement.[35] In the first production report submitted to Film Finances after Rosen had taken over as director, he outlined that the 'following steps have been taken, or are being effected':

1   A new storyboard based on the existing film is being constructed and into which will be included relevant material to restore the integrity of the story to the film. This will include a closer examination of the personal relationship between the characters, a stronger appreciation of the need to leave Sandleford Warren, and an intensified feeling of jeopardy throughout.
2   Those scenes that do not require new dialogue are being handed out to animators for revision and correction immediately.
3   Recasting of Hazel, Fiver and Blackberry is now in hand.
4   Establishment of bar sheets to effect liaison between all departments within the production.
5   Reappraisal of the music programme with particular emphasis on the underscore.[36]

It was also confirmed that Watership Productions agreed to extend the date of delivery to 30 December 1977.

Film Finances was now becoming increasingly concerned with the growing costs of the film, with Soames writing to Rosen: 'We are in receipt of your Cost Return to the 9th of January, 1977, and in view of the material we

---

[33] FFA Box 589: Richard Soames to Rosen, 7 September 1976.
[34] FFA Box 589: Film Finances to Nepenthe Productions, 14 September 1976.
[35] FFA Box 589: Film Finances to Nepenthe Productions, 14 September 1976.
[36] FFA Box 589: Rosen, 15 September 1976.

saw today, we feel that we should hold a meeting with you at these offices at the very first available opportunity.'[37] Discussion between Film Finances and Rosen continued in a similar vein over the following months, with Soames continuing to stress the guarantor's concerns with a lack of communication regarding the progress of the production and the rising costs of the film:

> In view of the present financial state of the picture and the importance of meeting the new delivery dates, I must ask you to keep us much more fully informed of your progress and forecasts to complete. If you recall the last two telephone conversations between us, you undertook to send me Progress Reports and these have not yet come to hand.[38]

In March, Soames was concerned particularly with the 'considerable disruption and delay', caused mainly by the 'call for a showing [of the animation reel] later this week'. Noting that this had been at the request of the distributors, Film Finances insisted that the costs incurred by the delay should be met by Nepenthe Productions: 'In view of the extremely tight schedule you are working to and the present financial status of the film, any such decision in the future that may affect the schedule or the costs should not even be considered without prior consultation with ourselves.'[39] Replying to Soames, Rosen explained that he was

> anticipating a major screening for a series of prospective buyers of the film at the end of May, i.e. just after the Cannes Film Festival. This has been a schedule for which I have been preparing since January and I do not believe that it will adversely affect our production flow. Indeed, I believe that as this has been a measured programme, the pressures attendant to preparation of the film should accelerate our schedule.[40]

Soames confirmed that Film Finances had no objection to the screening of the film at Cannes, on the proviso that 'this will be no cost to the picture and that it will in no way adversely affect your schedule', and questioned: 'Am I right in understanding that all animation will anyway be completed by that time?'[41] Rosen assured Soames that he was correct:

> We should have completed a substantial part of the animation by 30 May. Our average footage for the ten weeks since the beginning of the year is

---

[37] FFA Box 589: Soames to Rosen, 20 January 1977.
[38] FFA Box 589: Soames to Rosen, 17 February 1977.
[39] FFA Box 589: Soames to Rosen, 15 March 1977.
[40] FFA Box 589: Rosen to Soames, 16 March 1977.
[41] FFA Box 589: Soames to Rosen, 17 March 1977.

278 feet per week. If we meet this average over the ten weeks remaining until the end of May, we should be somewhat over our requirements. Naturally, this does not take into account major problems, which quite frankly I do not envisage.[42]

Matters came to a head on 11 May, after Film Finances received a cost statement for *Watership Down* reporting a current over-cost of £90,724. This prompted Soames to threaten that Film Finances would exercise its right to take over control of the production:

> We are in receipt of the Cost Statement dated the 4th of May 1977.... We have been informed by the Producer, Mr. Martin Rosen, that this cost is based on a schedule, which to date we have not seen and of which we were totally unaware. We understand this new schedule reflects a finishing date at the end of January 1978 and that the film is now running at 113 minutes of screen time. This situation is quite intolerable. Our contractual delivery date is 30th of December 1977 and it has always been understood that the film would be approximately 90 minutes and under no circumstances would it exceed 100 minutes.[43]

Rosen replied immediately to Soames, arguing that there was no new schedule, and shed light on the termination of Hubley's contract, writing that the latter's sacking was due to his 'failure to follow the storyboard and screenplay', and believed that this could financially assist the production overage: 'You are aware of the claim against Nepenthe made by Hubley for approximately $80,000. The successful defence of this case rests exclusively on my testimony. I am sure I need not remind you that these additional funds would be very useful to reduce the estimated overage defined in the last Cost Statement.'[44] Rosen further denied Film Finance's claims of a lack of communication:

> Since commencement of production in late 1975, I have made available to Film Finances all of the resources of the Company for examination. At no time has any question been raised or justification requested on any bills, statements or the general management of the Company during this period. As I have stated on numerous occasions, I welcome any suggestion which might reduce the Company's financial exposure in any area.[45]

---

[42] FFA Box 589: Rosen to Soames, 18 March 1977.
[43] FFA Box 589: Soames to Rosen, 11 May 1977.
[44] FFA Box 589: Rosen to Soames, 13 May 1977.
[45] FFA Box 589: Rosen to Soames, 13 May 1977.

Not surprisingly, Film Finances remained unconvinced by Rosen's somewhat erratic explanations of the problems affecting the production of the film, and the guarantor came to the decision to take over the production to ensure that the growing overcosts did not escalate further and that the film was delivered on time, citing their reasons as follows:

> We must put on record [that] we consider the conduct of this film highly unsatisfactory and unprofessional. We agreed to give a Guarantee on a film of a certain length with a budget we were told was adequate, and to be directed by a well-known Director, John Hubley. Later John Hubley was dismissed without proper consultation with us and furthermore we were not informed that all or a greater part of his work would be discarded. This meant the film re-started with a considerable deficit. Now within the course of one month we are informed the estimated cost has risen by £90,000, and the film is to be considerably longer than agreed and that there are to be certain 'improvements'.[46]

In the event, however, it was agreed between Nepenthe Productions, Watership Productions and Film Finances that the latter would be released and discharged from its obligation to guarantee the production, and on 23 August a Deed of Release was produced and signed by the three companies.[47] In the Deed, it was agreed between the three parties that Film Finances would pay the sum of £60,000 to the film's financiers in order to be released.

Due to the termination of the contract between Film Finances and Nepenthe Productions, the full extent of the final over-cost on *Watership Down* is not known as the guarantor did not continue to receive progress or cost reports. The film was released in the United Kingdom on 13 October 1978, where its distribution was handled by Cinema International Corporation (CIC), and in the United States on 1 November, distributed by Avco Embassy Pictures. The critical reception for the film was broadly

---

[46] FFA Box 589: Film Finances to Nepenthe Productions, 13 May 1977.
[47] *Watership Down* is not the only example of Film Finances being released from its guarantee. For instance, the successful *Tom Jones* (Richardson, 1963) had similar issues to that of *Watership Down* in relation to significant rising overcosts, leading to Film Finances threatening to take over the production of the film. A compromise was reached between Woodfall Productions and Film Finances, whereby the completion guarantor would pay £13,500 to be released from its obligations (FFA Box 346: Deed of Variation between Woodfall Film Productions Ltd and Film Finances, 22 February 1963). For further details on the troubled production history of this film, as well as *Isadora* (Reisz, 1968), where Film Finances was also released from its contract with Universal Pictures, see Llewella Chapman, '"They Wanted a Bigger, More Ambitious Film": Film Finances and the American "runaways" That Ran Away', *Journal of British Cinema and Television* 18, no. 2 (2021): 176–97.

positive. However, one reviewer, 'G. B.,' writing for *Time Out*, did question what Hubley's version may have looked like:

> All one can say about this animated feature is thank God for myxomatosis. The book is another matter: once you've got past fey footnotes explaining that rabbits can count up to five, Richard Adams presents a good solid story, ingeniously and effectively told from the rabbit's minuscule perspective. Had the original director John Hubley been allowed to persevere, maybe some of the virtues would have remained; but as rejigged by producer Martin Rosen, there is nothing. The 'camera' takes a conventionally objective viewpoint, perpetually rolling over rolling countryside, which effectively robs the plot of all its terror and tension. And the bunnies are a crudely drawn, charmless bunch, with the final nail provided by the soundtrack's famous voices, who help turn the film into a radio play.[48]

The production history of *Watership Down*, as revealed by the Film Finances Archive, does not answer that question. But it does bring to light the various tensions and difficulties that bedevilled the making of the film and in the process provides a rare example of a film where a troubled production history did not in the event affect its critical and popular success. As for the credited director of the film, Rosen was able to look back on the experience with humour. When Film Finances wrote to congratulate him on the release of *Watership Down*, his reply even acknowledged his own inexperience: 'Thanks for your note. If you ever need an animation expert (and believe me, I am now), my services are for hire, cheap!'[49]

Acknowledgements

Our thanks to all the staff at Film Finances, London, for allowing access to their archives, especially James Shiras, David Korda and Thoko Mavolwane.

---

[48] G. B., '*Watership Down*', *Time Out*, 20 October 1978: 48.
[49] FFA Box 589: Rosen to Robert Fennell, 18 October 1978.

CHAPTER 2

Revisiting the production of *Watership Down* through the Arthur Humberstone Animation Archive

Klive Humberstone, Nigel Humberstone and Chris Pallant

This chapter seeks to present new ways of thinking about the production history of *Watership Down* (Rosen, 1978), with the ambition being to expand the conversation, and, in doing so, cast light upon the contributions of a hitherto neglected yet long-serving member of the UK animation community: Arthur Humberstone.[1] We also aim to contribute to the overall project of this book, which is to enable a more nuanced appreciation of this important animated film. The intention here is not to lose sight of the collaborative nature of film production, which was a characteristic of the production of *Watership Down* with its crew of almost 100 individuals across a variety of roles; rather, it is simply to take advantage of a surviving archive and to

---

[1] Given the potential for ambiguity and confusion, throughout this chapter the initials K and N will be used in combination with the family surname, when relevant, to denote Klive and Nigel Humberstone, whereas 'Humberstone' presented without initials will refer at all times to Arthur Humberstone. For example: Humberstone, who worked on *Watership Down*, was the father of K. and N. Humberstone.

revisit the materials found within to establish fresh ways of understanding this production.[2] Drawing upon the autobiographical insight of Klive and Nigel Humberstone, Humberstone's sons, interviews with individuals who worked alongside Humberstone on the production of *Watership Down*, and working from the privately managed Arthur Humberstone Animation Archive (which contains a wealth of pre-production materials spanning his forty-five-year career), this chapter reveals the role played by Humberstone during the film's eventful production.

After a short discussion of the chapter's methodology, we will then provide a brief biographical account of Humberstone's working life, before engaging with a number of documents from the Arthur Humberstone Animation Archive. The archival documents consulted here, combined with the new key informant interview conducted during the preparation of this chapter, present new insights related to: the non-standard dialectical production practices employed on *Watership Down*; Humberstone's profound – yet hitherto overlooked – influence over the animal aesthetics found in *Watership Down*; and how the archive can be used to rebuild and deepen our understanding of the richly layered animation workspace.

A brief note on methodology

Given the mixed-method approach adopted when researching this chapter, it is worth highlighting a few key observations about the pros and cons of the methods employed, and how the combination of these methods goes some way to mitigating their individual shortcomings. The three research methods employed here are archival study, key informant interview and the interrogation of autobiographical memory.

Understandably, the privately held Arthur Humberstone Animation Archive has not benefitted from the many activities that support the accession, management and preservation of professionally curated archives. When working with an archive such as the one in focus here, it is essential to remain aware of the many forces – seen and unseen – that have shaped the archive in profound ways before your encounter with it. For example, what motivated Humberstone to keep these documents and, perhaps more importantly, what documents did he discard – either because he perceived little value in keeping them (notes to self, photographic reference, used pens and pencils, for example) or because their continued existence problematized the imposed sense of teleological draughtsmanship evident within those drawn works that were preserved (there is a conspicuous lack of rejected or

---

[2] Crew information gathered from Arthur Humberstone Animation Archive and IMDb listing.

crossed-out work). Then, in the intervening years between Humberstone's retirement and death, how was the original ordering preserved – or adjusted – as the material artefacts were moved between files, cabinets and storage sites? What is certain is that the archive in question represents just a snapshot of *Watership Down*'s production. With this in mind, the archival documents were treated with caution, and every effort has been made to triangulate our inferences by using the other methods noted here in an overlapping manner.³

The key informant interview was conducted with Humberstone's colleague from the production of *Watership Down*, Colin White, who worked as an animator on the production. As a qualitative information gathering tool, interviewing key informants has the potential to be a high-value research method. However, it must also be acknowledged that this approach carries a high potential for bias. For example, biases introduced inadvertently by the interviewer, whereby personal appearance, facial expression, tone of voice, misrecording of answers and ill-considered responses all have the potential to misdirect the informant.⁴ Additionally, failure of memory, given the time spans being covered, and the natural editorialization of memory that occurs as we recall details from the past stand as possible obstacles when interviewing key informants. As Stephen Frosh notes, the human subject is never a whole, since it 'is always riven with partial drives, social discourses that frame available modes of experience, ways of being that are contradictory and reflect the shifting allegiances of power as they play across the body and the mind'.⁵ Yet, when considered in combination with the archival record and the autobiographical memory of K. and N. Humberstone (discussed next) this potential for unconscious – and unhelpful – bias is reduced to an acceptable level.

Finally, the autobiographical memories of K. and N. Humberstone also proved a valuable source of information throughout the researching of this chapter, and also throughout the wider project of bringing this private archive to a wider audience (discussed in more detail later). As a research act, the parsing of K. and N. Humberstone's autobiographical recollections was done in a more organic manner, with notes taken at regular intervals based on unstructured, reflective conversations, but with several instances of more formal semi-structured interviewing taking place over the lifetime

---

³Many of these anxieties around archival research, particularly in the context of television studies, are covered in greater detail by the likes of Kristyn Gorton and Joanne Garde-Hansen, eds. *Remembering British Television: Audience, Archive and Industry* (London: BFI, 2019), Helen Wheatley, ed. *Re-Viewing Television History: Critical Issues in Television Historiography* (London: I. B. Tauris, 2007), and Christine Geraghty and David Lusted, eds. *The Television Studies Book* (London: Arnold, 1998).
⁴Geoff Payne and Judy Payne, *Key Concepts in Social Research* (London: Sage, 2004), 131.
⁵Stephen Frosh, 'Disintegrating Qualitative Research', *Theory & Psychology* 17, no. 5 (2007): 638.

of the research. At all times, the highly constructed and performative nature of memory was kept in mind. As Robyn Fivush writes, autobiographical memory 'is a socio-culturally constructed narrative of one's specific personal life, and as such, is culturally saturated and must be understood through the subjective lens of individual meaning-making'.[6] By remaining attuned to K. and N. Humberstone's place within the wider sociocultural collective, and vigilant of their own familial biases, the autobiographical insights gained were evaluated carefully before feeding into the mixed-method framework identified here.

Who was Arthur Humberstone?[7]

Given that a key objective of this chapter is to cast light upon the hitherto forgotten contributions of Humberstone to the UK animation industry, we must first establish a clearer biographical picture of Humberstone the man. Born in Derby, 1912, Humberstone was an avid film buff and hand-cranked home projection enthusiast with an early infatuation in Cameraless Animation.[8] Following this passion, Humberstone enrolled at Derby Technical College School for Arts & Crafts, learning art, fashion drawing, light and shade modelling but found it to be a piecemeal affair due to there not being an obvious route to a career in animation.

So, in 1942, after reading Robert D. Field's *The Art of Walt Disney*, Humberstone joined the Eagle Amateur Film Society with the intention of making cartoon films. Buying a couple of paint brushes, paints, an office letter punch from Woolworths, he then cut the ends off the brushes to fashion into two pegs to make a rudimentary but effective peg registration system, before punching holes in a wad of typing paper to match. Spurred on by his sister Mary, Humberstone sent some of his drawings to the Walt Disney studio in London, only to have the parcel returned a few days later with a covering letter informing him that the Disney offices were simply a British subsidiary business unit acting on behalf of the Californian parent studio, and that Disney cartoons were not made in this country. However, at their suggestion, he sent his drawings to J. Arthur Rank, as he was starting a new cartoon unit called G. B. (Gaumont British) Animation in the village of Cookham, Berkshire.

---

[6]Robyn Fivush, 'Autobiographical Memory', in *Research Methods for Memory Studies*, ed. Michael Pickering and Emily Keightley (Edinburgh: Edinburgh University Press, 2014), 13.
[7]The biographical detail presented in this section is informed by Humberstone's unpublished memoir and the recollections of K. and N. Humberstone.
[8]Following in the footsteps of contemporary filmmakers such as Len Lye, Norman McLaren and Harry Smith.

Humberstone was interviewed by the highly regarded American animator Dave Hand who, when shown his work, said, 'Yes, they have possibilities, when you come here we will be able to teach you how to draw but the ability to animate comes from in here' – with Hand indicating to Humberstone's head.[9] Hand, who was heading up the new G. B. Animation studio (which would became known in the animation community as Moor Hall), subsequently offered Humberstone his first professional employment as an animator.

In his unpublished memoirs, Humberstone recounts how Hand often attended the 'sweat-box' sessions and was present at the screening of one of Humberstone's early test sequences. As an exercise he had been asked to animate a sack of fertilizer marching over to a flower. The sack had arms and the bottom corners of the bag were made to act as feet. Upon reaching the flower, the sack put its hand into a pocket in its side and pulled out a handful of fertilizer to sprinkle on the plant. Immediately, the flower responded by growing tall and strong. When Hand saw his work, he declared this was not animation, and Humberstone had to do it all again. He was so chastened by Hand's reaction that he promptly telephoned his old firm in Derby and asked for his job back; they were very understanding and agreed. Meanwhile, Humberstone had another go at the offending sequence. This time he made all the movements bolder – the sack marched with a swagger, when the arm went into the pocket it went right down in an exaggerated manner, all rather overdone he felt, but then, he had nothing to lose. When Hand saw this new version the following Thursday, he declared, 'Now that's what I call animation!'[10] Humberstone was elated – he wrote to his old firm cancelling his request for reinstatement.

While Moor Hall produced two series of short animated films (nine *Animaland* cartoons and ten more *Musical Paintbox* shorts), they failed to find an audience and G. B. Animation folded within three short years of its launch. However, the studio's legacy was to live on through the draughtsmanship and quality of the animators it had created. Following Moor Hall's closure at the start of 1950, Humberstone returned to Derby, taking a job as newspaper cartoonist producing a regular strip for the sports page, but when the Halas & Batchelor studio started recruiting for *Animal Farm* (1954), one of his ex-Cookham friends recommended him to John Halas. At his interview, Halas asked Humberstone which animals interested him, to which he replied 'horses', prompting Halas to proclaim: 'Good . . . Then Boxer and Benjamin are yours!'

Moving to London in September 1951, Humberstone took up residence in a flat across the road from the studio in Paddington. When John Halas learnt of this, he said, 'In that case, you can have a key so that you can come back

---

[9]David Jefferson, 'Arthur Humberstone: Senior Animator', *Animator* 14 (1985): 25.
[10]Jefferson, 'Arthur Humberstone', 21.

in the evening to animate.'[11] *Animal Farm* was undoubtedly a hard slog for Humberstone, but whose enthusiasm saw him return to put in overtime most evenings, making countless corrections and winning best 'footage outputs', all helping to meet the target figures set by the American investors.[12]

After *Animal Farm*, Humberstone set up his own company undertaking a variety of freelance work including animated commercials for TV and cinema (Esso Oil, Surf Detergent, Kellogs Ricicles), shorts and TV series (Man of Action, Principle of X-Rays), working with companies such as Rank Screen Services, Shaw Films, Stewart Hardy Films and TV Cartoons. This was a period of prolific output and saw Humberstone amass over 100 titles including his self-initiated pilot *Noddy Goes to Toyland* (1964).

During the mid-1960s, when TV Cartoons (TVC London) were looking to enlist a team of national and international animators to realize the artistic vision of *Yellow Submarine* (Dunning, 1968), Humberstone was identified as an experienced member of the British community and someone to bring in for that production. Alongside feature productions and commercial advertising work, Humberstone still maintained his working relationship with John Halas, contributing to a number of Halas & Batchelor productions including *Dodo, the Kid from Outer Space* (1964), *The Jackson Sive* (1971–2), *The Osmonds* (1972) and *The Addams Family* (1973).

In 1976, Humberstone landed a job on *Watership Down* as Senior Animator.[13] Once again this was initiated by his pro-active nature as, purely on spec, he had sent some drawings of a fox to Martin Rosen, who then invited him to a meeting when John Hubley (the production's original director) would be present. They looked through the storyboard, then Dennis Gardiner (the studio personnel officer) arrived and Humberstone was invited to start work the same day! In the early days, Humberstone worked with Phil Duncan, a former Disney animator who had worked on *Bambi* (Hand et al., 1942). He recalls, 'There were just the two of us in the beginning. We walked the route the rabbits took in their flight to freedom, and a long trek it was, too, but a beautiful day. I shot some film, even obtaining shots of two hares.'[14] Other animators joined during the production, including Gordon Harrison, Alan Simpson, Peter See, Ted Pettingell and George Jackson, constituting a core team of three Layout Artists, three Background Artists, six residential animators and four freelancers.

Humberstone recalls in his memoir: 'Rosen would ask for criticisms. He sat on the floor cross-legged and invited comments. When you pointed out

---

[11] Arthur Humberstone, *Unpublished Memoirs*, in Arthur Humberstone Animation Archive.
[12] Humberstone, *Unpublished Memoirs*.
[13] During the production of *Watership Down*, Humberstone quite literally became a 'Senior Animator', by reaching retirement age in 1977.
[14] Humberstone, *Unpublished Memoirs*.

things to him he nodded wisely and said, "Oh yes! we noticed that – we're dealing with it".[15] 'He sent out appraisal sheets with questions followed by spaces for our comments, such as "what did you think of Hazel?" and "is the character of Big Wig [sic] developing?", and we submitted our thoughts on the matters'. It was a good idea, Humberstone notes, but there was never any follow-up to the questionnaires.[16]

While the film was in production, Humberstone kept twenty-six rabbits in his back garden. He filmed them on Super-8mm running up and down the grass banks and then used the recording of their movements to draw, frame-by-frame, their motion onto sheets of paper. These were then Xeroxed and circulated among the other animators so they could be used as a source of reference.

In 1979, following the completion of *Watership Down*, Humberstone relocated to San Francisco in order to join the rest of Rosen's team to make *The Plague Dogs* (1982).

Gradually winding down his career through the late 1970s and 1980s, Humberstone kept his hand in working with companies like Stewart Hardy Films and Bill Melendez on productions such as *The Lion, the Witch and the Wardrobe* (1979), *SuperTed* (1983–6) and *The Charlie Brown and Snoopy Show* (1983–5). His final big production, as key animator, was *The BFG* completed in 1989.

Looking at the archive

Dialectic production

Typically, animated feature production is a tightly regulated endeavour, whereby various department leads work together across various teams, coordinating the actions of junior staff and reporting back to the director and producer, thereby ensuring that very little energy – and budget – is wasted. As Chris Pallant has written elsewhere:

> In simple terms, live-action filmmaking is a subtractive exercise, while animation, by contrast, is necessarily additive. In almost every situation the live action filmmaker will seek to capture more raw footage than is required, with the foreknowledge that it is the post-production phase of editing that provides the opportunity to best assemble – through distillation – the already-imagined film. Contrastingly, the process of

---

[15]Humberstone, *Unpublished Memoirs*.
[16]Humberstone, *Unpublished Memoirs*.

animation typically sees the same pre-agreed narrative building blocks remade over and over, with increasing refinement on each pass, until what remains is the complete material artefact – the final film.[17]

However, in the context of *Watership Down* and after the departure of Hubley, Rosen's relative inexperience as an animation director created opportunities for less conventional working practices. Trusting his team, Rosen encouraged a more dialectic approach to production, whereby sequences evolved from a series of creative exchanges. Rosen remarks:

> The process in animation is that you give the script or the words that you want the artist to read, and you explain to them what you're looking for in the scene and you read a little before and a little after and read as much of the script as is formed. And then they record it. From that recording the animators then draw what's called line tests, which is a pencil test of the scene, and we film that. And I thought it would be useful to show that again to the voice artist and see if they could bring something else to it. And invariably they did, they brought something else which caused some additional animation to be done, but it was worth it. Because the second reading is always so much better.[18]

Reading Rosen's words, and the iterative process that he describes, it is tempting to see his inexperience as an animation director as a positive, given that this approach to production allowed him to work in ways not rigidly defined by prevailing animation production convention.

We can see that this approach to development recorded within the archive. In a production memo dated 22 August 1977 from Rosen to Humberstone, Rosen requests changes to be made to a previously completed sequence. Rosen writes:

> I would like this scene to open with the Chief Rabbit, full frontal view, answering Hazel's remark with his line 'A bad danger'. After that he should turn slowly around as if reaching to find some tidbit [sic] so that his entire backside is facing Hazel. Then, after a beat, his second line, 'How very upsetting,' which should link with the existing material, 'now what sort of danger I wonder?'[19]

Here, we see an example of Rosen relying on Humberstone's experience – and ability – to adjust the scene accordingly. For the sequence in question, the first

---

[17] Chris Pallant and Steven Price, *Storyboarding: A Critical History* (Basingstoke: Palgrave Macmillan, 2015), 53.
[18] 'Defining a Style', in *Watership Down*, Blu-ray (UK: Universal Features, 2013).
[19] Production memo (22 August 1977) from Martin Rosen to Arthur Humberstone, in Arthur Humberstone Animation Archive.

round of animation would have been created after – and been informed by – the initial sound recording. This was a fairly typical arrangement for hand-drawn animation production. However, Rosen then frequently encouraged the vocal performers to review this rough cut, and quite often this resulted in the audio for sequences being re-recorded, with the performers – in this case John Hurt (Hazel) and Ralph Richardson (Chief Rabbit) – adjusting their delivery based on the completed animation. This second round of review/re-recording/re-animation, which played a large part in the production of *Watership Down*, was – and is – a much less common feature of hand-drawn animation production given the added cost that it brings.[20] Returning to the archive, we see in Rosen's memo of August 1977, precisely this second round of re-animation being advocated, with the instruction being to revise the animation to take account of the updated vocal performance.

Another similar example can be seen in an earlier memo dated 13 December 1976, whereby Rosen explicitly instructs all animation staff to adjust their work on Silver. As Figure 2.1 reveals, as well as highlighting the new ways that Silver is to be characterized, Rosen also instructs staff to disregard the existing voice track, noting that the audio will be 're-shot as post sync'. Furthermore, the performance style of Terence Rigby in *Softly, Softly* (1966–9) is invoked as guide for the animation staff prior to the circulation of the new model sheet. Exchanges like this help to open up new ways of thinking about the chequered production of *Watership Down*. While the bumpy three-year production is well documented, with experienced animation director Hubley departing mid-production (causing a year of disruption), leaving the less experienced Rosen to steer the project through to completion, our examination of the Humberstone archive reveals how this directorial change paved the way for a more dialectical mode of production to develop.[21] This exchange-based production, as detailed earlier, invites a reconsideration of *Watership Down*'s production journey as one of creative freedom rather than directorial disorder.

Drawing from life

Given the subject matter of Richard Adams's original book, which does not shy away from the themes of violence and death, adopting a Disney-esque look,

---

[20]Colin White telephone interview with Chris Pallant, 19 March 2021.
[21]Whether Hubley left *Watership Down* due to creative differences is a contested point. Whereas John Pym, writing in the contemporary trade journal *Monthly Film Bulletin* (1978), suggests the departure was due to creative disagreement, Faith Hubley unambiguously stated when interviewed by Pat McGilligan in 1988 (*Film Quarterly* 42, no. 2: 2–18) that it had 'nothing to do with creativity', hinting that her own ailing health at that time, coupled with that of her husband's, might have played some part in his exit.

MEMORANDUM

TO:— All Animation Staff   cc: Tony Guy   DATE:—13.12.76.
                                Gordon Harrison
FROM:— Martin Rosen

You will be receiving new head model sheets on the character of Silver within the next day or two. We are changing his character from one of dumb and comedic-looking to a stronger, albeit slow-thinking, personality. Consequently, when you receive hand-outs which include Silver <u>do not interpret him according to the voice on the track</u>. This will be re-shot as post sync.

You might keep in mind the character of Terence Rigby, who plays Sgt. Snow in "Softly, Softly", as being representative of the quality of Silver.

Martin Rosen

MR:mpb

NEPENTHE PRODUCTIONS LTD.   SUFFOLK HOUSE, 1–8 WHITFIELD PLACE, LONDON, W1P 6HA. Tel: 01-387 5441

FIGURE 2.1 *Memo from Rosen to* Watership Down's *animation staff, 13 December 1976.*

as seen in contemporary features such as *The Aristocats* (Reitherman, 1970), *Bedknobs and Broomsticks* (Stevenson, 1971) and *Robin Hood* (Reitherman, 1973), would not have worked. However, in an early character line-up (Figure 2.2), we can see a Disney-esque aesthetic where the rabbits are all quite rounded with little attention given to visually distinguishing them based on their individual personalities. While not quite as doe-eyed as Disney's Thumper, these early rabbit designs did not fit the look needed for *Watership Down*.

As noted earlier in the chapter, Humberstone gained a comprehensive professional education working at large animation studios such as Moor Hall and Halas & Batchelor, as well as running his own animation studio, prior to joining the *Watership Down* crew. Consequently, his grasp of the production

FIGURES 2.2 AND 2.3 *Model sheets showing the development of* Watership Down's *characters.*

pipeline was such that he had a clear understanding of the need to use all of the available tools at his disposal to create the specific aesthetic required for *Watership Down*. In a revised model sheet signed with Humberstone's overlapped 'AH' initials and dated 1976, we can see a clear evolution in the character design (Figure 2.3). With more variety across the individual characters in terms of height, weight and demeanour, we can see a commitment to developing an aesthetic that is grounded in the real physical appearance of standard rabbits, with their more elongated faces, more expressive ears and arched bodies, which moves away from the more spherical facial designs, floppier ears and plumper bodies of the earlier model sheet.

When asked about the evolution of these character designs, Colin White recalled:

> I don't know who exactly did it. There was obviously a lot of pre-production stuff that had happened before the production started again [after the departure of Hubley] and looks like someone not so talented has done an earlier concept. So, they've then given this to Arthur to clean up, because his stuff is very anatomical, it is very precise, and he gives the muscles definition, so I think they gave it to him for that reason. The second one is definitely Arthur's style.[22]

White is in no doubt that the look of the rabbits seen in the final film stemmed directly from Humberstone's intervention. Noting how there were just two main animators in the production, Humberstone and George Jackson, White notes how Humberstone 'very much wanted to be the big gun in town, the best', before observing that, while their styles were different, 'Arthur was always trying to make his stuff the very best. He would shoot reference ... he would use this reference and research, and try really hard to be Walt Disney, really.'[23]

Consequently, Humberstone created many pencil and ink sketches of animals such as badgers, rabbits, ducks, horses while working on the film, so, by the end of the 1970s, he had generated quite a large number of animal studies. This study of animal life proved particularly useful when animating the scene where we see the curious farmer's dog sniffing along the bank of the river Enborne. After filming the Humberstone family dog (Ranger) on 8mm, he then projected it back to analyse it. Working from the reference footage he created the sequence we can see in Figure 2.4, which shows how the movement of a dog can be broken down into smaller connected motions. By working in this way, he was able to get a feel for the weight of the dog, how it shifted its weight between its legs and how its tail moved while he sniffed the air with his nose.

What is now apparent, given the triangulation of the new archival- and interview-based research presented in this chapter, is the profound influence that Humberstone had over the film's final aesthetic. Singlehandedly giving definition to the rabbits and Kehaar, as well as informing many of the other

---

[22]Colin White telephone interview.
[23]Colin White telephone interview.

FIGURE 2.4 *The breakdown of a dog in motion, by Arthur Humberstone.*

animal design choices by virtue of his extensive reference and research work, it is time that Humberstone's contributions received greater attention and credit.

Recovering lost workspaces

Given the richness of the Humberstone archive, a key objective in recent years has been to bring these materials, and the insights they provide about the production of *Watership Down*, to new audiences. Picking up momentum in 2018 and feeding into the British Film Institute's focus on animation that year, Humberstone's 1963 short *Noddy Goes to Toyland* was selected for inclusion as one of the season's free-to-view films hosted on the BFI Player. As part of this initiative, Klive and Nigel granted Jez Stewart,

Curator of the BFI's Animation Collection, access to their family archive to help inform the retrospective that was installed at the BFI's South Bank exhibition space that year.

In November of 2018, the authors of this chapter gave the Keynote presentation at the conference 'The Legacy of *Watership Down*: Animals, Adaptation, Animation' held at the University of Warwick. Then, in June 2019, Nigel Humberstone delivered a paper entitled 'Noddy Goes to Toyland (1963): A Case Study from the Arthur Humberstone Archive' at the Society for Animation Studies annual conference. The objective of this conference activity was to bring into focus the contributions of Humberstone by unearthing the narrative exposition, background information and historical context behind the ten-minute *Noddy Goes to Toyland* pilot produced by Humberstone. As a result of changing finance criteria and sales inertia, the film was effectively shelved upon completion, remaining dormant and unseen for years. The presentation featured a rich collection of visual materials, production insight and accounts of correspondence between Humberstone, Enid Blyton and the executive producer Victor Broadribb.

More recently, in 2021, insights from the archive were shared at Canterbury Anifest, with members of the public. As part of this presentation, a recreation of Humberstone's workspace was staged, drawing upon photographs taken during the production of *Watership Down*. Rather than simply treating this in some totemic sense, the curatorial process that supported the recreation of the workspace actually allowed new associative connections to be considered. Several documents from the Humberstone archive contain visual jokes or playful notes written on company paper, which, when taken in isolation, hint that Humberstone may well have been a source of levity within the production. By considering how these seemingly disposable materials might have been displayed for varying lengths of time within the workspace, these documents are granted additional meaning.

To date, little focussed effort has been made to recover the history of the hand-drawn animation workspace. While references to these spaces proliferate animation scholarship, when reference is made to them it is often matter of fact, being just background detail in a discussion focussed elsewhere. The consequence of this neglect is that the social, industrial and individual histories of the hand-drawn workspace, during the form's most pervasive era, are in danger of being lost to time. You might wonder why we should care, but to follow that logic overlooks the layered nature of this particular animation workspace and the extra-textual perspectives they afford.[24]

---

[24] Arguably, stop-motion and CG animation workspaces offer a less concentrated focal point for study, given the fact that many stop-motion animators work standing up, by virtue of the

Examples of the storied nature of the workspace can be found across the world of hand-drawn animation. Writing in his book *Sharing a House with the Never-Ending Man: 15 Years at Studio Ghibli*, Steve Alpert, who worked as Head of International Sales at the studio, writes:

> For a long time at Ghibli, even after the success of *Princess Mononoke*, anybody could just walk upstairs and stand in front of Hayao Miyazaki and watch him work. Miyazaki is an iconic figure in Japan. . . . At work on a film, Miyazaki would sit in a tiny corner of the animators' area at an animator's desk that was identical in every way to any other animator's desk in the room, though the aura emanating from him identified him at a glance as someone unique and special.[25]

While Tom Sito, writing in *Eat, Drink, Animate: An Animators Cookbook*, tells a story about Eric Abjornson, who he worked with on several productions, actually cooking at his animation desk with a convection oven that he kept under his desk.[26]

In the context of *Watership Down*, documents such as this fake production memo (Figure 2.5), this caricature (Figure 2.6) or this model sheet (Figure 2.7) reveal instances of humour, centred around Humberstone's work or demeanour that were situated within his workplace. As a senior figure within production, but with a tolerant personality, Humberstone was evidently seen as a safe individual at which to direct such well-meaning exchanges. By elevating these documents from their current situation, arranged in a decontextualized folder within an organically arranged private archive, and considering them once more as artefacts situated in space – the workspace of Humberstone – draws our attention to small, yet important details.

Looking more closely at Figure 2.5, for example, we find three small holes at the top of the document. While we cannot know with absolute certainty, it is likely that these holes were made by noticeboard pins, perhaps the same pin, as the document was re-mounted on three separate occasions. There is a possibility that only one of the holes was made by the pin that initially fixed the memo to the noticeboard, and that the other two holes were made when other documents were pinned over the top of the memo; this is unlikely given the photographic records of Humberstone's workspaces across his

---

materials employed, and therefore the concept of a workspace morphs more into the concept of a workshop or studio space, while CG animation encourages (with some exceptions, such as Disney and Pixar, for example) a less personalised or invested approach to the workspace habitat.

[25]Steve Alpert, *Sharing a House with the Never-Ending Man: 15 Years at Studio Ghibli* (Berkeley: Stone Bridge Press, 2020): 86.
[26]Tom Sito, *Eat, Drink, Animate: An Animators Cookbook* (Boca Raton: CRC Press, 2019), 36.

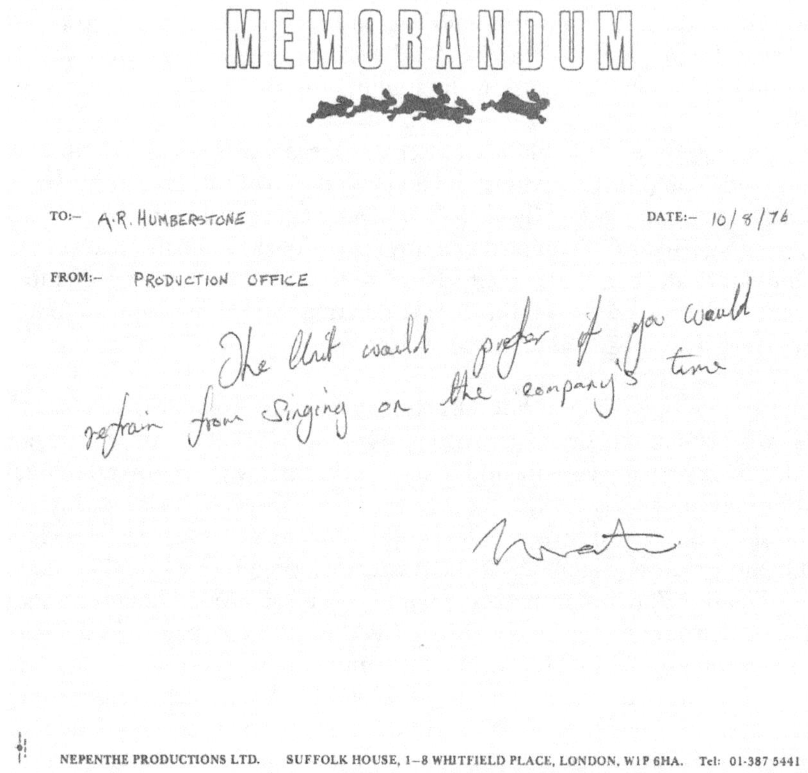

MEMORANDUM

TO:– A.R. HUMBERSTONE   DATE:– 10/8/76

FROM:– PRODUCTION OFFICE

The Unit would prefer it if you would refrain from singing on the company's time

NEPENTHE PRODUCTIONS LTD.   SUFFOLK HOUSE, 1–8 WHITFIELD PLACE, LONDON, W1P 6HA.   Tel: 01-387 5441

FIGURE 2.5 *A fake production memo addressed to Humberstone from the production office, requesting that he 'refrain from singing on the company's time'.*

career, which show consistently orderly arrangements with little or no overlapping documents (Figure 2.8), and it is also unlikely that these were made by adjacent pins given how closely the holes are grouped, thereby indicating that it would have been difficult, if not impossible, to fix three pins in such close proximity.

By the fact that this document resided in private possession, in an undisturbed state until after the death of Humberstone in 1999, we may also judge with some confidence that these pin holes originated when the documents were in active circulation, and not at some intermediate moment of review.[27] Our inferences then, which appear reasonably plausible, suggest

---

[27]For a thoughtful consideration of the acts – and hazards – of archival inference, see Jennifer Meehan's 'Making the Leap from Parts to Whole: Evidence and Inference in Archival

FIGURE 2.6 *A playful caricature of Humberstone.*

that although the memo might well have been intended as a throwaway joke, once in Humberstone's possession this artefact became a treasured possession, which, given the puncture pattern, seemingly moved around his workspace as the production developed and his pinboards become more crowded.

When asked about the nature of the *Watership Down* workspace, White recalled:

> It was a bunch of creative people working in the same space, so it was like a little society. Once you're working on a common project when you're 'in house', you can hear feedback from all the other people there, it was tremendously good! It doesn't happen anymore, really. Nobody was plugged into a Walkman, people would walk around and chat to each other, forming friendships. There was a real sense of community and a common project. . . . We'd be sitting in our cubicles working, but we'd get up and move around a lot more than when you work in a digital

FIGURE 2.7 *A fake model sheet depicting a cartoon Humberstone.*

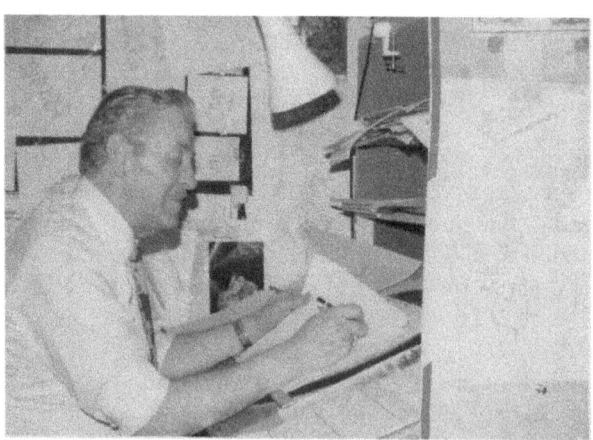

FIGURE 2.8 *Humberstone at work during the production of* Watership Down *at Nepenthe, London.*

studio, there was more interaction. In your cubicle you'd have shelves, space to pin things for reference, or just things you liked, and it created a nice atmosphere.[28]

---

[28]Colin White telephone interview.

White's words neatly capture the richness of the workspace, as well as offering a reminder of Norman McLaren's oft-rehearsed statement about the collapsible temporality of animation production, whereby McLaren proposes that 'animation is not the art of drawings that move but the art of movements that are drawn; what happens between each frame is much more important than what exists on each frame; animation is therefore the art of manipulating the invisible interstices that lie between the frames'.[29] Therefore, the workspace-specific documents found in the Humberstone archive not only point towards the filmic text, but they also present a fresh perspective on the past, or the past-present, of the production moment – and the many in-betweens experienced in that moment. The recreation of Humberstone's workspace represents an attempt to spotlight the material flow of *Watership Down*'s production and the active curation of personal workspace that took place.

Conclusion

Having discussed the value of this privately held archive and having only scratched the surface of the materials held within it, the challenge that lies ahead is ensuring the long-term preservation, management and access of this archive. Furthermore, while this chapter has increased our understanding of the role played by Humberstone both within the production of *Watership Down* and as a respected figure within the UK animation community, and in doing so helped to add greater nuance to our sense of UK animation history, there remains more work to be done – far beyond the scope of this chapter – to reclaim the personal narratives of Humberstone's many colleagues whose personal archives and professional contributions have yet to be studied with the level of detail offered in this chapter.

---

[29]Georges Sifanos, 'The Definition of Animation: A Letter From Norman McLaren', *Animation Journal* 3, no. 2 (1995): 62.

CHAPTER 3

'Trying to eat grass that isn't there':

Unearthing a Lapine Corpus in Richard Adams's *Watership Down* and its film adaptation

R. Grider

In 1978, after many years of challenging developmental hurdles (see Chapter 1 of this volume), the Nepenthe Productions adaptation of Richard Adams's *Watership Down* premiered in the Empire theatre in Leicester Square.[1] The film is notorious among people that grew up with it and among BBFC employees who must still field complaints contesting the film's U rating forty years later. To many, the film captures the grim reality of animal existence that was present in the book and represents the world Adams built with a great degree of fidelity. To others, it is a story grimly out of place among other animated fare: offering little in the way of explanation for its tone, its violent imagery or the more fantastic elements of its world-building. Adams's rural English countryside becomes

---

[1] Ben Simon, 'A Conversation with Terry Rawlings', *Animated Views*, 22 May 2015. https://animatedviews.com/2015/conversation-with-terry-rawlings/ (accessed 18 October 2021).

vast from the viewpoint of a little rabbit, the setting for an epic journey about building a new home in the face of cataclysm. Thus, Adams's Down becomes the home of an entire culture existing in parallel with but hidden from our own – a rabbit culture with its own stories, lessons, values and crafted language specifically for the rabbits to use. Having been a unique feature of the book, the language was given life in Nepenthe's adaptation: a move that had the potential to be met with confusion by viewers who were not as familiar with the original work.

The use of constructed languages (conlangs) in television, literature and film was not an unknown concept at the time of the film's premier, with *Star Trek*'s Klingon serving as perhaps the most widely known example of such outside written works – a constructed language mentioned in passing within the original series (1966–9) but first *heard* by viewers in the 1979 film, used to carry cultural material for an alien species of the same name.[2] However, unlike Lapine's fragmentary and translated state, Klingon's lexical corpus is much more extensive, its syntactic systems made much more transparent to the interested fan. Indeed, this conlang is now so extensive and widely studied that an opera entirely in Klingon exists, and academic conferences are held annually with Klingon as their primary language for content delivery. Aside from functionally crafted artificial languages like Esperanto, it is rare for conlangs built for artistic purposes (artlangs) outside the realm of J. R. R. Tolkien's works to be treated with such levels of interest, validity and academic acceptance. Lapine in particular, due to its fragmentary existence, is often considered as more of an art project than a linguistic one – a quirky footnote in the history of constructed fantasy languages, constructed by a non-expert, an outsider in the field of linguistics.

Languages, even fictional ones, do a lot more work than simply allowing communication between users. Language conveys prestige or loyalty or even identity, making moving between two languages in a text a delicate balancing act between literal meaning and cultural weight. When we view Adams's text as a vessel to hold cultural material – animal cultural material – it and its subsequent adaptations demonstrate that this is true even for Lapine, a language previously described as underdeveloped. Despite the language's fragmentary state, there is a lot more evidence for its presence beyond the directly glossed words that most give it credit for; and through this language, the *Watership Down* rabbits possess the means and the agency to describe their experiences outside the colonizing species' frame of reference, and outside their very language – something a lot more powerful

---

[2] A. Overbeeke, 'Fictional Languages in Film and Television', *Academia.edu*, 22 December 2014. https://www.academia.edu/12472592/Fictional_Languages_in_Film_and_Television (accessed 18 October 2021).

than simply 'serving the narrative'. In this text, where bilingualism is at the heart of the undercurrent of many rhetorical encounters, we – the humans – are the outsiders looking in. In this chapter I examine Hazel's story, Fiver's story and all of the rest of the stories in *Watership Down* as stories for rabbits, made available to humans via translation and, as is the case for all other translations, the influence of the source language cannot be fully removed in translation whether the finished product be a book, a film or something else entirely.

The linguistic landscape of Adams's *Watership Down*: From page to screen

To gain an understanding of how Lapine functions in translation, one must understand the ecosystem that it exists in, and how it interacts with other languages that it comes into contact with. On pages 19 and 20 of *Watership Down*, Adams establishes the language hierarchy present for the rest of the novel; here, we learn which languages the characters know, which languages they do not know and who they use those languages with. When this scene begins, rabbits Hazel and Fiver are talking idly and grazing in the fields beside their home when they come across a strange new object in their environment, surrounded by the foreboding smell of human beings.[3] This object is a sign announcing an upcoming construction project that will certainly destroy their home. Both rabbits express confusion at the presence of the new object and at the markings that cover it but leave the area with a non-specific sense of danger.[4] The sign itself is illegible to them, and it reminds the reader that the rabbits in Adams's text do not speak or read English, but Lapine – a rabbit language steeped in rabbit cultural material and its own rabbit rhetoric. This is not an isolated incident, but it is merely the first; throughout *Watership Down* and Adams's second text within the same universe, *Tales from Watership Down* (1996), the rabbits repeatedly are able to communicate with other wild animals but note their inability to understand human speech, writing or thought processes. Beyond this point in chapter one, we may consider any dialogue in Adams's work between rabbit characters to be a viable source for information on Lapine substrate post-translation, drastically increasing the corpus size usually attributed to the conlang.

Additionally, it becomes clear that Lapine is not only unintelligible to humans but that proximity to human culture and domestication seems to

---

[3] Richard Adams, *Watership Down* (New York: Avon, 1975), 19.
[4] Adams, *Watership Down*, 20.

alter if not remove an animal's capacity for animal–animal communication – the rabbits rescued from the hutch on Nuthanger farm seem to speak strange but fully intelligible Lapine[5] while the mute farm cats from the book speak in sinister, clipped utterances in the film.[6] These animals occupy a border space, both in terms of language and level of belonging to the world of wild animals. Kept rabbits are outsiders to wild rabbits, their speech inherently coloured by their interactions with humans. Similarly, cats are even further alienated from the world of rabbits by both their contact with humans and their status as *elil*, or predatory species that threaten wild rabbits; even when Hazel taunts the Nuthanger farm cat in Hedgerow, the text points out that it does not reply while hinting that it could have.[7] The farm dog, an example of a fully domesticated creature, is shown not to speak at all; he becomes a silent killing machine, single-mindedly harrowing wild animals once he is set free from his chain. The rabbits are able to communicate with other wild animals, such as Kehaar the gull and the mouse in chapter twenty, but it is illustrated to be difficult.[8] The language at play in these exchanges between different wild species is not Lapine, but a second, entirely unrepresented conlang called Hedgerow that serves as a bridging language between Lapine and a more universal form of wild animal speech. The rabbits' interactions with the character Kehaar and the clipped, streamlined syntax structure they use in these exchanges illustrate the difference between how the rabbits talk to each other and how they talk to other animals via Hedgerow; at the textual level, Adams represents this with a kind of eye-dialect for Kehaar's speech grounded in what S. P. Corder describes as 'foreigner talk'.[9] In the film, Zero Mostel's memorable performance as Kehaar and the rambling musical overtones that seem to follow him around carry this into the adaptation, setting his speech patterns apart from the rest of the Lapine speaking cast. This shared linguistic landscape between both texts provides us with a level ground not only for comparing the two but for drawing conclusions about the use of translated Lapine as it evolved from original text to adaptation. To build a base for this, I used the method of qualitative data gathering, cataloguing and analysis described in the following section.

---

[5] Adams, *Watership Down*, 202.
[6] Adams's use of the cat as an animal that is between tame and wild has precedent both in literature and in the field of animal studies. Consider T. S. Eliot's 'The Naming of Cats' (1939) where all cats have three names, including one humans use, one cats use and one they only know themselves: to Eliot, no one truly knows or owns a cat. Similarly, cats find themselves uniquely in between languages and levels of agency here.
[7] Adams, *Watership Down*, 204.
[8] Adams, *Watership Down*, 149.
[9] S. P. Corder, 'The Language of Kehaar', *RELC Journal* 8, no. 1 (1977): 1.

Cataloguing instances of translation: Method and data examples

As William Labov points out in 'The Study of Language in its Social Context', the identity- and community-building power that language wields is equally as powerful as its ability to spread and share ideas.[10] The power of language to communicate respect, intimacy and prestige in speech cannot be ignored when exploring the discourse of a closed group, and the presence of a unique lexis must be noted if a text is to undergo a translation. For a working definition of translation types and functions, we will refer to Christiane Nord's work in *Translating as a Purposeful Activity*.[11] What is the *purpose* of the translation present in Adams's novel? If the purpose of the Lapine conlang is to preserve rabbit identity, then the purpose of translation is for narrative ease for a non-rabbit audience. The search for a cultural substrate in translated casual dialogue is mirrored in Klaus Krippendorff's method for content analysis, where he notes that the methodology excels in exploring discourse and cultural material because of its focus on contextualizing the data collected by the researcher and the ability of language to hold, preserve and transmit culture across time and space.[12] As content analysis can be used on a wide range of media, this method will also allow us to explore the same guiding questions and collect the same sort of data from both the novel and its subsequent animated film adaptation in 1978 to determine if there has been a transfer of rabbit culture between the two texts. This content analysis seeks to answer the following questions:

1 In what contexts is Lapine used in the narrative?
2 Which rabbits are more likely to use Lapine?
3 What types of words remain untranslated to English?
4 Can we identify translated Lapine substrate in English passages of the text?

Content analysis as a method seeks to answer questions by utilizing both quantitative and qualitative data. Through content analysis and computer-aided qualitative analysis, all instances of rabbit dialogue, monologue and

---

[10]William Labov, 'The Study of Language in its Social Context', in *Advances in the Sociology of Language Volume 1: Basic Concepts, Theories and Problems: Alternative Approaches*, ed. Joshua A. Fishman (The Hague: Mouton & Co: 1971), 152–216.
[11]Christiane Nord, *Translating as a Purposeful Activity: Functionalist Approaches Explained*, 2nd edn (New York: Routledge, 2018).
[12]Klaus Krippendorf, *Content Analysis: An Introduction to its Methodology* (Thousand Oaks: Sage, 1980), 75–7.

inner reflection in the text and film were collected, recorded, and catalogued according to the following closed coding protocol:

Purely Lapine words, utterances and phrases – sub-categories

1. Singular words [LAP:W]
2. Phrases and idioms [LAP:P]
3. Character Names [LAP:N]

'Moments of translation' – sub-categories

1. Dialogue with highly English construction – translated for ease of access to plot [lENG:D]
2. Translated Lapine Idioms and phrases – non-traditional use of English words [lENG:I]
3. English half of an English/Lapine pair – English versions of rabbit names, etc. [lENG:P]

These tags allow for data points to be grouped together and for the frequency of various words, grammatical constructions and word relationships across the entirety of the text to be determined and represented visually – especially when additional data is associated with each point.[13] For this analysis, all entries will also include associated page numbers (if applicable), scene numbers (if applicable), which characters are listening to each utterance and which characters are speaking. The frequencies of specific character interactions while using Lapine, word correlation and word type can all be calculated from the saved contextual data.[14] While simple word frequency calculations can be limiting, the context-based approach of this method allows for more meaningful conclusions to be drawn, particularly when qualitative data is also paired with frequency.[15] Krippendorff's methodology for content analysis allows for an iterative approach to data collection and provides advice for observers on recording and organizing their data. To ease data transfer between recording and the qualitative analysis software, all raw data collected from the text was kept in a Microsoft Excel document.

---

[13]Krippendorf, *Content Analysis*, 15.
[14]Krippendorf, *Content Analysis*, 59.
[15]Krippendorf, *Content Analysis*, 413.

After applying this method to the primary text, we are left with over 300 individual data points across all coding categories. Table 3.1 displays a partial selection of data from the novel: the number of datapoints as organized by chapter and tag. Likewise, Table 3.2 displays available data from the 1978 film.

Even before analysing the raw data with the qualitative analysis software, we can see obvious spikes in Lapine usage in particular chapters of the text, namely chapters six and ten; this is noteworthy, particularly chapter six, because it has an unusually high frequency of singular Lapine words including names, honorific titles and words for other concepts (mostly nouns). This is a common occurrence in translation for names are, as Maria Tymoczko describes, 'often the semiotic elements of a text that are most urgent and at the same time the most problematic to be translated,

Table 3.1 Lapine Language Data from the Novel *Watership Down* (1972) by Chapter and Data Tag, Chapters 1–10

Chapter	LAP:W	LAP:P	LAP:N	LENG:D	LENG:I	LENG:P
1	3			12	1	6
2	4	1		19	1	8
3	5	1		12	1	12
4	6			17		2
5	1			5		2
6	42			6	3	
7	3	2		12	1	2
8	2	1		32	1	8
9	9		1	18		2
10	17			46	7	3

Table 3.2 Lapine Language Data from the Film *Watership Down* (1978) by Section and Data Tag

Section	LAP:W	LAP:P	LAP:N	LENG:D	LENG:I	LENG:P
Intro	14		3	8	2	2
Feature	21	5	12	26	14	26

especially due to their semiotic significance which is often culture-bound'.[16] This chapter corresponds to the part of the film that has been labelled 'Intro' in Table 3.2; this particularly memorable section depicts a creation myth of sorts for the Lapine culture.

In chapter ten of *Watership Down*, we are confronted with a heavy reliance on an unusual amount of dialogue; this makes sense when we consider the fact that chapter ten has the group of protagonists confronting a road and a car for the first time, and this prompts an extended discussion between the rabbits. From the data collected, there also appears to be a strong correlation between the use of Lapine words and storytelling. Major outlier chapters like chapter six are almost wholly dedicated to sharing Lapine myth, and they are shared orally as a story within the overarching narrative; thus, characters that are credited with being particularly gifted storytellers tend to exhibit a more frequent use of the conlang. These chapters boast a large number of untranslated rabbit names and words for other animals, as well as one of the largest numbers of translated phrases and idioms – not to mention a number of life lessons taught by the folk hero El-ahrairah. Dandelion, the member of Hazel's group that tells the majority of these stories, carries a certain kind of prestige among the other rabbits, and they call upon him to tell a story when everyone is in particularly low spirits, or when they meet another group of rabbits that do not seem to share the same cultural practices.[17] In this section, they ask Dandelion to tell a story that will impress the outsiders; the unusual rabbits from Cowslip's Warren express disinterest in traditional rabbit culture – a response that Hazel's rabbits find disconcerting. The newcomers instead share a kind of free-verse poem unlike anything the others had ever heard before that use much less of the Lapine language cues that we come to see from our main characters. Hazel and the other rabbits find the poem to be unfamiliar and almost alienating, and after a series of nearly deadly incidents they soon take their leave of the place.[18] While the hidden dangers of Cowslip's Warren can be read both as a comment on the complete rejection of traditional culture and as further evidence to the dangers of living close to humans, this scene also serves as a good demonstration for what Walt Wolfram and Natalie Schilling outline as the ability of language to serve as an identity marker for both overt and covert prestige, not just a communication tool.[19] While the two groups of rabbits communicated fairly well, the differing levels of regard that they held for their language and the cultural practices contained within it inevitably put them at odds. Even in its

---

[16]Maria Tymoczko, *Translation, Resistance, Activism* (Amherst: University of Massachusetts Press, 2010), 224.
[17]Adams, *Watership Down*, 102.
[18]Adams, *Watership Down*, 127.
[19]Walt Wolfram and Natalie Schilling, *American English: Dialects and Variation* (Hoboken: John Wiley & Sons, 2015), 175.

fragmentary state, Adams's conlang clearly serves multiple functional roles within the text at both a base communicative level and at a deeper level of cultural interaction – not only between groups of rabbits but between rabbit characters and human readers.

The interconnection between one's perception and how one uses language to describe experiencing life is uniquely centre stage when looking at animal language and experience, made further visible by the use of constructed words that defamiliarize the rabbit experience from the human. While we as humans will never truly know what it is like to be as low to the ground as a rabbit, the way Adams uses both his conlang and defamiliarizing language severs the reader's reliance on human perception. Instead, readers are left to build a meaning from context or to speculate on the meaning on their own by further engaging with the animal world portrayed in the rest of the text. This is even discussed in chapter eighteen, albeit in a roundabout way, when the rabbits compare their perception of the sky (rather, the horizon, which they can most easily see) to that of a taller animal like a human. But perhaps the most fitting example of this is the rabbit idiom on page 340, where Fiver works to convince Hazel to step back from his desire to get work done while he waits for a leg injury to heal: 'you're trying to eat grass that isn't there.' On the one hand, we might try to negate this example by pointing out that we as English speakers have a similar adage – you're 'grasping at straws' or looking for connections between events or ideas that do not actually exist – yet at the same time, that does not quite fit the meaning if we look at the context in which Fiver is using it. The rabbit idiom is more about being patient and waiting for things to grow, the similarity in form to our idiom representing a false cognate or false equivalency in a translation setting. Doesn't acknowledging this connection between our world and theirs confirm that there is an undercurrent of a culture that is not quite our own permeating even the English of the text, even though it is never explicitly confirmed? The paradox of the grass idiom is just one example that illustrates the subtlety that this translated Lapine can take on and is at its most visible if we approach the document from the vantage point of a translator, both as a reader and as a scholar.

Film implications

When I first embarked on this project in late 2018, I was not convinced that the film, which spent many years languishing in production troubles under many different sets of hands, would align itself as closely to the linguistic model presented in the book. Where the book has the opportunity to rely on translation aids, like footnotes, asides and a glossary, these genre conventions that are possible in a textual medium would not be possible to implement in an audio/visual experience without distracting the viewer from the story. To reach a general audience, the Lapine conlang stood at risk of being cut, subtitled or explained in an introductory passage. Upon watching it in full, I was fascinated to see that it did neither of those things.

Much like parts of the translation itself, the film's choice to depict its rabbits, though animated, as realistically as possible extended also to its treatment of their language as it was represented in the original book. The Lapine words chosen to appear in the film were treated as part of reality – used without gloss, explanation, subtitle and sometimes without context in a way that made the viewer pause and reevaluate what they were hearing. Where the novel made an attempt to ease the reader into Lapine language learning, the film chose to throw viewers into the deep end of the pool, using the ambiguity of the presentation of the conlang to produce the same defamiliarizing effect that places focus on a rabbit's rather than a human's perspective that Adams's attention to the language in the book initially produced. Adaptation is, in some senses, a sort of translation all its own, and the move from book to film represented another step in the translation process that chose a unique way to continue to represent and preserve rabbit culture.

A film is a fully curated experience, and in *Watership Down* the first thing the audience experiences is the foregrounding of rabbit culture; before the opening scene of the book, before the name of the film or the credits are shown, the prologue presents the audience with a Lapine myth heavy with Lapine dialogue. The origin story of the Lapine folk hero El-ahrairah is also present in the book, but not until chapter six. Not only does the folk tale foreshadow what skills the protagonists will need to survive the dangers of the story and pay tribute to the late John Hubley, the original director and animator for the film prior to his early departure from development due to disagreements, but it is an excellent example of introducing new viewers to an unfamiliar culture via cultural material. Before we get to meet any of the protagonists at all, we first meet their culture and – specifically – the significance of their traditional names. After all, this genesis story of a sort is how the rabbit hero *El-ahrairah* gets his name: 'Prince with a Thousand Enemies' when translated directly from Lapine. In translation, names are known for carrying a lot of cultural weight and for posing unique challenges for translators who must choose between preserving the original name and the cultural material that goes with it or choosing an equivalent in the target language to make the meaning clearer for the reader.[20] Adams's novel and Rosen's film consistently show the fluidity and situationality of such translation choices, choosing when to refer to rabbits with their English name and when to use their Lapine name. As is the case for rabbits with paired names like Fiver/*Hrairoo*, the use of the traditional name by a trusted rabbit functions as a uniquely rabbit auditory expression of intimacy.

---

[20]Lincoln Fernandes, 'Translation of Names in Children's Fantasy Literature: Bringing the Young Reader into Play', *New Voices in Translation Studies* 2 (2006): 46–7.

Beyond the base level of speech, Rosen's film uses a number of other strategies to replace the function of the glossary that are more appropriate for film as a medium, including visual symbolism. An early example of this in the film occurs when Hazel and the other rabbits narrowly escape the dangers of Sandleford Warren. Bigwig cautions Hazel against making the survivors run too far on the first night or 'They'll go *tharn*' – a Lapine word to describe a state of catatonic, paralysing fear that prey animals sometimes experience when faced with their own mortality. In this case, the conlang is not decorative but functional, not a veneer of imagined culture but a direct symbol for a concept that lies outside the human experience as a non-prey animal. As we explored within the text, a reader might encounter this word and immediately turn to footnotes or the glossary for an explanation; *tharn* in the film, in contrast, is never explained or questioned by another character. Another example that we might explore is *hrududu*, a Lapine word for a motorized vehicle that means to imitate the sound a motor makes when it runs, very likely to be the main way a hearing-reliant animal like a rabbit might experience a car. Here, the film chooses to show signifiers and signified visually; when the rabbits encounter a road – a structure they are less than familiar with – Bigwig, a more well-travelled and knowledgeable rabbit, explains that the road is a path for a *hrududu*. When another rabbit makes a puzzled noise, it prompts an explanation as dialogue: 'You know, a *hrududu* – it runs faster than we can, but they don't mind us.' At this moment in the film, the *hrududu* in question speeds by, scattering the rabbits from where they stand on the road and directly relating the Lapine word with the image of the familiar object (Figure 3.1).

This scene is also noteworthy for its use of the translated Lapine phrase 'Man-thing', which appears throughout the novel and seems to be a stand-in blanket term for human-crafted objects for which rabbits have no context. While things like cigarettes and bullets can be related to familiar-looking objects – 'white sticks' and 'black stones' respectively – something like the car holds no familiarity to anything the rabbits have context for. In these situations, only an invented phrase like 'Man-thing' will convey the right idea to an animal audience. Humans, on the other hand, might be left wondering just which 'Man-thing' they mean in any given situation. Both the film and the novel decenter the human point of view with this defamiliarization technique and make us pause to question just how much of our own perception as human we project onto stories that might not even be for us.

Conclusion: The value of the animal, the outsider and art

Clearly, the use of Lapine is equally sophisticated in the novel and film versions of *Watership Down*, yet it is generally sidelined or excluded from

FIGURE 3.1 *The car's appearance.*

scholarly discussions of conlangs. In the end, questions surrounding animal texts, constructed languages and animal culture representation across media all come down to a question of value: How do we determine the scholarly value of a creative endeavour, how do we promote the representation of experiences beyond the human as valuable and how does a piece of art's distance from our own experience as scholars or as humans affect our ability to see value within it? The question of value and how we see it in the experience of the Other has remained a steady presence throughout humanities scholarship and is one of those questions rooted in individual ambiguity that tends to defy a concrete, well-defined answer. *Watership Down* itself has faced this same line of questioning on multiple fronts: Can animated films be considered in scholarship? Are animal stories intended only for children and therefore exempt from the study? Can a human writer or audience place value on the animal experience without exploiting the animal? Is a project created by a non-expert inherently unvaluable because of the author's lack of accredited experience? To answer each of these questions for Adams's works would be an entire book in itself. But for the case of Lapine culture, I would like to return briefly to the Lapine artlang itself and to the similarities it and other similar animal-centred projects share with the world of Outsider Art. Defined by Roger Cardinal in 1972, Outsider Art is now often erroneously applied to all art produced by the untrained, outside the mainstream, professional art world. But more accurately, Outsider Art is closely related to *Art Brut* and is often produced by marginalized groups that are not only not participating in the mainstream art world but completely cut off from it and from major society as well. The art of children and of asylum patients were first considered in this way, and the term has expanded since then to include other marginalized groups.[21] Both interpretations of the term are poignant when we consider an art language as a piece of art, particularly an art language meant to represent a marginalized, voiceless group like that of an animal. They become even more poignant when we consider the disagreements Outsider Art can spark within the larger community, particularly in terms of value, prestige and gatekeeping into the greater art world; while many outsider artists experienced no prestige during their lived lives, their work enjoyed relative popularity upon its post-mortem discovery for its difference from the contemporary modernist movement. Now consider the parallel. Adams was not a professional linguist, and though he did briefly correspond with one while creating his conlangs for *Watership Down*, he did not engage in the discourse of the community at large or retain scholarly background in linguistics as Tolkien did, for example. When browsing texts related to the history of conlangs and their function or creation, the section dedicated to Lapine is often a handful of statements, even a footnote while other conlangs like Klingon and Quenya receive chapters, essays or even entire books dedicated to analysing their role and function in their respective works. Should Lapine be considered less worthy of study simply because it is small and elusive? Is Adams's work less valuable than a linguist's? While it is an overstep to ascribe a label to a creator, particularly in a genre outside the one in which he works, the parallels here surrounding acceptance and community gatekeeping have notable ramifications when considered through the lens of humanities scholarship. After all, Adams himself was no stranger to humanities scholarship as a holder of a BA in modern history from Worcester College, Oxford. If we begin to make judgement calls regarding art based on the creator's academic experience or prestige, not only are we cutting out large swathes of well-studied, extant works by marginalized creators denied access to such institutions, we are wilfully ignoring and discouraging new works by enthusiasts that might lack the prestigious backing of organized education. Conlangs have always been an enthusiast's project, so closely associated with fantasy worlds and science fiction and the social outsider groups that enjoy them. To say that they are less worthy of study than other more grounded works is to ignore this inherent aspect of their existence.

And what of the animals represented by Adams's work? If we were to take the comparison one step beyond and consider the speakers of Adams's conlang, through translation, the true users and owners of that cultural material, what does the act of gatekeeping Outsider Art based on the values of the established art world imply for marginalized animal narratives within the realm of the academic? Perhaps this is me grasping at straws or 'trying to eat grass that isn't there', but I think it is a grave situation that needs considering.

---

[21]John Maizels, *Raw Creation: Outsider Art and Beyond* (London: Phaidon, 1996), 113.

PART II
Animal stories

CHAPTER 4

Animating utopia:

Aesthetic instability and the revolutionary gaze in the film adaptation of *Watership Down*

Lisa Mullen

'It's only a made-up story,' Richard Adams told a radio journalist in 2007. 'It's in no sense an allegory or parable or any kind of political myth.'[1] He had made similar pronouncements regularly since the publication, in 1972, of his novel, *Watership Down*.[2] The story follows a group of principled rabbits, led by their resourceful leader, Hazel, as they reject the feudal stratifications of the society into which they were born and embark on a cross-country journey to found a warren of their own, based on Hobbesian principles of rationality and justice. Hazel's enlightened social prospectus is yoked to the millenarian prophecies of his dreamy brother Fiver, who foresees blood, shadows, death and danger if they should fail in their mission. Adams may have dismissed the idea that his story harboured an ideological or theological agenda, but its archetypal motifs continue to invite allegorical readings; one

---

[1] 'Interview: Richard Adams', *BBC Berkshire*, 16 March 2007. http://www.bbc.co.uk/berkshire/content/articles/2007/03/16/richard_adams_interview_feature.shtml (accessed 22 September 2020).
[2] Richard Adams, *Watership Down* (London: Puffin, 1973).

recent example suggests that the rabbits' flight from Sandleford Warren, and the search for a promised land on Watership Down, reflects biblical accounts of the Exodus from Egypt, for instance; another interprets the rabbits' quest as a political pilgrimage in defence of the virtues of liberalism, with the freedom-loving bunnies navigating a workable pathway between the twin perils of decadence and totalitarianism.[3]

This temptation to anthropomorphize has been conditioned by centuries of fairy tales, from Aesop's fables to George Orwell's 1945 novel *Animal Farm*, in which animals make conveniently simplified avatars for individual human traits and tendencies and provide imaginative space in which to reveal, and perhaps dismantle, the status quo. As Orwell remarked, 'a "perfect" society only becomes thinkable if the human mind and even the human physiology are somehow got rid of.'[4] Indeed, this practice is so widespread across history and culture that perhaps it is impossible to write a story about talking animals *without* creating an allegory, wittingly or otherwise. Later in this chapter, I will consider the residual rabbit-ness of the Watership rabbits and the eco-biological imperatives which Adams implicitly posited as the 'real' engine of his narrative in his various denials of allegorical intent.[5] I will, however, delve unapologetically into the symbolic earth which the author preferred to leave unburrowed. Rather than proposing yet another interpretative key with which to unlock the rabbits' symbolism, I want to consider how the narrative's semantic procedures work to prompt, or disrupt, such interpretations, and how the novel's already apparent porosity was compounded by its adaptation into film. The 1978 animation, I argue, not only re-reads the utopian message of the original text but reveals the instability of the utopian impulses of narrative as such – that is, as a category of political as well as aesthetic discourse.

Black zigzags: Animation, affect and politics

In her 1926 essay 'The Cinema', Virginia Woolf argued that the adaptation of novels into films was an animalistic activity, red in tooth and claw. 'What

---

[3]Nathan Abrams, 'The Secret Jewish History of Watership Down', *Forward*, 15 June 2018. https://forward.com/culture/film-tv/402920/the-secret-jewish-history-of-watership-down/ (accessed 18 October 2021); Ross Douthat, '*Watership Down* and the Crisis of Liberalism', *New York Times*, 22 October 2019. https://www.nytimes.com/2019/10/22/opinion/watership-down-liberalism.html (accessed 18 October 2021).
[4]George Orwell, 'Review of *An Unknown Land* by Viscount Samuel' (1942), *Complete Works*, Vol XIV, ed. Peter Davison (London: Secker & Warburg, 1998), 254.
[5]R. M. Lockley's *The Private Life of the Rabbit: An Account of the Life History and Social Behaviour of the Wild Rabbit* (London: Corgi, 1976) is cited by Adams as a source of inspiration in the 'Acknowledgements' of *Watership Down*.

could be easier, what could be simpler?' she asks with mock innocence. 'The cinema fell upon its prey with immense rapacity and to this moment largely subsists upon the body of its unfortunate victim. But the results are disastrous to both.'[6] The problem, according to Woolf, was that film had yet to understand the power of its own, purely visual, devices; she surmised that affect might be conveyed, not on actors' faces and bodies but in the pulsing shapes of expressionist animation. 'Terror', she wrote, 'has besides its ordinary forms the shape of a tadpole; it burgeons, bulges, quivers, disappears. Anger might writhe like an infuriated worm in black zigzags across a white sheet.'[7]

The idea that animation, more than any other film technique, might unlock a new kind of narrative and imaginative space was later taken up by Theodor Adorno and Max Horkheimer, although for them, the squirming, counterfactual figures on screen would be loaded not just with emotional but with political freight. In *Dialectic of Enlightenment*, written in 1944, they proposed that Donald Duck was not (or not only) an amusingly luckless, spluttering blowhard but an effective training tool for capitalist oppression. Cartoons, they wrote, confirm 'the old lessons that continuous friction, the breaking down of all individual resistance, is the condition of life in this society. Donald Duck in the cartoons and the unfortunate in real life get their thrashing so that the audience can learn to take their own punishment.'[8]

Adorno and Horkheimer understood animation to be a radical new art form, one that forged its own distinct relationship with the post-Enlightenment, realist norms of eighteenth- and nineteenth-century narrative. All forms of modern art and popular entertainment, they reasoned, including the products of Hollywood, were inevitably shot through with the ideologies of the technology that created them. These technologies were in the process of cracking open a tradition of aesthetics based on Kantian critique and a stable, indexical relationship between human mark-making and the observed world. Film, especially, created fissures in this system of looking and seeing, and from such cracks powerful, revolutionary energies might emerge. Moreover, these must arise, partly, from the sense of embodied kinship an audience feels towards figures made of flickering light and shadows on a screen: the viewer winces and flinches in response to the character's intangible discomforts, as if to repair the deficit of their disembodied state. A similar exchange of sensory consciousness would later

---

[6]Virginia Woolf, 'The Cinema', in *Selected Essays*, ed. David Bradshaw (Oxford: Oxford University Press, 2008), 172–6, 173.
[7]Woolf, 'The Cinema', 174.
[8]Theodor W. Adorno and Max Horkheimer, *Dialectic of Enlightenment*, trans. John Cumming (London: Verso, 1997), 138.

be theorized by Roland Barthes as photography's punctum, while a core concept of interpenetration also informs Jean-Pierre Oudart's description of the cinematic suture which binds the viewer into the film, via the spatial organization of the hegemonic camera eye.[9] However, in the materialist analysis of Adorno, Horkheimer and others aligned with the Frankfurt School, the sympathy pains of interpellation were understood primarily as a call to, or a longing for, praxis. In this reading of Marxist theory, political action and reaction must always begin and end as embodied phenomena; material conditions raise consciousness, and only then can theoretical and structural ramifications emerge. Thus, it is the body which populates abstract nouns like power and freedom with their content. The hectic Disney shorts which lampooned modern life took the physical clowning of vaudeville and early live-action cinema and redrew them as impossible contortions within a fantastical space of the imagination, reminding us that the outcome of politics always manifests, like slapstick, in and on a body which has already been denaturalized by capitalism.

This was not just a question of failing to see the funny side of Donald Duck: Adorno and Horkheimer considered laughter – especially the forced laughter of popular entertainment – itself to be inherently political, describing it as the 'echo of power as something inescapable', a 'medicinal bath' prescribed by the pleasure industry and a 'disease which has attacked happiness'.[10] And they were not alone in taking the funnies seriously. Their gloomy critique of Disney cartoons was, in part, a response to Walter Benjamin's optimism about the revolutionary potential of the medium of animation.[11] For Benjamin, the very flatness of early cartoons, in other words their lack of – or more accurately their refusal to concede to – naturalism, should be read not as the technological limitation of a bourgeois form but, rather, as an avant-garde counterpoint to the supposedly immutable laws of rationalism, economic hierarchies and social control. In cartoons, these laws are revealed as convenient myths which entrench power and privilege – because in cartoons everything we can ourselves experience, the whole of what we call reality, is seemingly encompassed by another, infinitely extensive, realm of possibility. Such extravagant moments of awakened imagination are, according to Benjamin, precisely what is required in order to critique political and societal norms. Early cartoons – with their exaggerated movements, slapstick pratfalls and violent dismemberments suffered by strange beings endowed with stretchy, indestructible bodies –

---

[9]Roland Barthes, *Camera Lucida*, trans. Richard Howard (London: Vintage, 2020); Jean-Pierre Oudart, 'Dossier Suture: Cinema and Suture', *Screen* 18, no. 4 (1977): 35–47.
[10]Adorno and Horkheimer, *Dialectic of Enlightenment*, 140–1.
[11]See Esther Leslie, *Hollywood Flatlands: Animation, Critical Theory and the Avant Garde* (London: Verso, 2002).

provide a blueprint for revolutionary rupture. Freed from the photograph's dependence on a world of objects which already exist, animated films are the perfect vehicle for utopian what-ifs, and *animal* cartoons in particular, because they draw attention to our own human animality. Like fairy tales, these excessive animal antics expose uncomfortable truths about human sadism and violence.

First, they must catch you: Animal bodies, cartoon physics and trickster tales

Clearly, *Watership Down* was not conceived according to the precepts of Marxist theory, but it does respond to the same fairy-tale paradigm of fantasy, violence and fear which interested the Frankfurt School. The aesthetic of the film is closer to naturalism than the rubbery excesses of Disney's early cartoon shorts, but it is a fragile naturalism which always teeters on the brink of destruction. In his examination of 'cartoon physics' and 'cartoon biology', Scott Bukatman sets out a series of laws which 'propose an alternative set of means by which [cartoon] bodies navigate space: momentum trumps inertia, gravity is a sometime thing, solid matter often isn't'.[12] The utopian potential of the cartoon arises within 'a magic circle with its own rules and codes of behaviour'.[13] Rosen's *Watership Down* adaptation explicitly accesses a similar kind of animated dream realm but brackets this off from the main quest narrative. It does so, first, through the introduction of a set of visually distinct, simplistically drawn religious stories and beliefs, which exist in parallel to the rabbits' everyday reality and guide their political and ethical decision making: this mythology concerns the sun-god Frith and the trickster rabbit El-ahrairah. Second, it foregrounds Fiver's psychic ability to see signs and portents of the future and to intuit danger via some mysterious and ineffable rationale. And third, it alerts the viewers at crucial moments to the tricks and aporetic inconsistencies of its own production as a piece of animation – emphatically not a live-action imprint of the material world but an artefact entirely constructed out of painted cels, paper backgrounds and a static camera lens. As Bukatman points out, in a Wile E. Coyote cartoon, a tunnel through a cliff-face may be created with a tin of paint and brush, but while a roadrunner will pass through the tunnel

---

[12]Scott Bukatman, 'Some Observations Pertaining to Cartoon Physics; or, the Cartoon Cat in the Machine', in Karen Beckman, ed. *Animating Film Theory* (Durham: Duke University Press, 2014), 301–16, 309.
[13]Bukatman, 'Some Observations Pertaining to Cartoon Physics', 309.

unscathed, a coyote will smash into the rock.¹⁴ The trickster is thus tricked by the unstable aesthetic conventions of realism, revealing them to be a deception rather than a reliable epistemological framework. Rosen's utopian rabbits evade such obvious technological snares by slipping between worlds and between aesthetic registers, in order to brace the threshold between them and facilitate the emergence of dream into reality.

Reading Adams's book, it is easy to elide the distinction between the rabbits-as-rabbits and the talking, feeling, reasoning, quasi-human characters who capture our sympathy. In the film, though, this disjunction is harder to ignore, as the rabbits switch rapidly from wide-shot scenes of naturalistic grazing and other Lapine behaviours to close-ups of quasi-human facial expressions and speech. Benjamin, in 'The Storyteller', originally published in 1936, notes the power of fairy tales to access deep truths which can sidestep the habitual thought-structures of society. Animal tales told to children, he argued, made direct links between humanity and nature, leaving social expectations out of the equation: 'The wisest thing – so the fairy tale taught mankind in olden times, and teaches children to this day – is to meet the forces of the mythical world with cunning and with high spirits.'¹⁵ Here, this particular strain of Marxist optimism intersects cleanly with the sun-god mythology of *Watership Down*. In the mythological prologue to the film, Frith instructs the rabbits to be cunning:

> All the world will be your enemy, Prince with a Thousand Enemies, and whenever they catch you, they will kill you. But first, they must catch you. Digger, listener, runner, prince with the swift warning: be cunning and full of tricks, and your people will never be destroyed.

This cunning is an aspect of rabbit-ness which has more to do with human storytelling than Lapine reality. Folk traditions surrounding the character of the trickster Br'er Rabbit, for instance – deployed as a symbol of African American resistance to slavery in work by Nella Larsen, Ralph Ellison, Toni Morrison and others – have been theorized as 'hidden transcripts' of a hybridized network of resistance politics, acting as the coded records of deceptive tactics which might evade the expropriative bodily incursions of an oppressor, even when open rebellion is not possible.¹⁶

---

¹⁴Bukatman, 'Some Observations Pertaining to Cartoon Physics', 306.
¹⁵Walter Benjamin, 'The Storyteller', in *Illuminations* ed. Hannah Arendt, trans. Harry Zorn (London: Pimlico, 1999), 101.
¹⁶Nella Larsen, *Passing* (New York: Norton, [1929] 2007); Ralph Ellison, *Invisible Man* (London: Penguin, [1952] 2001); Toni Morrison, *Tar Baby* (London: Vintage, [1981] 2004); James C. Scott, *Weapons of the Weak: Everyday Forms of Peasant Resistance* (New Haven: Yale University Press, 1985), 241. See also Emily Zobel Marshall, *American Trickster: Trauma,*

Frith's gift of trickery, then, gestures towards a quality belonging to rabbits understood in a cultural, rather than ethological, system. Yet it is crucial for the utopian project of Adams's *Watership Down* novel that neither cunning nor culture should be the end of the story. Indeed, an excessive interest in culture is the key marker of the eerie death-cult which Hazel's group encounter in Cowslip's Warren, just before they arrive on Watership Down. Here, a few fat and melancholy rabbits have accepted the plentiful free food laid down by the local farmer, refusing to talk about the wire snares which surround their burrows and never mentioning the comrades who regularly end up in the farmer's pot. Instead, they 'found out other marvellous arts to take the place of tricks and old stories. They danced in ceremonious greeting. They sang songs like the birds and made shapes on walls . . . though these didn't help them at all.'[17] The sturdy truths of folk wisdom are dismissed by Cowslip as 'very charming' while his arid solipsism is revealed via his quasi-Romantic ode, which takes nature to be the mirror of the poet's soul: 'Where are you going, stream? Far, far away / Beyond the heather, sliding away all night / Take me with you, stream! Away in the starlight.'[18]

For Adams, who threads stories of Frith and the trickster El-ahrairah into his narrative throughout the novel, mythology is the armature defining Hazel's political quest; in the film, on the other hand, a dichotomy is established between the ancient lore and the new utopia, both ideologically and aesthetically. Rosen locates the mythology firmly outside the main narrative, as an imaginary frame within which the naturalistic escapades of Hazel, Fiver and Bigwig take place. These mystical sequences remind the viewer of the rabbits' status as anthropomorphized spectres with allegorical work to do, but as the film progresses, this work becomes increasingly uncomfortable. Fiver's dreams and visions unlock a more explicit mode of horror than anything found in the ultra-violent but ludic safe spaces of Hollywood's animated shorts. The film's famously terrifying scenes of inter-rabbit murder are sharply in tension with the stylized realm of Frith and his harmonious distribution of power and vulnerability among species. Thus, these scenes confront the human viewer with an image of our own 'unnatural' propensity for genocide and atrocity. Likewise – and in accordance with Benjamin's cartoon theory – when we acknowledge that our sense of horrified recoil derives from mere images of painted blood dripping from painted rabbit-fur, yet find ourselves recoiling nevertheless, we are also confronted with the truth that abstract ideas have material, embodied, results.

Tradition and Brer Rabbit (London: Roman and Littlefield, 2019) and Bryan Wagner, *The Tar Baby: A Global History* (Princeton: Princeton University Press, 2017).
[17] Adams, *Watership Down*, 125.
[18] Adams, *Watership Down*, 125.

The aesthetic instability of *Watership Down* is exemplified, and partly explained, by the change of director which occurred when the film's producer, Martin Rosen, sacked John Hubley and took over the role himself. As a director, Hubley's instincts veered towards the avant garde; his 1970s work was characterized by a fashionably flat and simplified style, as can be seen in *Everybody Rides the Carousel* (1975), the psychedelic oddity which he was still making, even while work was supposedly beginning on *Watership Down*. In the end, Hubley was responsible only for the opening 'Frith' sequence of the finished film, and although the jarring effect of the stylistic transition was more unavoidable than intentional, the chasm between Hubley's and Rosen's aesthetic preferences effectively sets up the film's ongoing tension between allegory and naturalism. In practice, the visual switch between styles was achieved via two match-cuts on either side of the opening credits, the first fusing Hubley's stylized sun with the hazy orb shining down on Rosen's congenial Berkshire countryside and the second dissolving the Berkshire sun into its own reflection in a complex, photorealistic close-up of a rabbit's eye. Having established the primacy of the all-seeing, Apollonian gaze in the narrative that will follow, the camera zooms out to position the viewer comfortably within the apparently innocent, and cosily familiar, perspective of naturalistic animation.[19]

Yet because these reassuringly solid, snuffling, nibbling, furry creatures of the warren have burst out of the opening sequence's mythological register and into an appearance of three-dimensionality, they have already begun the process of jamming up the mechanism of animal allegory; shortly afterwards, the tension between the two realms is re-established by the persistence of the supernatural, represented by Fiver's mystical access to visions of blood and death, which pushes back against the comforting consistency of the orderly hillside scene. In a 'Confidential Production Report' dated 28 June 1976, Rosen emphasized the importance of these dream sequences to the meaning of the film. Much of this report concerns emergency measures he has put in place to 'forestall a possible whiplash effect' among the design team, prompted by the tight production schedule and the necessity of arranging a work-in-progress screening for the film's investors. Nevertheless, he insists on adding to this workload, in order to restore a key section of the film which had been provisionally cut:

I have asked that 'FIVER BEYOND' (Chapter 26), not included in the storyboard, be reinstated in the film. The macabre realisation of the fate of Sandleford can be highlighted much more effectively through

---

[19]For the 'Apollonian gaze', see Dennis Cosgrove, *The Apollonian Eye: A Cartographic Genealogy of the Earth in the Western Imagination* (Baltimore: Johns Hopkins University Press, 2001).

this scene, than reliance upon exposition. It will also confirm Fiver's visionary characteristics.[20]

The sequence he refers to comes at a moment of emotional and political crisis in the film: Hazel has been shot by a farmer and is missing, presumed dead; the rabbits fear that their experimental society on Watership Down is failing. Fiver, led by the hovering wraith of the Black Rabbit of death, enters a mist in which colourful, silhouetted rabbit shapes swirl and morph into leaves and abstract forms, while blood spills across the land and dark foliage tangles itself into nets. The effect is strikingly reminiscent of the quivering, expressionistic tadpoles imagined by Woolf; as Rosen realized, by making Fiver's emotions visible to the viewer, he could also make his 'visionary' characteristics emphatically *visual*. Fiver emerges from his dream having 'seen' the impossible; his certain conviction that Hazel is alive leads to a rescue mission; the wounded hero returns from the dead, naturalism is re-established and Watership Down is saved.

Such aesthetic junctions might, to a politically minded critic, be signposts for the hidden work of fetishization and reification which govern social relations in a Marxist analysis. It is fitting, then, that the organization and exploitation of labour have been the rabbits' most pressing concern as they embark on their quest to create a new and better society for themselves. We see clearly, in the various kinds of society which the rabbits experience, that body-work – the getting of food, the guarding of territory, the rearing of young – is generally done by a proletarian class of workers and doe-rabbits, who are rendered powerless by their lack of agency while a privileged and bloated male elite control the community's key resources. Yet a conceptual problem arises as soon as the animals edge too close to human political reality. If *Watership Down* is to be understood as an allegory for human politics, then the rabbit-ness of the rabbits' embodied experience must not be established too assertively, lest the physical sympathy which binds us politically into their predicament begin to fail.

Outlandish speech: Language, translation and utopia

The *Watership* rabbits' problematic animality surfaces clearly when the rabbits interact with another non-human species. Language – a primary

---

[20]Martin Rosen, 'Confidential Production Report', 28 June 1976. From the private archive of Arthur Humberstone, Senior Animator on *Watership Down*. Reproduced by permission of Nigel and Klive Humberstone.

marker of humanity – is inconsistently available to the creatures within this particular fairy-tale realm. The rabbits encounter a farm cat who speaks English just as they do, while the farm dog only barks. Rodents and birds of prey do not communicate audibly at all and encounters with them seem to render the rabbits temporarily mute too, as in the eerie scene in the dark, rat-infested barn where a silent ballet of attack and survival unspools in the shadows. Meanwhile, rabbits, despite speaking in 'human', must devise their own names for technological 'man-things' such as the hedgehog-flattening 'hrududu'. This sense of linguistic contingency may be a convention of fairy tales about talking animals, but the film's knowing sense of its artificiality also highlights the flaws in the rabbits' totalizing, rabbit-centred point of view.

This is pointedly apparent when the seagull, Kehaar, appears in the film. This comical bird – inheritor of Donald Duck's perpetually affronted self-importance and clumsy dignity – is alone among the film's (and the book's) characters, in that he speaks English with a noticeable, though unidentifiable, non-standard accent and idiom. Adams's novel explicitly links this language difference with the rabbits' narrow and earthbound perspective:

> Kehaar's speech was so outlandish and distorted at the best of times that it was only too common for the rabbits to be unsure what he meant. The vernacular words which he used now for 'iron' and 'road' (familiar enough to seagulls) his listeners had scarcely ever heard. Kehaar was quick to impatience and now, as often, they felt at a disadvantage in the face of his familiarity with a wider world than their own.[21]

Kehaar is a denizen of the oceans – the 'Peeg Vater' as he refers to it. He is marked as 'outlandish' not only by his transnational status and mode of speech but by his pelagic purview, his ability to fly and see the world from a broad and lofty perspective. Just as, in the opening section of the film, a naturalistic rabbit's eye brings Hubley's stylized sun down to earth, so Kehaar's eye performs an opposite translation, transporting us back into the realm of the sky, from where a map-like, Apollonian omniscience can solve problems which are impenetrable at the level of grass and burrows. Kehaar's allyship arises from his unwilling sojourn on the ground, when he resides with the rabbits while recovering from an injury to his wing. His comical attempts to boss the rabbits around, and to learn to fly again, gesture back to the slapstick and laughter of the early animal cartoons, where creatures habitually interacted across species gaps and burst out of their natural element. Hazel is compassionate, but he is also astute in his willingness to give asylum to this avian refugee; the nascent political system he is beginning

---

[21] Adams, *Watership Down*, 201.

to establish is predicated on the idea that the differing talents and insights of individuals combine to produce a stronger collective. Narratively, though, Kehaar punctures the rabbits' pompous Lapine exceptionalism and expands the scope of the story. The rabbits, who have hitherto considered themselves to be the centre of the universe and the subject of all meaningful culture, become suddenly conscious of their own limitation by seeing themselves through Kehaar's unimpressed eyes; rabbit society, even with its complex oral history and theology, is suddenly revealed as insufficient to describe the world. Just as animation unsettles the viewer by suggesting that naturalism is a mere set of restrictive conventions, so Kehaar's scopic range and linguistic hybridity create a zoom-out effect both in his diegetic encounters with the rabbits and for the audience watching the screen. Crucially, Kehaar's disorderly physicality and clownish antics drag Hazel's drily bureaucratic version of a well-tempered utopia into a realm of imaginative possibility which must also encompass the physical – as when he points out that Hazel has managed to found an all-male society with no reproductive future. Here, as elsewhere, the clockwork moral machinery of the Aesopian fable winds down, and a more complex array of narrative imperatives is revealed to be at work.

These intimations of fairy-tale failure point to the unavoidable tension operating within all utopian literature, which attempts to describe and contain an actually existing problem by positing a fantasy solution which must always remain tantalizingly incomplete. In her analysis of twenty-first-century 'fictions of the not yet', Caroline Edwards traces the development of utopian literature and (following Louis Marin) identifies a quality of 'figurative totality', staged within the alternative space-time of 'cartographic otherness' as the key marker of a utopian text struggling against its own impossibility.[22] She goes on to trace the turn against utopianism which occurred in the post–Second World War period, inspired by the anti-fascist work of Karl Popper and Hannah Arendt. According to Edwards, this developed into the anti-authoritarian stance taken by the radical activists of the 1960s, whose disillusion with all kinds of systemic thinking was based on the valid observation that a contorted utopianism could all too easily tip into fascism, as it had in Nazi Germany. Inspired by post-structuralists like Jean Baudrillard and Jean-François Lyotard, the student protestors in Paris in 1968 wanted to problematize and fragment all kinds of 'grand narratives' and included Marxism within that definition. Lyotard, in particular, linked the 'diegetic structures and topographies of "traditional" or "classical" utopian voyages' with 'the teleology of global capitalist expansion' with its

---

[22]Caroline Edwards, *Utopia and the Contemporary British Novel* (Cambridge: Cambridge University Press, 2019), 40–1; Louis Marin, *Utopics: The Semiological Play of Textual Spaces*, trans. Robert A. Vollrath (New York: Humanity Books, 1990).

'colonialist passages into the uncharted territories of the New World'.[23] Such critiques of all and any metanarrative discourses would find their apotheosis with the fall of the Berlin Wall and the rise of neoliberalism.

Adams, working in the early 1970s against the twin backdrops of insurgent youth activism and the postmodern turn against materialism, imagined a less threatening utopian praxis which could be neatly contained within a rational, hierarchical structure – and the model he chose for this was 'nature' – understood naively, as an unspoilt, self-regulating and changeless ecosystem. *Watership Down* solves the problem of utopian impossibility by stepping outside the confines of narrative naturalism into another kind of 'natural' order, where anthropomorphic animals could exist beyond the murky semiotics of postmodernism, and where place, culture and language could be reconceived and reclarified from first principles. The novel is thus essentially conservative: it attempts to fold together an idealized vision of human society with an element of respect for the natural rabbit-ness of the rabbits. In doing so, Adams rejects equality among animals as the defining principle of his utopia; the promised land of Watership Down offers a home for old constructs of gender and caste, and a society which organizes itself according to unexamined assumption rather than political theory, defining itself only as the reasonable counterexample to various extremist positions. The film, on the other hand, revolts against such reactionary narrative strategies by injecting visceral terror, not enlightened opposition, into the rabbits' encounters with extremism. A sense of fear and estrangement is triggered by the spectacle of anthropomorphized animals acting like beastly humans, particularly in the violently dystopian realm of Efrafa.

Darko Suvin has identified a similar impulse in post-war science fiction, where post-human or extra-terrestrial utopias form a radical 'literature of cognitive estrangement' which provides a platform for critique.[24] This was essentially the same impetus which had been apparent to the post-Marxists to whom Mickey Mouse revealed the absurdity of human (and Western-liberal humanist) exceptionalism. Similarly, in Rosen's film, the political occlusion of the rabbits' non-humanity fails to survive the ineluctable visual presence of their animal bodies. In Cowslip's death-cult, rabbits trade their bodies, in the form of meat, for a short life of comfort and ease, and overcome their cognitive dissonance by ignoring the abrupt disappearances of their fellows. In contrast, Hazel's group must confront, and solve, Bigwig's entanglement in one of the deadly snares set by the farmer. This moment is one of the fulcrums of the film: a test of the rabbits' Br'er-like cunning

---

[23]Edwards, *Utopia and the Contemporary British Novel*, 38.
[24]Darko Suvin, *Metamorphoses of Science Fiction: On the Poetics and History of a Literary Genre* (Oxford: Peter Lang, 2016) quoted in Edwards, *Utopia and the Contemporary British Novel*, 42.

and the fulfilment of Fiver's original prophecy, establishing the relationship between his extra-sensory vision and the privileged perspective of a cinema audience watching events unfold. As Fiver has explained to the Chief Rabbit in the first act, his knowledge of impending doom is based on an empathic ability to feel with the suffering he 'sees' on the cinema screen of his mind. 'I can feel the danger like a wire round my neck – like a wire!' he shouts. Contemplating, in gruesome detail, the fate of Bigwig, both the other rabbits and the audience recoiling from the gore can at last feel what Fiver felt, ensnared by the visual power of a violent scene, even though it is happening in an impossible, imaginary otherwhere.

Yet, just as Fiver's stylized visions of fields stained with red come to be replayed in the physical blood and pain experienced by the rabbit refugees, so the idealized dreamworld of Hazel's social utopia must be tested against the hard facts of life and death. As we have seen, this collision of alternate realities is mirrored precisely in the clash of the film's visual registers: the more the animation strives for frictionless naturalism, the more deeply the supernatural dreamworld embeds itself in the story's flesh, reminding us to critique the lofty perspectives of all those who seek to offer us a 'vision'. If Fiver's vision of blood references Cassandra's unheeded warnings about the destruction of Troy in Greek mythology, they also tacitly gesture towards the infamous 'rivers of blood' speech given by the right-wing nationalist Enoch Powell in 1968, in which he referred to Vergil's account of an Apollonian prophecy that war would be the outcome of the founding of Rome by Aeneid. Egregiously misquoting and misreading Vergil, Powell claimed, 'like the Roman' to see 'the River Tiber foaming with much blood', cynically deploying a third-hand vision of doom to stoke up racism and anti-immigrant sentiment in a society which was attempting to navigate its post-imperial responsibilities and the demands of post-war modernization. Unlike the novel, the film *Watership Down* suggests a riposte to Powell by issuing another type of warning: myth-inflected dystopianism should be distrusted as incendiary fear-mongering, unless it can be attached to a well-formed sense of a decency and justice. Thus, though Fiver's originary vision appears to be the trigger for a simple quest for a homeland, this is revealed to be only half of the story. On Watership Down, the rabbits must physically inhabit a hopeful future, rather than merely reacting blindly to fear of what might come to pass. As Ernst Bloch writes in his analysis of utopian art and culture: 'Hope, superior to fear, is neither passive like the latter, nor locked into nothingness. The emotion of hope goes out of itself and makes people broad instead of confining them.'[25]

---

[25]Ernst Bloch, *The Principle of Hope* Vol. 1, trans. Neville Plaice, Stephen Plaice and Paul Knight (Cambridge, MA: MIT Press, 1986), 3.

Conclusion

In the 1960s, Bloch and Adorno were brought together to discuss utopian fiction.[26] Adorno's argument was that utopianism had been rendered banal by the fulfilment of so many technological, medical and scientific promises: many of the things that previous generations had considered impossible dreams were now humdrum reality, and this was experienced as a terrible feeling of having been deceived. Bloch, on the other hand, felt that this 'melancholy residue', as he put it, which pervaded modern life, was evidence of the impoverishment of utopian longings, which never, in his view, went far enough. The essence of utopia, he argued, was defined by its very inaccessibility. Social, medical and technological utopias are all too easily translated into reality, but 'the essential function of utopia is a critique of what is present. If we had not already gone beyond the barriers, we could not even conceive them as barriers.'[27] Part of his argument is that death itself, and our fear of it, puts utopias properly back into the realm of the impossible and opens the door to a spiritual dimension in political thinking. And again, here, we find the film *Watership Down* offering a visual image of this idea. Death hovers constantly over the rabbits, from the earliest depiction of the mythology of Frith to the Black Rabbit who comes to relieve Hazel of his worldly responsibilities.

Why does *Watership Down* conclude, not with the culmination of the quest but with Hazel's death and his re-entry into the mythological world of Frith? This can only be, it seems to me, a Blochian gesture towards the insufficiency of utopia. Just as the rabbits' reproductive instincts kick in at the point where they have finally achieved their theoretical sunny uplands, so the next-level utopia – Watership Down plus – must be tainted by the inevitability of death, in order to preserve the sense of loss and longing which has been the engine of the plot. Death anchors politics into the mechanisms of time and embodiment: Hazel's translation into disembodied spirit imbricates the utopian dreamworld with the brusque imperatives of ecology. By noting this emphasis on somatic longings and the limits of life, then, we can perhaps begin to formulate questions which bring the animal fables of the twentieth century into dialogue with contemporary utopian fictions, which deploy narratives of critical posthumanism to challenge the 'naturalistic' dreamwork of the Anthropocene. *Watership Down*'s uncertain traversal of the boundaries between the constructs of aesthetic naturalism and the priorities and imperatives of more-than-human nature reminds us that political praxis is always rooted in embodiment, and that bodies are an essential corrective to the utopianism of the merely possible.

---

[26]'Something's Missing: A Discussion between Ernst Bloch and Theodor W. Adorno on the Contradictions of Utopian Longing' in Ernst Bloch, *The Utopian Function of Art and Literature: Selected Essays*, trans. Jack Zipes and Frank Mecklenburg (Cambridge, MA: MIT Press, 1988).
[27]'Something's Missing', 12.

CHAPTER 5

'Whenever they catch you, they will kill you':

Human–animal conflict in 1970s British children's cinema

Noel Brown

Beaten to death with a shovel; bludgeoned by poachers; torn to pieces by a hound; devastated by mechanical diggers. These are the fates that befall the animal protagonists of several of the most iconic British children's films of the 1960s and 1970s. The four films discussed in this chapter, *Ring of Bright Water* (Couffer, 1969), *The Belstone Fox* (Hill, 1973), *Watership Down* (Rosen, 1978) and *Tarka the Otter* (Cobham, 1979), foreground bleak, often realist evocations of human–animal conflict that contrast sharply with the sentimentalism of mainstream Hollywood animal films, particularly those produced by Disney. Today, however, most of these films have slipped out of the popular consciousness. If they are remembered at all, it tends to be with a vague combination of nostalgia and something approaching dread, as relics of a less consumerist era of British children's media culture and as loci of childhood trauma.

In this chapter, I would like to situate *Watership Down* in the context of the broader preoccupation with animals and nature in British children's cinema of the period.¹ Between the late 1960s and late 1970s, the animal film was the most important British children's film cycle. The four films discussed in this chapter are linked by recurrent features: an emphasis on an ultimately ungovernable, untameable nature; humankind figured as an intrusive and destructive force, diametrically opposed to the 'natural' order; a tendency both to embrace and to repudiate anthropomorphism and sentimentality; punctuating moments of brutal realism; and implicit or explicit criticisms of modernity.

The animal film and 1970s British cinema

While it may be tempting to regard children's movies containing animals as a distinct, formally coherent subgenre, these four films have very little in common with the most common form of Hollywood animal film as encapsulated by classical-era family films such as *National Velvet* (Brown, 1944) and *Old Yeller* (Stevenson, 1957): a sentimental maturation narrative that develops a simpatico relationship between a child and a beloved animal, and which reaffirms deep, almost spiritual interconnectedness between humans and the natural world. In this tradition, the union between humankind and the natural world is unalterable, and rarely tainted by ambiguity, much less by the possibility of mutual destruction.

The very different attitude to nature – and to humanity's relation to it – in the four films discussed here is neatly encapsulated by a passage of dialogue in the late-1960s British animal film *Run Wild, Run Free* (Sarafian, 1969), in which John Mills's character, the Moorman, explains to Mark Lester's child protagonist the wondrous yet unfathomable and potentially lethal qualities of the natural environment:

> That's the wonderful thing about the moors. The whole thing heaving and bursting with new life in the spring, yet it's almost invisible. Now, look around. What can you see? You can't see anything, can you? But it's there, just the same. . . . The moor's alive, Philip. Sleeps and breathes and eats and drinks. Sometimes it's serene and peaceful. Feels kindly towards us. Other times it's angry and dangerous. It can even kill us sometimes, if it takes a notion to it. And right now, in the centre of the moor, deep down in the black peat, there's a heart beating. You can feel it, sometimes.

These films tend to view the relationship between modern humans and nature as antithetical. Indeed, their inter-species interactions present a clear

---

¹This chapter builds on work previously published by the author in *British Children's Cinema: From The Thief of Bagdad to Wallace and Gromit* (London: I. B. Tauris, 2016).

metonymy for the current trajectory of Western society. Arguably, they show the children's film at its most progressive, presenting barbed criticism of modernity and its structures of advanced capitalism and industrialization and gesturing to the increasing dangers of ecological collapse.

Children are conspicuously absent from all four films. In *Ring of Bright Water* and, to a lesser degree, *Watership Down*, animals are cast in the role of symbolic child; their basic drives and emotions are roughly analogous to the needs and reactions of young children. In *The Belstone Fox* and *Tarka the Otter*, though, the animals belong to a harsh, untamed natural world that, in its brutal excesses, is anathema to normative social constructions of childhood as a realm of innocence and unfettered play. Similarly, the children's film is traditionally associated with a rather different set of tendencies: brightness and colour, lightness of tone, the foregrounding of children and their experiences, an emphasis on family and friendship and community and happy endings.

Instead, a pervasive air of miserabilism permeates these films. The same can be said for a good deal of British children's and youth visual culture of the late 1960s and 1970s, including the Ken Loach films, *Kes* (1969) and *Black Jack* (1979), the post-apocalyptic drama *Survivors* (1975–7), and even a notorious series of public information films produced by the Central Office of Information (COI) that warned children, in the starkest terms, of the lethal dangers of fireworks, electricity pylons, ponds and agricultural machinery. All share a similarly bleak tone, murky visual aesthetic and (mostly) dysphoric endings. Given their clear incongruity within the larger patterns of children's film (in Britain and elsewhere), it is important to explore the factors that allowed such films to be produced and to be received with such enthusiasm.

In many regards, these four films are products of their time. If the brightness and extravagance of late-1960s mainstream British children's musicals like *Yellow Submarine* (Dunning, 1968), *Oliver!* (Reed, 1968) and *Chitty Chitty Bang Bang* (Hughes, 1968) resemble a narcotic high, with money flowing in from Hollywood, the 1970s certainly looks – and, more importantly, *feels* – like a comedown. Investment in British family-oriented extravaganzas ground to a halt after Hollywood's financial crisis of 1969, beginning a downward spiral that was cemented by the government's withdrawal of financial support to the National Film Finance Corporation – established in 1948 to stimulate production of British features – in 1971, and the financial difficulties of several major studios. In 1974, the *Observer* grimly noted that 'for years, the [British] film industry has been playing out a death scene besides which the most lachrymose Hollywood weepies would seem indecently cock-a-hoop'.[2] British children's films thus reverted

---

[2] Brian Bell, 'Can the Film-Makers Carry On', *The Observer*, 11 August 1974: 11.

from a populist transatlanticism to a more characteristically 'British' style: low-budget, unformulaic, naturalistic; and now entering new territory, sometimes quixotic, obscure and confoundingly downbeat, yet buoyed by greater levels of creative freedom.

These changing institutional contexts coincided with burgeoning political activist movements, including ecological conservationism and animal rights. Both were causes célèbres of British liberal-socialism that had begun to move beyond fringe activism into the left-wing mainstream of political discourse. Certainly, Richard Adams's novel, *Watership Down* (1972), was widely viewed on publication as a political allegory, even if the author disavowed this interpretation. It is also worth noting that, in 1978, otter numbers had declined to such an extent that they were added to the list of UK-protected species, bringing the centuries-old practice of otter hunting to an end. While this had nothing to do with the film adaptation of *Tarka the Otter* (which was not released until late 1979), Henry Williamson's 1927 novel had played a major role in bringing the practice of otter hunting to national scrutiny. The point is not that these films are underpinned by an explicit polemical agenda, but rather that they reflect ideologies and cultural trends that were very much 'in the air' in 1970s Britain.

British children's cinema of the 1970s operated as something of a cottage industry. The Children's Film Foundation (CFF), which had produced children's shorts and features since the 1950s and was funded indirectly by the state through a mandatory levy on all cinema admissions in Britain, produced some of its most creative work during the 1970s, but its films reached ever fewer children. Commercial children's film was at an even lower ebb, but it did support the endeavours of a handful of entrepreneurial producers and directors.[3] One of these was James Hill, a documentary producer who became a key player in British animal films during the 1960s and 1970s. Having directed the transatlantic hit *Born Free* (1966), the production that reinvigorated the long-moribund animal film, Hill went on to direct notable later releases such as *An Elephant Called Slowly* (1967), *Black Beauty* (1971) and *The Belstone Fox*. Although *Born Free* and *Black Beauty* tend more to anthropomorphic cutesiness, all of Hill's films share a simple, naturalistic style that conveys both the splendour and the desolation of Britain's landscapes. This simple visual aesthetic, married to an apparent conviction to represent nature as it really is, strongly characterizes *Ring of Bright Water*, *The Belstone Fox* and *Tarka the Otter*.

---

[3]Noel Brown, '*The Railway Children* and Other Stories: Lionel Jeffries and British Family Films in the 1970s', in *Family Films in Global Cinema: The World Beyond Disney*, ed. Noel Brown and Bruce Babington (London: I. B. Tauris, 2015), 120–36.

Humans and animals in conflict: *Ring of Bright Water, The Belstone Fox* and *Tarka the Otter*

Ring of Bright Water can, in retrospect, be seen as a midpoint between the optimism of the 1960s counterculture movement and the increasing disillusionment of the 1970s. One of the film's main selling points was its reuniting Bill Travers and Virginia McKenna, the stars of *Born Free*, in the lead roles. After their experiences making that film, the couple had become heavily involved in animal rights (they eventually established the Born Free Foundation in 1991) and closely associated with children's films focussing on animals. Travers, in particular, had prominent roles in *An Elephant Called Slowly* and *The Belstone Fox* and was producer-director of the documentary films *The Lions Are Free* (co-directed with Hill, 1969), *The Lion at World's End* (1971) and *Christian the Lion* (1976). While Hill was a jobbing director who happened to specialize both in children's films and documentaries, Travers and McKenna apparently viewed their crusading children's films and nature documentaries as two sides of the same coin forming part of a larger project that combined political pressure on governments to stamp down on the mistreatment of animals in captivity with the moral imperative of educating children to be enlightened, compassionate future citizens.

Based on Gavin Maxwell's bestselling autobiography of 1960, which centres on his domestication of an otter, *Ring of Bright Water* draws much of its pathos and authenticity from its rooting in real life. Its human protagonist, Graham Merrill (Travers), begins the film as a frustrated office-based administrator, appalled that he has become 'A code number that gets a pension, an expectancy of life calculated in years and days', and that 'we've been computerized – by our own computers'. Graham spots an otter through a pet shop window, and they exchange a lingering glance. His voice-over narration tells us that

> From that first day, I imagined that the otter had somehow singled me out from all the thousands of people who passed the pet shop window every day.... Every time I passed he seemed to be watching me, and me alone. At first I thought it was only my imagination, but whatever I did he seemed to sense that I was there, and fixed me with his beady eyes. Clearly, I was the chosen one.

Graham's impulsive purchase of the otter, which he names Mij, expresses itself as tacit rebellion against the joyless regimentation of his city life. Mij's predictable ransacking of his London apartment cathartically releases Graham from the materialism and consumerism embodied by the post-industrial city. Unable to keep the otter in London anymore, Graham takes Mij to a zoo to try and find him a home but is dismayed by the sight of the caged animals and quickly turns on his heels, observing that 'I hadn't just bought myself an otter. I'd taken a step which was to change the whole course of my life. This otter had become a part of me.'

Later, Graham reads a classified ad that appeals to him: 'Escape the rat-race. Exclusive old-world cottage, west coast of Scotland.' On a whim, he buys the house in Scotland, taking Mij with him, and decides to live as a beachcomber. As with many dissatisfied city slickers during the individualist movement of the late 1960s, Graham retreats to the wilderness in search of spiritual fulfilment. However, his need for an intimate relationship (previously frustrated by a recent divorce) is only partially fulfilled by his friendship with the kindly Mary MacKenzie (McKenna). Mij offers Graham the affiliation with nature (or the appearance of it) that he yearns for.

The otter is a peculiarly British animal to use as the centre of a family film. Savage, not adorable in the accepted sense, unsuitable for domestication, widely regarded as a pest and hunted mercilessly for sport, the otter bridges the divide between humanity and nature more than conventionally domesticated animals, displaying adaptability to land and water, possessing intelligence and playfulness, but remaining thrillingly untameable. However, audiences are denied an ingratiating happy ending. There is a disturbing portent of Mij's fate when Graham briefly returns to London and notices an otter-skin coat in the window of the same shop he had purchased Mij. In the following scene, unaware that Mij is a beloved pet and driven by received ideas that otters are vermin, an amiable roadside digger beats him to death with his spade. Reacting to Mary's horror, the man responds, bemusedly, that Mij was 'just an otter'.

Mij's death is presented in deliberately prosaic fashion, with none of the prolonged suspense of similar scenes in *The Belstone Fox*, *Tarka the Otter* and *Watership Down*. The fact that the killer blow is delivered by an apparently pleasant person in the course of their everyday work seems curiously appropriate, since what the film continually questions – and ultimately laments – is unempathetic thoughtlessness rather than active maliciousness. Despite such traumatic episodes, these films place greater emphasis on the cyclicality of nature – and the dialectic between its beauty and barbarism – than on the lives of individual animals. Mij, like the mother goose whose goslings Graham adopts after she is shot by poachers, successfully procreates, thus ensuring natural continuity. This fact is perhaps intended to make his violent death somewhat bearable. Mary's assertion in the film's final scene that 'wild otters' (i.e. Mij's cubs) swimming in the burn is 'the way it ought to be' perhaps serves as a reproof of Graham's removing the animal from its natural habitat for his own ends.

The Belstone Fox, described by the *Daily Mail*'s David Lewin as 'the most original film I have seen in years', is even less optimistic about the possibilities of inter-species accord.[4] The film opens with a brutal scene in which two men in search of foxes dig into the ground, uncover a burrow in which a vixen is guarding her cubs and bludgeon the animals to death. The voice-over narration intones: 'And so begins the strange and terrifying story of the Belstone fox.' No explicit reason is given for the killing of the animals beyond one character's matter-of-fact observation that 'some people don't like foxes'. This immediately places the species on the same level as the otters of *Ring of Bright Water* and *Tarka the Otter* and the rabbits of *Watership Down* as animals under constant threat from human incursions into their natural territory. A surviving cub is rescued by professional huntsman Asher (Eric Porter), who names it Tag. Asher's decision to spare the cub and wean it with a hound dog is viewed with scepticism by the squire, Kendrick (Jeremy Kemp), who permits it only on condition that he 'keep [the fact] quiet'. The film's opening sections develop a tripartite relationship between Asher, Tag and the hound Merlin, with whom Tag is happily paired as a cub. The film's major reversal is Asher's decision, under pressure from Kendrick, to make Tag the quarry in a fox hunt. By this stage, Tag has become famous in the local hunting fraternity for his boldness and cunning.

In the film's most gruesome sequence Asher, fervently leading the hunt against Tag, is thrown from his horse and badly wounded. Pursued by the pack of hounds, Tag leads them across a railway track. Tag and Merlin cross safely, but the rest of the pack is killed by an oncoming train. The camera quickly cuts between the carnage on the tracks (where limbs and bloodied bodies fly through the air) and Asher's face as he shields his eyes and cries out in anguish. Having been forced to shoot one of the crippled survivors, he then mutters to himself, 'damn him'. Subsequently, Asher hardens to the obsessive pursuit of vengeance; he rationalizes this to Kendrick by claiming that, if left alive, Tag will use the same strategy to escape the pack again. He refuses Kendrick's suggestion of hunting Tag with guns, insisting it 'wouldn't be right' and that they must kill him 'traditionally' through the hunt. Unusually, for this cycle of films, *The Belstone Fox* ends not with the animal's death but the human's. Increasingly ailing, Asher follows Merlin into the mountains, where he discovers Tag and Merlin peacefully side-by-side in a cave. Intending to kill Tag, he pulls out a knife but suffers a fatal heart attack. Asher's body is later discovered with Tag and Merlin loyally having remained by his side, keeping vigil. The final shot sees Tag alone, indefatigable, on top of the barren mountain.

Ironically, it is the decent but compromised Asher, a master of the hunt with forty years' experience, who imposes human qualities on the animal. His decision to spare the fox cub and wean it with a hound dog is viewed as quixotic by Kendrick. It is hinted that his kindness stems from a weakening of his faculties as a hunter – an individual supposedly divorced from

---

[4] David Lewin, 'The Hound and his Best Friend . . . The Fox', *The Daily Mail*, 26 October 1973: 6–7.

sentimental attachment to (and anthropomorphism of) animals. Ageing, and increasingly indulgent, Asher acts against his hunter's instinct to kill the young animal and feels personally betrayed when Tag leads his pack across the rail track. But the real culprit is Asher himself, who insists on casting Tag as symbolic child and then hunting him, secretly hoping, as a point of personal pride, that the fox will escape. Ultimately, the human tendency to anthropomorphize is revealed as a dangerous misreading of nature's true essence, which is characterized by amorality, spontaneity, hardness and endurance.

In contrast, the changeability of human civilization is highlighted. Asher's daughter, Jenny (Heather Wright), proclaims herself anti-hunting. One of the film's most potent images is of a young child, having been taken on her first fox hunt, being 'blooded' – that is, having the hunted animal's blood smeared on her face to initiate her to the practice. The camera slowly zooms on her blank face as the music becomes discordant, and she reaches her hand up to her bloodied cheek. The child's horrified incomprehension, coupled with the youthful and progressive Jenny's ethical objection to the hunt, and Asher's transformation from decent family man to bloodthirsty obsessive suggest that traditional pursuits such as fox hunting have become outmoded.

Tag's ability to survive and evade his pursuers rests on his own innate skills. Indeed, for Asher, it is important that the animal is afforded the opportunity and the means of survival, but not the certainty of it. The philosophy is similar to that of the sun god in *Watership Down*, who warns the rabbits that 'All the world will be your enemy. . . . And whenever they catch you, they will kill you. But first they must catch you.' The sentiment is echoed here when the hunter, Tod (Bill Travers), remarks of Tag: 'You can hunt him as much as you like, but you'll never catch him. . . . Never.' These films imbue their animal protagonists with natural defences (cunning, endurance) against a world of manifold dangers, where comfort, reassurance and safety are unknowable. Equally, their defences are often insufficient. Even the seemingly indefatigable Tag survives only because Asher keels over before he is able to deliver the death blow.

Both *The Belstone Fox* and *Tarka the Otter* are predicated on exposing the savagery and injustice of blood sports. *The Belstone Fox* takes deliberate aim at fox hunting (which was finally banned in Britain in 2005), and *Tarka the Otter* does the same for otter hunting. With a screenplay by naturalist and author Gerald Durrell, *Tarka the Otter* is a starkly brilliant riposte to the sentimental, sanitized Disney nature documentaries of the 1950s, and one of the bleakest and most brutal children's films ever made. The film follows the dog otter Tarka, interspersing documentary-style footage of wild animals and staged sequences shot on location with a sparse narration by Peter Ustinov. It presents various episodes in the otter's life, including his birth, the violent deaths of his mother (shot by a hunter) and father (savaged in a hunt), the honing of his predatory instincts, his finding a mate and his eventual apparent death at the hands of Deadlock, the leader of the pack of hounds who possesses 'an insatiable lust for otters'. Although unstinting in its distressing details, the film shows many scenes of animals engaged in pleasurable activities. In an early scene, Tarka's mother and father are seen mating underwater. Later, we see Tarka delightedly taking a shower in a stream, the narration reminding us that 'Like all otters, Tarka revelled in falling water, going wild with joy, rolling in ecstasy as he tried to catch the twisting rope of water.' Tarka's predatory inclinations are never denied. There are various scenes of him catching and eating fish, and the voice-over explains: 'The more he killed the more he wanted to kill, and he feasted on them till his jaws were tired.' There is no implied tension in the film's alternate representations of its animal protagonist as symbolic child and vicious predator.

Again, humans are always malign: the salmon poachers, illegally stealing from the estate's streams under cover of night; the fishermen who trawl the sea and attempt to catch Tarka in their net, asserting that his skin will fetch 'a few bob'; the rabbit hunters who take a pot shot at Tarka; even the old woman who unwittingly throws a bucket of water over him from her window above. Anthropomorphism occasionally asserts itself. Towards the end of the film, Tarka sleeps with White-Tip and their cubs, dreaming, we are told, of travelling 'to a strange sea, where otters were never hungry and never hunted'. It is characteristic of the film's weighing the joys and beauty of nature against its viscerality that this yearning fantasy is juxtaposed by the return of the otter hunters. For the hunters, 'the first meet of the otter-hunting season was a grand social occasion.' They toast their anticipated success with glasses of sherry, interspersed with polite, genteel conversation. Then the hounds, who 'loved the huntsmen, who called each of them by name', arrive and the hunt finally commences. The cruelty of the hunt is in the protracted chase as much as the kill itself. The huntsmen allow Tarka a four-minute head start, 'a sporting chance' that serves only to instil fear in the quarry and build pleasurable anticipation in the hunters as, inexorably, the exhausted otter is brought down.

Neither the hunters nor the spectators, who observe with curiosity, are despicable people; the fault is with the arrogant assertion of 'natural dominion' over animal kind. Tantalisingly, during the climactic, fifteen-minute hunt, it seems at several points that Tarka may elude his pursuers, but once again there is no happy ending. In the final scene, Tarka is cornered by Deadlock, and they struggle underwater. Deadlock's dead body rises to the surface, but there is no sign of Tarka. Do the three bubbles that appear on the surface in the moments that follow suggest his escape upstream, or merely his final breaths? Perhaps they symbolize White-Tip's and the two cubs' escape? Is a hopeful interpretation of this scene permissible, given the film's harshly pragmatic interpretations of life in the wild, or merely a self-delusion that stems from its status as a 'children's film'?

'They'll never rest till they've spoiled the earth': *Watership Down*

If *The Belstone Fox* and *Tarka the Otter* espouse a common philosophy, it is that human beings, despite technological advancements and the hubristic assumption of moral and spiritual sophistication, are still animals in all senses of the word. The rabbits in *Watership Down* reside in a society ridden by recognizable social structures, rituals, fears and conflicts. In so doing, the film approaches the same theme from the opposite angle: whereas the other films depict humans barely having progressed beyond animal savagery, *Watership Down* shows an animal civilization that in almost every regard mirrors the human world. It allegorically centres on rabbit civilization, delineating a society with its own laws, customs and language, though bound by earthly preoccupations and threats.

There is much that could be said about the film's allegory of human civilization, but I am more concerned here with its occasional, fleeting, but always disruptive interactions between rabbits and humans. Whereas the narratives of the live-action films described earlier proceed via startling realistic images of animal slaughter and suffering, the animated *Watership Down* is much more expressionist in style – closer, at times, to 'abstraction' than 'mimesis'.[5] In its own way, the results are equally unsettling. The humans' impending arrival at the Sandleford Warren early in the film is described by Fiver as 'something oppressive, like thunder'; human footmarks in the mud and a still-burning cigarette confirm that a 'terrible thing is coming', and Fiver then has a vision of blood gushing over a nearby cultivated field. A large wooden human sign overlooking the field that warns that the land is to be redeveloped for a housing estate offering 'high class modern residences' is introduced with an ominous low-angle shot as Fiver looks at the structure from ground height, making it look like gallows. Expressionist shots of this kind add considerably to the film's portentous tone, but they serve another important function. By allowing us privileged access to the rabbits' subjectivity, the film externalizes the actions of the humans (i.e. us) and presents humanity as Other, just as *The Belstone Fox*, *Tarka the Otter* and (to a lesser degree) *Ring of Bright Water* do. This is a far cry from the presentation of human–animal encounters in classical animal films, which invoke pastoral images of humans and nature in perfect synchronicity. The only such images here occur after the rabbits have found the Arcadian habitat of Watership Down, whose bucolic perfection is explicitly predicated on its isolation from the human world.

---

[5]See Sam Summers's chapter in this volume for a delineation of these concepts.

Elsewhere, audiences are repeatedly shown nightmarish visions of natural habitats compromised by human activity. In Cowslip's Warren, where the few remaining rabbits are cowed into fearful submission and forced into willing collaboration by the human farmer with the promise of abundant food, the atmosphere is described as heavy, 'like mist'. Holly's recollection of the destruction of Sandleford is particularly evocative, describing 'runs blocked with dead bodies' and 'warrens, earth, roots, grass all pushed into the air'. Holly concludes that 'They just destroyed the warrens because we were in their way', and Fiver responds, 'They'll never rest till they've spoiled the earth.' Holly's traumatized description is accompanied by a montage sequence that contains one of the film's most potent images: a mechanical digger raking a field, leaving blood-red claw marks scarred into the landscape. The shot is disturbingly (and intentionally) evocative of various sequences in which rabbits claw one another and, invariably, draw blood. In both cases, the effect is equally dissonant: the image is of nature brutalized and defiled. Moreover, the fact that no humans are seen during the destruction of Sandleford is an artistic choice that seems, deliberately, to evoke the mindlessness of the machine, the seemingly reflexive, amoral tyranny of late modernity.

The theme of nature and animals being 'in the way' of human progress is a recurrent one. The rabbits are forced to cross a busy country road (with a dead rodent flattened on to the surface of the tarmac), and later a speeding train mows down a group of rabbits escaping Efrafa, in a sequence that recalls the slaughter of the hounds in near-identical circumstances in *The Belstone Fox*. Human characters themselves are barely glimpsed. The pair of farmers who shoot Hazel are seen only in silhouette with their shotguns, and although we hear snippets of conversation, the point-of-audition remains with the rabbits, rendering it almost inaudible. The only exception to the film's overwhelmingly hostile depiction of humans is the young girl on the farm who reprimands the cat ('cruel thing!') for chasing after Hazel and Pipkin and later saves Hazel from being killed by it. We might interpret this character in a number of ways. Most basically, she reflects a broader convention in children's fiction for children to have greater affinity with animals and nature, and to be relatively innocent and untainted by the ethical compromises of adulthood. However, her presentation perhaps offers the possibility (but no more) of a more thoughtful, compassionate and enlightened future, much in the way that *The Belstone Fox* presents Asher's daughter, Jenny, as actively rejecting the methods and the prejudices of earlier generations.[6]

---

[6] Adams's novel is more explicit in this regard: the child, Lucy, plays a much more actively sympathetic role, helping to nurse Hazel back to health after he is attacked by the cat and then releasing him close to the Watership Down Warren.

Watership Down also shares with the other three films discussed in this chapter a pervasive funereal tone. As with *Animal Farm* (Halas and Batchelor, 1954), Britain's first feature-length animation (and in obvious contrast with Disney), the muted, often drab colour palette is matched by the often doom-laden orchestral score. Comedy, a staple of children's animation, is mostly localized to the figure of Kehaar, a black-headed gull portrayed by Broadway legend Zero Mostel. Kehaar remains anomalous for several reasons. First, he is voiced by an American among an otherwise uniformly British voice cast. Second, he remains a comical figure (even when flapping his wings in defence of the rabbits escaping Efrafa for Watership Down) with his outrageous European accent and his obsession with finding 'big water'. Third, he is freed (both by his wings and his demeanour) from the oppressive threat constantly hanging over almost every other character.

Watership Down, whose Royal World premiere was attended by Prince Charles, was a major commercial hit, becoming the sixth most popular film of 1979 in British theatres.[7] But the film also attracted controversy. The debate began when the BBFC awarded *Watership Down* a U rating, reasoning that 'Animation removes the realistic gory horror in the occasional scenes of violence and bloodshed'.[8] This decision is among the most complained about in the history of the BBFC and was immediately condemned by the film's director, Rosen, who personally requested that the BBFC assign it the 'A' rating.[9] Rosen believed that only in Britain was *Watership Down* considered a children's novel; in the United States, it was viewed as an adult allegory.[10] Contemporary British critics did not agree. *The Spectator*'s Ted Whitehead saw it as 'a straightforward children's adventure story', and while *The Guardian*'s Derek Malcolm asserted that it is 'as appealing to adults as children and, just possibly, to people who don't normally go to the cinema', and he insisted that 'It is not true . . . that the film is too violent and disturbing for children.'[11]

Today, by contrast, the film has passed into the collective folk memory as a nightmarish, almost inexplicable aberration within the history of children's film, a genre that (in Britain, at least) has since become far more innocuous.

---

[7] Paul Donovan and Douglas Thompson, 'Booming Bunnies', *The Daily Mail*, 17 October 1978, 24; Justin Smith, 'Cinema Statistics, Box Office and Related Data', in *British Film Culture in the 1970s: The Boundaries of Pleasure*, ed. Sue Harper and Justin Smith (Edinburgh: Edinburgh University Press, 2012), 273.
[8] 'Watership Down', *British Board of Film Classification*, 15 February 1978. https://darkroom.bbfc.co.uk/original/1b0cb7188e02ac62c6cdcce5f2d1b928:2199e5760ab7c37b5b037fdee3a35735/watership-down-report.pdf (accessed 25 October 2021).
[9] Glenys Roberts, 'The Rabbits of Warren Street', *The Times*, 19 October 1978: 11.
[10] Roberts, 'The Rabbits of Warren Street'.
[11] Ted Whitehead, 'Cinema', *The Spectator*, 20 October 1978: 30; Derek Malcolm, 'The Buck Stops Here', *The Guardian*, 19 October 1978: 12.

Hyperbolic it may be, but this view of *Watership Down* as 'unsuitable for children' requires some consideration. First, it bears pointing out that both *The Belstone Fox* and *Tarka the Otter* were classified as 'A' films on account of their punctuating moments of gruesome action and the bleakness of the milieu. Those ratings have escaped scrutiny, since neither film is especially well-remembered today, but standards of acceptability in the children's film (in Britain at least) have clearly changed since the 1970s. In some regards, attitudes have liberalized; mild swearing, sexual content and relatively strong violence are now considered 'suitable' for children's consumption. However, it is hard to imagine the punctuating moments of gruesome action and the clearly polemical social discourse at work in all four films being viewed as palatable in contemporary British children's cinema (which is characterized, in part, by the strategic avoidance of any hint of political contentiousness).

Freed from the comparatively rigid institutional parameters of mainstream Hollywood and post-1990s British cinema, the producers of these films worked under fewer constraints than their latter-day counterparts. There are various reasons why this might be so, and a full answer would require more space than is possible here. However, it does seem clear that a confluence of social, political, stylistic and industrial factors were at play. The lingering controversy over *Watership Down*'s status as a children's film is not purely a result of ongoing popularity, though, but also stems from its status as an animated film. Its sequences of rabbits being savaged to death are apparently more disturbing than instances of violent mayhem in, say, the *Indiana Jones* (1981–2008) or *Harry Potter* (2001–11) films. Presumably, this is largely because *Watership Down* presents psychologically disconcerting incongruities in the fictional realm of anthropomorphized animals, which runs contrary to the domineering, sentimentalized Disney image. Whereas real-life experiences of nature might prepare viewers (even children) for the dysphoric elements in the live-action films, representation of animals and the natural world in children's animation are enmeshed in the ideology of Western childhood. As Rosen explains, violent rabbits created problems 'because of the legacy of the Disney studio'.[12] Nonetheless, it is important to remember that all four films *perform* animality for ideological and aesthetic purposes. While the live-action films present the appearance of unmediated reality, their often unstinting representations of nature 'red in tooth and claw' (as Tennyson has it) no less reflect the cultural and political contexts of 1970s Britain than *Watership Down*'s more abstract, but equally troubling, encounters between humans and animals. Of the four films discussed in this chapter, only *Watership Down* retains a prominent place in the popular cultural consciousness. To some degree, this reflects the enduring popularity of Adams's novel, which still sells hundreds of thousands of copies per year

---

[12] Roberts, 'The Rabbits of Warren Street'.

worldwide, as well as its striking, occasionally expressionist visual style and the seemingly indelible mark it made on contemporary audiences.[13] In contrast, the neglect of its live-action counterparts (despite their clear virtues) adds weight to Terry Staples's claim to the ephemeral nature of British children's cinema.[14] These films are long overdue for rediscovery; their critiques of human aggression and self-absorption, and their implicit demand for a greener politics – one less marked by speciesism – remain pertinent today. All four films work to expose the brutality that lies behind the veneer of human civilization, showing us that the savagery of the natural world was never truly left behind.

---

[13]Sandra Beckett, *Crossover Fiction: Global and Historical Perspectives* (London: Routledge, 2009), 107–8.
[14]Terry Staples, *All Pals Together: The Story of Children's Cinema* (Edinburgh: Edinburgh University Press, 1997), 195–6.

CHAPTER 6

They watered ship down: Eco-doom and ecopedagogy in adaptations of *Watership Down* and *The Animals of Farthing Wood*

Hollie Adams

Living in rural Devon, a daily excursion often entails sightings of various species of birds, insects and mammals. These sightings are usually expected in rural areas; however, sightings are now all over the UK as the natural world more frequently meets the industrialization of the human world: foxes skulk through car parks; rabbits dart out onto pathways and deer get caught in headlights. These human encounters with wildlife are a stark reminder that we share our earth, and that we need to be respectful as we cross each other's paths. However, with increased industrialization and a rising population, the natural world and the space non-human animals inhabit are being encroached upon by industries who may feel we need housing, farmland, factories, etc. The consequences of this are a declining biodiversity with animals left displaced or worse, destroyed. This daily occurrence is something we need to raise awareness and educate about as so many turn a blind eye or do not even realize it is happening.

As a secondary school English teacher, I am in the unique position to educate young people and raise awareness about current issues. A writing prompt in a Year 7 class asked the eleven-to-twelve-year-old students to write a descriptive piece based on the destruction of a forest. Students chose their own narrative perspective that they felt fit the piece. As I read the pieces, I noticed that a large majority of students had written from an animal's point of view, highlighting the devastation, and the innate emotions they felt as their home was destroyed. These pieces were emotional, and the students wrote in great detail. I was intrigued to find out my students' reasoning and so asked during a feedback class. Eighteen of my thirty students said that they felt animals would suffer the most from the destruction, and they wanted to give them a voice. A small percentage mentioned how animals were vulnerable and could not speak for themselves. Using this as a discussion point, I asked students about examples where we see an animal's narrative voice and where we see vulnerability in media featuring animals; *Watership Down* (the 1978 film by Martin Rosen) was mentioned after a few Michael Morpurgo books. Students were divided about *Watership Down*. Many commented on the terror that they felt when watching the film; however, some students, after hearing their classmates mention terror, said that perhaps it was full of terror and trauma to educate about the impact humans have on animals and how important this is.

Since its release in 1978, *Watership Down* has become known as 'one of the greatest British animated films of the past 50 years'; however, it has also most notably been labelled as one that 'terrified an entire generation', which can be seen from my classroom discussion.[1] It is a film that 'plunges down a rabbit hole of distressing imagery from the start and rarely lets up'.[2] When Rosen's film is mentioned, horror and trauma often surround the topic. Indeed, it is no surprise then that parents/carers have shielded their children from the film due to the fear that they will be traumatized by any extreme and harrowing portrayals of destruction, devastation and bunny violence. Interestingly, some of my Year 7 and Year 8 students (aged between eleven and thirteen) divulged that they were still not allowed to watch the film and had only seen advertisements for it when aired on TV. It is perhaps no surprise, then, that when a new television adaptation of the novel was announced to be in production by the BBC and Netflix, producers clarified that this version would not be 'as harrowingly violent as

---

[1]Ed Power, 'A Piercing Screen: How Watership Down Terrified an Entire Generation', *Independent*, 20 October 2018. https://www.independent.co.uk/arts-entertainment/films/features/watership-down-film-bright-eyes-rabbits-disease-martin-rosen-richard-adams-disney-a8590226.html (accessed 1 February 2021).
[2]Power, 'A Piercing Screen'.

the original' 1978 film.³ However, one could argue that depicting the horror of fraught human–animal relations is beneficial in educating and raising awareness about wildlife displacement, ecological disaster and humanity's destructive actions towards non-human animals. By erasing the trauma, we create yet more animal stories where animals are used for entertainment. Film and literature often show trauma narratives from a human perspective and are not watered down; so why, when it comes to animals, do we feel the need to shield? Perhaps it is because some feel that these narratives cause 'eco-doom', generating a type of fear that parents have recently started to question.⁴ Eco-doom, or eco-anxiety, is the 'fear of environmental damage or ecological disaster' at a large scale, as defined by Medical News Today.⁵ While not officially listed as a mental health disorder, it has become prevalent among all ages over the past decade. These fears raise the question whether narratives like *Watership Down*, *The Animals of Farthing Wood* (1992–5) and other texts fill the viewer with this sense of dread. Perhaps they do, but based on my direct experience with young people, they also have the ability to raise awareness and educate. Those that fear the decline of biodiversity, mass extinctions and mass environmental catastrophes may already be tuned in to the issues we see in these visual representations, but those that are not inclined to believe in the decline of the natural world may think twice when watching texts that deal with the human impact on the natural world. This chapter will discuss later the importance of our representations of human–animal relationships in children's media specifically, and how they raise awareness and educate about environmental issues, while also questioning if they are simply trying to inspire 'eco-doom'.

In 2008, Steven Wolk argued that 'the time is urgent for all schools and teachers to awaken their students' consciousness to the world and help them develop the knowledge and inspiration to make a better world'.⁶ This argument echoes an approach to education called ecopedagogy. Emerging in the 1990s, ecopedagogy is 'literary education for reading and rereading human acts of environmental violence' and is prevalent to this day.⁷ The approach

---

³Julie Raeside, 'Watership Down Without the Claws? You Shouldn't Have Bothered', *The Guardian*, 29 April 2016. https://www.theguardian.com/commentisfree/2016/apr/29/watership-down-remake-without-claws (accessed 1 June 2021).
⁴Patrick Barkham, 'Tears at Bedtime: Are Children's Books on Environment Causing Climate Anxiety?' *The Guardian*, 27 February 2020. https://www.theguardian.com/books/2020/feb/27/tears-at-bedtime-greta-thunberg-effect-behind-boom-in-childrens-climate-crisis-books (accessed 1 February 2021).
⁵Jennifer Huizen, 'What to Know About Eco-anxiety', *Medical News Today*, 19 December 2019. https://www.medicalnewstoday.com/articles/327354 (accessed March 2021).
⁶Steven Wolk, 'Reading for a Better World: Teaching for Social Responsibility with Young Adult Literature', *Journal of Adolescent & Adult Literacy* 52, no. 8 (2008): 664–73.
⁷Greg William Misiaszek, *Ecopedagogy: Critical Environmental Teaching for Planetary Justice and Global Sustainable Development* (London: Bloomsbury Academic, 2021), 1.

'is centred on better understanding the connections between human acts of environmental violence and social violence', especially related to 'domination over the rest of Nature'.[8] This approach can be used to argue for the realistic depictions of human–animal relations in literature and media, and as a secondary school teacher, it is an approach I often take in my own pedagogy when choosing resources. Wolk's argument was posed in 2008, and over ten years later the general public has seen a surge in the modern environmental movement. 2018 to the present-day pandemic in 2021 have become banner years for this movement. Social media has been ablaze with impassioned content about humankind's impact upon the earth, inspiring many to act. Alongside social media, other forms of media may also inspire the public to take action. The general public may have been inspired to take environmental action, change their dietary lifestyle and become a spokesperson for animal welfare, but authors and creators have also been inspired to depict realistic human–animal relationships. They believe it is important to not shield children and adults from the impact humanity has upon the earth. In addition to Richard Adams, the author of the *Watership Down* novel (1972), authors include Gill Lewis, Piers Torday and Sita Brahmachari.

In this chapter, the film adaptation of *Watership Down*, the TV adaptation of Colin Dann's book series *The Animals of Farthing Wood* and the most recent *Watership Down* adaptation, co-produced by Netflix and the BBC in 2018, will be analysed to discuss the way they show the destructive nature of humans. *The Animals of Farthing Wood*, while not directly inspired by Rosen's film or Adams's novel, shares striking parallels with *Watership Down*, namely in its uncompromising portrayals of human–animal relations. As a result, both texts have prominent places within British cultural memory, and they are often raised in the same breath in discourses surrounding British children's environmentally themed media. This allows for a productive comparison between the two texts.[9]

Background

Before analysing these case studies, it is important to first look at the sociopolitical contexts of the 1978 film *Watership Down* and the

---

[8]Misiaszek, *Ecopedagogy*, 1.
[9]While there was also an animated television adaptation of *Watership Down* broadcast from 1999 to 2001, I find *The Animals of Farthing Wood* to be a more effective spiritual successor to 1978 film. As the 1999 series of *Watership Down* significantly toned down the novel and 1978 film's violent content in order to meet dominant perceptions of 'suitability' in children's television, much of my arguments regarding the 2018 television adaptation are also applicable to the 1999 series.

2018 television remake. The changing perceptions of Green Party UK provide a useful case study to demonstrate how environmental attitudes have developed in British society.

In 1972, the Green Party in the UK described itself more as a 'political movement rather than a party'.[10] The party was formed by 'the merging of two organisations' – The PEOPLE party and the Movement for Survival.[11] In late 1972, founders Tony and Lesley Whittaker, Michael Benfield and Freda Sanders established the PEOPLE party after becoming terrified over Paul R. Ehrlich's predictions of famine, due to rapid population growth.[12] The second organization, the Movement for Survival, was established by Teddy Goldsmith, who focussed on the 'unsustainable nature of indefinite economic growth and argued for de-industrialisation and decentralisation'.[13] These parties officially merged in 1973 and launched the 'Manifesto for Survival'. This focussed on the survival of the human race rather than all inhabitants of the world. However, this newfound realization about the destruction of industrialization can be linked to how views changed to realize the negative impact of humans on the natural world, providing an illuminating sociopolitical backdrop to the production of *Watership Down*. Despite these legitimate fears, these parties were deemed too radical and led them to change direction to reflect a new 'green' focus under the name 'The Ecology Party'.[14]

The choice of name at the time was not entirely understood, as the word 'ecology' was quite obscure.[15] However, the party shifted their thinking towards values related to humans and non-humans, which reflect the values of the Green Party today. The Ecology Party situated themselves within animal rights, education and health, and from this, the party began to grow in the late 1970s and early 1980s. Activists began to join, and they looked to become the fourth biggest political party in the UK. More people were inspired by the green focus on both humans and animals, highlighting the importance of all factors of the natural world. This finally led, in 1985, to the party adopting the name the Green Party. Unfortunately, they did not find the same success as other Green parties in Europe as they found that they could not connect with others who supported environmental issues as

---

[10]David Taylor, 'Early History: Green Party Origins', *UK Green History: The Green Politics Movement 1972 to 1989*, 18 August 2016. https://green-history.uk/articles/opinions/early-history#article-info (accessed 31 March 2021).
[11]Taylor, 'Early History'.
[12]Tom Bawden, 'The Green Party: A Short History', *Independent*, 23 November 2014. https://www.independent.co.uk/news/uk/politics/green-party-short-history-9878649.html (accessed 1 February 2021).
[13]Bawden, 'The Green Party'.
[14]Bawden, 'The Green Party'.
[15]Taylor, 'Early History'.

these people did not want to be associated with what they saw as a 'political party'. This has widely led to poor election outcomes. In recent years, the Green Party have emerged with a slight increase in votes. In 2019, they almost doubled their votes in the general election. However, they only won one seat.[16]

This slight increase in interest could be seen as a response to the escalating climate emergency. In 2019 it was reported that 'more than two-fifths of UK species including animals, birds and butterflies have seen significant declines in recent decades'.[17] 'Thousands of acres of habitats are being lost to development' and due to this, 'nearly 700 species . . . have seen populations decline since 1970', and '15 percent are threatened with being lost from Britain'.[18] Young conservationist Sophie Pavelle stated that 'she had felt the loss of nature more acutely this year than any other', and this is how many others, including myself, have felt.[19] This is where the media can step in. As we see a rise in media usage, the public see more media than ever, especially young people. Using this screen time to show movies or series that deal with the issues of biodiversity that the world face may empower young people to take positive action against climate change.

The news outlined earlier has reached far and wide and inspired climate change strikes across the globe with thousands in attendance. UK students have staged Friday school walkouts to protest about the impact of humans on the natural world and the 'unjustifiable' lack of action taken by our government on climate change.[20] Headed by Swedish activist Greta Thunberg, 'large crowds and brightly coloured placards of the school climate strikes became some of the defining images of 2019'.[21] This movement has even moved online during the Covid-19 pandemic with Thunberg hosting 'mass video calls' with placards decorating screens, dubbed 'Fridays for

---

[16]Donnachadh McCarthy, 'National Politics is over for the Green Party – The Only Way it Can Fight the Climate Crisis is to Radicalise', *Independent*, 29 January 2020. https://www.independent.co.uk/voices/climate-change-crisis-green-party-lucas-bartley-general-election-first-past-post-a9307731.html (accessed 2 February 2021).

[17]Emily Beament, 'Biodiversity Collapse in UK Continues', *Ecologist: The Journal for the Post Industrial Age*, 4 October 2019. https://theecologist.org/2019/oct/04/biodiversity-collapse-uk-continues (accessed 3 November 2020).

[18]Beament, 'Biodiversity Collapse in UK Continues'.

[19]Beament, 'Biodiversity Collapse in UK Continues'.

[20]Ian Johnston, 'Government's Own Environment Experts Slam its "unjustifiable" Lack of Action on Climate Change', *Independent*, 29 June 2017. https://www.independent.co.uk/climate-change/news/government-climate-change-experts-unjustifiable-lack-action-environment-global-warming-fossil-fuels-committee-a7813741.html (accessed 1 December 2020).

[21]Jessica Murray, 'Climate Strikes Continue Online: "we want to keep the momentum going"', *The Guardian*, 22 April 2020. https://www.theguardian.com/environment/2020/apr/22/climate-strikes-continue-online-we-want-to-keep-the-momentum-going (accessed 2 December 2020).

Future'.[22] This movement, despite the pandemic, has kept 'the momentum going' so that interest will remain high.[23] While these online protests are beneficial for education, they are also keeping the conversation going and 'giving the strikers a unique opportunity to connect with people they would not normally get the chance to meet'; it gives an international perspective to those around them, that this is not just a national issue, it is global.[24]

From this, it is evident that the youth today are interested and inspired to take action that the government may otherwise not; but what about those who are perhaps unaware of what is going on in the world around them? This is where film, TV and books can raise awareness and educate. It is pertinent that the interest in environmentalism and creation of the Green Party emerged concurrent with *Watership Down*'s original release in the 1970s, and that a similar wave of climate change awareness and activism also surrounds the remake of *Watership Down* as a television series in 2018.

Watership Down (1978)

Written by Adams to entertain his two young daughters on a car journey, *Watership Down* is widely considered a children's book despite its controversial themes. Animals have always been 'pervasive in children's literature', and this is perhaps why *Watership Down* is categorized as 'children's literature'.[25] In children's animal literature, 'child readers accept talking animals as equally worthy beings who, like them, are struggling to forge relationships and gain acceptance.'[26] These books help children escape school, parents, bullies and other childhood worries. They are invited to become one with the characters and live their experience. Due to this, 'novels can play a special role in ethical education' and so can films.[27] However, these types of novels – and later, films – have rarely focussed on the harrowing effects humans can have on animal experiences. Instead, positive human–animal relationships are usually explored. Films like *Flipper* (Clark, 1963) and *The Call of the Wild* (Annakin, 1972) follow a pattern of a human saving an animal, developing a bond, and a climax causing the human to depend on the animal to save them.

Adams's novel and Rosen's adaptation do not follow this traditional pattern as they criticize humans and their harmful actions; there are very

---

[22]Murray, 'Climate Strikes Continue Online'.
[23]Murray, 'Climate Strikes Continue Online'.
[24]Murray, 'Climate Strikes Continue Online'.
[25]Catherine L. Elick, *Talking Animals in Children's Fiction: A Critical Study* (Jefferson: McFarland & Company, 2015), 7.
[26]Elick, *Talking Animals in Children's Fiction*, 6.
[27]Elick, *Talking Animals in Children's Fiction*, 10.

few positive human–animal relationships in *Watership Down*. The animated film shows the mix of human industrialization with the natural life of the rabbits and when these come together, disaster occurs. The rabbits are seen as powerless; they have no way to stop the oncoming onslaught by the humans. However, although the rabbits have no power, they are given a voice, which helps educate the audience about the effect humans have upon wildlife. In this section, I will discuss two scenes in the film version of *Watership Down*, which have consistently appeared in conversations with my colleagues and students as scenes that have had a lasting impression: the rabbits crossing the road and Captain Holly's recount of the collapse of Sandleford Warren.

From the beginning, *Watership Down* does not hold back when the audience are immediately introduced to the devastating consequences of human actions. After the opening prologue the film begins with beautiful pastoral imagery, lulling the audience into a false sense of security, which is quickly decimated when we meet Fiver, who has a terrifying premonition of a field covered in blood and the destruction of Sandleford Warren. The urgent music and the speed at which the blood covers the field emphasize how the rabbits must quickly abandon their home or face impending doom. While the rabbits blindly follow, Rosen presents the human audience with the truth with a wide shot of a large, wooden sign, stating that 'six acres of excellent building land is to be developed with high class modern residences'. The language here is insensitive, corporate and uncaring. It provides the audience with understanding and allows them to connect to the fear and urgency of the rabbits, rather than their own human selves. Here, the 'audience's emotional identification with literary characters leads to his or her experience of sympathetic imagination – the extent to which we can think ourselves into the being of another'.[28] The audience, feeling the fear and urgency through the music and imagery, may realize the true horror of the scenario and come to terms with what will happen. They may also recognize these scenes from around them too as housing developments and new businesses are frequently constructed on fields in the UK.

The audience's sympathetic imagination is triggered constantly by the film's tragedies, which subject the viewer to the devastation humans cause. This devastation is often shown in passing, perhaps to highlight the normalization of these tragedies from our human perspective. For example, on their exodus from the warren, the rabbits must cross a road. During this scene, the viewer can see the corpse of a hedgehog, previously run over. The hedgehog's corpse is shown in passing, perhaps reminding the viewer that this is a constant in the natural world. The scene then frightens the viewer as

---

[28] Barbara Hardy Beierl, 'The Sympathetic Imagination and the Human-animal Bond: Fostering Empathy Through Reading Imaginative Literature', *AnthroZoos* 21, no. 3 (2008): 213–20.

Bigwig is almost knocked down by a speeding car; we never see the car nor the human driving. Humans are faceless, ever-present dangers in the world of the rabbits, and here, we are reminded of the carelessness of our own species. This scene, despite being short, is important in educating children and adults further about humanity's impact on animal lives. Roads are man-made, unnatural to the animals. Most animals are unaware of the dangers, and so humans must be mindful. Naturally, accidents happen but most times, they are avoidable. This heartless, hurried attitude is what threatens our biodiversity to this day. This scene encourages the human viewer to see this common, daily exercise of driving from an animal's perspective so we may think differently about our country drives.

The film constantly shows humans as unfeeling, unthinking, cruel, selfish and violent to both the rabbits and the human audience. We (as humans) 'blatantly conceal the living world from our conscience, which allows us to dominate, expand and develop the land at our will' with no emotions.[29] This is perhaps most evident from Captain Holly's description of the warren's destruction:

> Men came. Filled in the burrows. Couldn't get out. There was a strange sound. Hissing. The air turned bad. Runs blocked with dead bodies. I couldn't get out. Everything turned mad. Warren, herbs, roots, grass, all pushed into the earth.

The imagery paired with Holly's words is particularly horrifying as we see flashing clips of red-eyed, suffocating rabbits, struggling as they are gassed by men, who tear up the earth with bulldozers, leaving red tracks that represent the blood spilled. The soundtrack that accompanies this scene is haunting, horrifying and evokes disgust. However, the rabbits' words here are the most poignant. They state matter-of-factly that 'men have always hated us', 'they'll never rest until they've spoiled the earth'. Holly rebuffs this saying that 'they just destroyed the warren because we were in their way'. The frank dialogue reflects reality. The rabbits to humans are nothing but 'an obstacle, a nuisance, which hinders their progress'.[30] The viewer may be left disillusioned, thinking about their own actions and the actions of those around them. In previous research completed in a school, I found that reading fiction with key issues at the heart of them helped students understand the world, made them more aware and made them feel discomfort at what they had learned. Jacqueline Glasgow states that 'good books unsettle us,

---

[29]Christine Battista, 'Ecofantasy and Animal Dystopia in Richard Adams' Watership Down', in *Environmentalism in the Realm of Science Fiction and Fantasy Literature*, ed. Chris Baratta (Cambridge: Cambridge Scholars Publishing, 2012), 163.
[30]Battista, 'Ecofantasy and Animal Dystopia', 164.

make us ask questions about what we thought was certain; they don't just reaffirm everything we already know'.[31] These students and the audience perhaps found the contents of their viewing unsettling because they had been previously shielded from these experiences. With *Watership Down*, the audience are given the opportunity to be a part of a new experience, seeing life through a rabbit's eyes.

Media can offer an important way in which we explore the connection of the human and natural world and 'can transform our attitudes towards the land, towards the nonhuman world'.[32] Used within the framework of ecopedagogy, we can then teach about environmental issues and change the way younger generations or, indeed, older generations think. In *Watership Down*, the audience sees the trauma and impact humans have upon the environment through the eyes of non-human inhabitants, and Adams and Rosen urge 'us to identify with the nonhuman world so that we might begin to transform our anthropocentric orientation into a more ethical, ecocentric perspective'.[33] These narratives could be seen as purely trying to create eco-doom and traumatize a nation, but these adaptations are what keep environmental messages topical for young people. These texts may be key in educating those who have never thought of our impact on the world.

The Animals of Farthing Wood

The Sandleford rabbits are not the only non-human protagonists that have the potential to challenge an audience's thinking. Colin Dann's book series *The Animals of Farthing Wood* was first published in 1979 and was later adapted to television in the 1990s. Like *Watership Down*, the catalyst of the events in the series is the displacement of multiple species of animals from their habitats due to the development of new houses. In contrast to Rosen's rabbit-filled adaptation, the species portrayed in Dann's series span a wide variety of wildlife found in Britain, such as badgers, weasels, adders, shrews, pheasants and foxes. The great variety of non-human protagonists provides the viewer with the opportunity to see through the perspectives of multiple species and their unique experiences.

At the beginning of *The Animals of Farthing Wood*, the pastoral, idyllic vision of the British countryside we first see in *Watership Down* is absent; the viewer is immediately immersed into construction work. The atmosphere is ominous, the music eerie as the animals watch the devastation

---

[31]Jaqueline Glasgow, 'Teaching Social Justice through Young Adult Literature', *The English Journal* 90, no. 6 (2001): 54–61.
[32]Battista, 'Ecofantasy and Animal Dystopia', 158.
[33]Battista, 'Ecofantasy and Animal Dystopia', 159.

of their habitat. Unlike Sandleford Warren, the animals are aware of what is happening. They echo Holly and Bigwig as one of the protagonists, Badger, states that the humans are 'chopping away at us every day and still they are not satisfied', once more critiquing the ruthlessness and selfishness of humans. The audience is presented with the idea that humans may never stop encroaching on natural habitats and leaving behind devastation. While we see the destruction of animal habitats throughout the series, we also are shown the true horror of man versus nature and nature versus nature. The audience's sympathetic imagination is activated as the series portrays the non-human experience of death, tragedy and grief, particularly through the twenty-four characters killed in just thirty-nine episodes. Memorable examples of these deaths are the death of the Pheasant and the Hedgehog families. In series 1, episodes 3 and 4, while sleeping near a farm, Mrs Pheasant is shot, plucked and roasted. Her husband, Mr Pheasant finds her, roasted and being enjoyed by the humans. In his surprise, he sobs loudly, showing a raw human emotion of grief, which helps the audience sympathize with him. Sadly, his sobs alert the humans to his presence, and he is also shot. The audience here are encouraged to sympathize with Mr Pheasant and think about their own choices. In episode 10, an episode that almost directly parallels *Watership Down*, the Hedgehog family cross a busy motorway. When they get scared, their instincts take over, they curl up and are both struck by a truck. Both *Watership Down* and *Animals of Farthing Wood* use these scenes to critique human ignorance and modernization. However, while *Watership Down* shows the blatant cruelty displayed by humans to non-humans, *Animals of Farthing Wood* highlights that humans can be ignorant towards each other too. For example, when a careless human throws a cigarette into dry grass, a fire breaks out threatening non-humans and humans alike. Like *Watership Down*, humans are depicted as faceless, unfeeling, selfish and ruthless. However, there is a chance of redemption for the humans in both film and TV series. Lucy the farmer's daughter in *Watership Down* will be discussed in the next section. In *Animals of Farthing Wood*, there are the naturalists, who set up nature reserves, such as White Deer Park. The naturalists are different from all other humans and are an exception to the negativity previously portrayed. In this regard, the audience is not entirely disillusioned by the way in which humans treat animals.

    This series may be concerning to parents to put children to bed with fears for the earth's future fresh in their heads, but this series also provides hope for the future. It presents the viewer with the opportunity to live alongside animals, peacefully. Barkham states that the environmental book boom has been driven by 'a genuine interest and passion from children' and they allow children to 'think about what they can do'.[34] The opportunity to read these

---

[34] Barkham, 'Tears at Bedtime'.

books gives 'children power and agency in all sorts of ways' and makes them feel that they can make a difference.³⁵ *The Animals of Farthing Wood* helps children see this with the introduction to the naturalists. These despairing tales filled with 'eco-doom' may create fear, but they allow viewers to see the possibility of living in unison with animals without creating fraught interspecies tensions.

Watership Down (2018)

This brief excursion into *Animals of Farthing Wood* leads us straight back to Sandleford Warren. The BBC and Netflix's announcement of their 2018 remake of *Watership Down* brought with it questions about the gore and violence, the age certification, and its environmental message. It also brought with it the question of why remake this 'traumatic' story into a new series. On the one hand, it could be argued that the BBC and Netflix wanted to make a more universal and child-friendly adaptation of Adams's famous tale. Ben Travers, in his review, confirms that the series is 'less ghastly' and that 'the gore has been toned down', but in his opinion, it still is not appropriate for small children.³⁶ The fact that the BBFC later applied an age rating of 12 to the series corroborates this view. It thus seems more likely that this remake was produced not just to provide a more 'child-friendly' version but also to resonate with the rise in recent environmental awareness. This is confirmed by the writer for the series, Tom Bidwell, who states that 'the environmental message is crucial' and that he doesn't mind 'if it's very on the nose because what's happening to the environment is one of the most important crises of our time and this story reflects that'.³⁷ It is therefore illuminating to compare the depiction of environmental messages in the series to the 1978 film, especially given the similarity in each text's sociopolitical contexts that are strongly characterized by climate anxiety.

After a mythological prologue (as in the 1978 film), the series opens with the familiar pastoral imagery of Sandleford Warren. Quickly juxtaposed with Fiver's vision, time stands still, and the scene becomes dark. The warren is crumbling, and we see dead rabbits throughout as we follow Fiver's point of view. These dead rabbits show no signs of injury or blood, and it is only through Fiver's terror that we realize they are dead, not sleeping. The vision

---

³⁵Barkham, 'Tears at Bedtime'.
³⁶Ben Travers, 'Watership Down Review: Netflix Makes a Stunning, Scarring Story a Hare Too Ugly', *IndieWire*, 20 December 2018. https://www.indiewire.com/2018/12/netflix-watership-down-review-2018-miniseries-1202029873/ (accessed 4 March 2021).
³⁷Sarah Hughes, 'Watership Down – The Film Traumatised a Generation Gets a Gentler update', *iNews*, 23 December 2018. https://inews.co.uk/culture/watership-down-film-new-bbc-remake-review-238429 (accessed 5 March 2021).

ends with a digger; however, unlike in the film, we do not see the bloody claw marks it leaves. Later, Fiver has another vision of the blood over the hills; the field turns red with no streams or trickles to depict blood. The string music is eerie and more mournful than suspenseful. Instead of startling and worrying the viewer, it evokes sadness. This sadness lessens the sense of the urgency of the film, evoking sympathy for the rabbits but not a sense of horror at the humans who are responsible.

The next scene furthers this by presenting an almost positive portrayal of humans, while still trying to produce an environmental message. As the rabbits make plans to leave, they sit by a river. The scene is dark, eerie and quiet until a tin can washes up on the riverbed and startles the rabbits. At this point, we hear humans mentioned for the first time. The rabbits state that the item comes from humans and has been sighted more frequently lately. This is a new environmental angle for the *Watership Down* story. Litter is not predominant in the film; the series uses this scene to possibly remind the audience that our thoughtless littering affects wildlife and burdens their homes. However, although this tin can seems sinister at first, the litter serves as a useful tool for the rabbits. This undermines the message that litter can be harmful. As the Sandleford runaways come to the river, they realize they must cross or be captured. At this point, a dustbin lid sails by. The rabbits' quick thinking leads them to jump on the lid, using it to float to safety, instead of the driftwood in the film. With this, viewers can argue that litter may be beneficial to wildlife and somehow manages to portray this positively. In the 1978 *Watership Down*, humans are consistently depicted as a negative influence on the natural world, with the brief exception of Lucy. This scene in the 2018 series begins with raising awareness about the negativity of littering, but instead, awareness is forgotten when the litter is presented as though it is not a threat.

Despite this, humans are then depicted negatively throughout, especially in the two key scenes: the road scene and the return of Captain Holly. The road scene is very similar to the one in the film. Bigwig steps onto the road, claiming it is harmless until a car speeds by and Bigwig flattens to the floor. At first, it looks like he has been run over, but he quickly jumps up and realizes the danger. This is when the camera pans to a hedgehog dead on the road. Bigwig, at this point, uses verbs such as 'crush' to suggest the violent, aggressive nature of the hedgehog's death. It is a relief that the series has shown this scene as it highlights again the careless, selfish nature of humans. Then in Captain Holly's description of the warren's destruction, we hear the screams of female and young rabbits, alongside the rumbling of the digger. We hear scrabbling and see the rabbits trying to escape. The scene shows the digger digging into the rabbits, yet there is, unrealistically, no gore. Although this still depicts the faceless humans negatively, Captain Holly recalls that it was friends and family who killed each other in blind panic as they scratched and scrabbled their way out of the warren. This highlights that while humans can harm rabbits, they can also harm each other.

Perhaps the most enlightening scene in the series though is when Fiver returns from being attacked by the farmer's cat. We see him let out of a car by who we can infer is Lucy, the farmer's daughter. Fiver reunites with his warren, and Hazel has a realization, saying, 'maybe some humans do understand that all living things suffer, that all living things deserve respect'. This, like the naturalists in *Animals of Farthing Wood*, reassures the audience that we are not all bad; a 'have your cake and eat it' approach to raising environmental awareness that seeks to excuse human behaviour while also seeking to change it.

In all, the 2018 *Watership Down* series still depicts humans negatively and highlights their impact on animal lives through a bloodless, less violent manner. However, the lack of blood and violence almost eradicates the 'eco-doom' that the 1978 film created. My students enjoyed the series, finding it less frightening than the original, but they also stated that they would not have identified environmental aspects had I not mentioned it to them. They personally felt they would choose the series over the film as they preferred less traumatic viewing but said they could not see an educational benefit and understood the 1978 film's importance. These comments, while anecdotal, highlight that 'eco-doom' can be an effective way of communicating environmental messages and that the series, while valuable in its own way, may lose its educational benefit by toning down the violence and trauma.

Conclusion

Exposing young people to violent depictions of human–animal relationships worries some, especially as we leave children with despairing ideas about what the world is or could be like. However, texts are a way to start conversations and provide messages to the reader/viewer. They have the opportunity to educate and to be realistic in what it depicts. In doing so, it may inspire other creators to be brave and creative in the way that they portray our world.

Watership Down and *The Animals of Farthing Wood* can be upsetting and traumatizing. They can lead the audience down the metaphorical rabbit hole of despair, but it could be argued that they are necessary viewing material. Through literature and film, children learn ways to sympathize and empathize with characters, stop stigmatization, and are made aware of issues. Today's children 'will face huge environmental challenges': they are going to witness rising sea levels, polluted oceans, and they will feel the lack of bird song in the air or insects buzzing by.[38] It is a harrowing reality, but fiction 'can help children deal with these grim eventualities'.[39] By being realistic and remaining hopeful in some ways, children (and other audience members) may 'engage with nature in profound ways' and realize a new connection with the natural world.[40] It has long been known that 'story has the power to develop empathy and build knowledge', and although 'children's books alone cannot save the nature world', they may teach, raise awareness, and provide possible solutions for change.[41] While leaving children to watch texts like the *Watership Down* film alone with no context could lead to feelings of 'eco-doom', it is possible for adults to lead a conversation, framing these depictions as educational. These books and films provide vehicles for such discussion and change, and we should not be shielded away from them.

---

[38] S. F. Said, 'Where the Wild Tales Are: How Stories Teach Kids to Nurture Nature', *Nature* 556 (2018): 434.
[39] Said, 'Where the Wild Tales Are', 434.
[40] Said, 'Where the Wild Tales Are', 434.
[41] Said, 'Where the Wild Tales Are', 435.

CHAPTER 7

Watership Down Under: When rabbits came to Australia

Dan Torre and Lienors Torre

In the British animated film *Watership Down* (Rosen, 1978) rabbits are portrayed favourably and serve as direct metaphors for human society. In Australia, however, rabbits have frequently generated more complicated representations as a result of their equally complicated status in Australian culture. In light of this difference, this chapter considers the contrasting attitudes towards rabbits in Australian and British culture; contextualizes *Watership Down* among the depiction of both rabbits and native animals in Australian animation; and subsequently directs special attention to *Watership Down*'s promotion and reception 'down under'. To consider *Watership Down* from an Australian perspective reveals surprising links between the film and the Australian animation industry, despite the film's British roots.

Invasive species

Rabbits are very prolific creatures (after all, they do breed like rabbits); they are also quick, intelligent and highly adaptable to changing conditions. These abilities are clearly articulated in the opening creation myth sequence of the animated film, *Watership Down*. Often described as having an Indigenous-Australian aesthetic (a point that will be returned to later), the opening sequence describes how assertively 'the rabbits wandered everywhere, multiplied and ate as they went'. As a result of this unrestrained behaviour, the sun god Lord Frith warns El-ahrairah, 'if you cannot control your people, I shall find ways to control them.' But, as the rabbits make no effort to control their appetites (or their population growth), Frith subsequently declares:

> All the world will be your enemy, Prince with a Thousand enemies. And when they catch you, they will kill you. But first they must catch you; digger, listener, runner, prince with the swift warning. Be cunning, and full of tricks, and your people will never be destroyed.

Although Frith did not directly curtail the rabbits' ability to proliferate, he did establish feasible countermeasures by emboldening and increasing the numbers of their natural predators. However, it could be argued (imagining that such a tale was true) that Frith failed to account for the extraordinary degree by which human intervention could disturb this equilibrium, especially with regard to the Australian continent.

Humans, particularly non-Indigenous settlers to Australia, have managed to greatly disrupt the continent's natural environment; and there are numerous instances in which introduced flora and fauna species have quickly evolved into highly invasive pests. Probably the most recognized species of invasive plant life has been the prickly-pear cactus,[1] and by far the most invasive animal species has been the European rabbit (*Oryctolagus cuniculus*). In fact, the spread of the European rabbit in Australia has been regarded as the rapidest of any invasive mammal in the world.[2]

Rabbits were initially brought to Australia with the first British fleets in the late 1700s; these rabbits, however, remained in captivity and were bred chiefly for their meat and fur. The first significant introduction of *feral* rabbits would not occur until the following century when the wealthy landowner, Thomas Austin, received thirteen wild rabbits from a relative in England. On Christmas Day, in 1859, he released these feral rabbits onto his property (located just outside of Melbourne) to provide his guests with some festive sport-hunting.[3] Some of these original thirteen rabbits evaded the hunters, and they soon multiplied exponentially; within just 10 years, over 14,000 rabbits were shot by guests staying at his estate. Some of the guests that Austin entertained included members of the British royal family.

In December 1867 Queen Victoria's son, Prince Alfred, visited Australia. He stayed at the Austin's homestead and went shooting there. In three

---

[1] Dan Torre, *Cactus* (London: Reaktion Books, 2017).
[2] 'Rabbits Introduced', *National Museum of Australia*. https://www.nma.gov.au/defining-moments/resources/rabbits-introduced (accessed 3 February 2021).
[3] 'Rabbits Introduced', *National Museum of Australia*.

and half hours over 1000 rabbits were shot by the party. The Prince alone shot 416 and was so delighted with the shoot another was arranged for the Prince's return visit to Victoria the following February.[4]

Austin was well known for his generosity and would give live pairs of rabbits to anyone who requested them. As a result, within just fifty years, rabbits had spread to more than two-thirds of the Australian continent, and by the 1920s it is estimated that there were as many as *ten billion* feral rabbits residing in Australia. One writer has pointed out that 'the ultimate irony' of this rabbit invasion was that some of the original British convicts had been sent to Australia as punishment for the very crime of 'poaching rabbit'.[5]

Although the rabbits initially provided hunting sport for wealthy landowners (as well as comforting reminders of their beloved English countryside), the animal's spread also led to the destruction of millions of acres of farm and grazing lands. It is estimated that just nine rabbits can eat more vegetation than a sheep.[6] Thus, many people grew to abhor rabbits and would attempt everything from poisoning and trapping the animals to the blasting of their underground burrows. 'Rabbit-proof' fences were also built to try to stop their spread across the continent; the largest of these fences spanned 1,700 kilometres, the entire north to south length of the Australian continent. These fences, however, proved to be mostly ineffective as the rabbits inevitably spread far beyond the fence lines before they could be completed.[7] Less publicized was the vast destruction that these rabbits caused to natural vegetation and native fauna.[8]

One interesting development, however, was that the rabbit infestations provided low-cost and plentiful meat sources for much of the human population, especially during the depression of the 1930s and during the years of the Second World War. By far, the least expensive meat available at the local butcher was rabbit; alternatively, one could enter virtually any vacant lot or paddock and quickly shoot or trap a rabbit or two for supper. An enterprising man from Melbourne, Jack McCraith, created an enormously successful business empire by selling wild-caught rabbit meat – at first for domestic consumption and later for international export as well. To supply the increasing demand for wild rabbit meat, a number of collection

---

[4]'Barwon Park Mansion', *National Trust*. https://www.nationaltrust.org.au/places/barwon-park/ (accessed 3 February 2021).
[5]Bruce Munday, *Those Wild Rabbits: How They Shaped Australia* (Adelaide: Wakefield Press, 2017), 6.
[6]Peter West, *Guide to Introduced Pest Animals of Australia* (Melbourne: CSIRO Publishing, 2018), 59.
[7]Mike Braysher, *Managing Australia's Pest Animals: A Guide to Strategic Planning and Effective Management* (Melbourne: CSIRO Publishing, 2017), 81.
[8]West, *Guide to Introduced Pest Animals of Australia*, 59.

stations were set up across the country. Independent trappers would sell their locally caught rabbits to these facilities, which would freeze-store the rabbit carcasses and then ship them to Melbourne to the McCraith canning factory. Through this business model, after just 10 years of operation, Jack McCraith had exported over 130 million canned wild rabbits to the rest of the world.[9] As a result, he managed to corner the global demand for rabbit meat – and in a rather ironic reversal, effectively 'flooded the British market'[10] with cheap canned rabbits from Australia (which were of course distant decedents of British wild rabbits). The plenitude of rabbits also generated an unexpected sub-industry, the production of rabbit-fur felt hats. In parallel to McCraith's rabbit success, several major hat manufacturers in Melbourne produced and sold tens of millions of these felt hats (which were made entirely from processed rabbit-fur fibres) to both domestic and international consumers.

In the early 1950s, in an effort to cull their numbers, the myxoma virus (*Myxomatosis cuniculi*) was intentionally introduced to rabbit populations in Australia. The virus had originated in South America at the turn of the century, but it had a much more benign effect on those populations. Scientists in Australia had been experimenting with the virus for several years before it was determined that it normally requires intermediary insects (such as mosquitoes and fleas) to facilitate its spread. Within six months of its release in Australia, over 500 million rabbits succumbed to the disease.[11] Myxomatosis causes a slow and cruel death with horribly apparent inflammation and visible lesions, and as a result many people became critical of the project. Many also began to fear for their own safety, worrying that the virus would jump to human populations. Because of these worries, the virus also quickly destroyed the rabbit meat industry – as nobody wanted to eat infected and potentially dangerous rabbit meat. The collapse of the meat industry also led to the collapse of the sizeable rabbit-fur felt hat industry. In an attempt to calm public fear, the top Australian scientists working on the virus project held a press conference where they publically injected themselves with the virus in order to prove that it was safe. This stunt, however, seemed to have had little effect on entrenched public

---

[9]Catherine Watson, *The Rabbit King: Jack McCraith and His Rabbit Empire* (Melbourne: Morning Star Publishing, 2015).

[10]John Martin, 'Case Study of a Changing Human–Animal Relationship: Wild Rabbits in Britain from the Nineteenth Century to the Onset of Myxomatosis', in *Shared lives of humans and animals: Animal agency in the global north*, ed. Tuomas Räsänen and Taina Syrjämaa (London: Routledge, 2017), 84.

[11]'How European Rabbits Took over Australia', *National Geographic*, 27 January 2020. https://www.nationalgeographic.org/article/how-european-rabbits-took-over-australia/ (accessed 9 February 2021).

opinion.¹² After a few years, many rabbits began to develop an immunity to the myxoma virus and rabbit populations began to increase. In 1996, an even more deadly virus, the RHDV (Rabbit Haemorrhagic Disease Virus), was officially introduced to rabbit populations in Australia, which killed up to 90 per cent of rabbit populations – particularly in dry areas where the myxoma virus had been less effective.¹³ In more recent years, much of the remaining Australian rabbit populations have also become resistant to the RHDV viruses, and so further virus research and introductions have occurred.

As with Australia, Britain also experienced an exploding rabbit population. However, the difference most certainly rests within the magnitude of the spread; it took rabbits some 700 years to spread across Britain, while it took only 50 years for the species to inhabit over two-thirds of the Australian continent (an area more than 25 times larger than Britain).¹⁴ As John Martin notes, the rabbit experienced a 'transformation in Britain from being a historically highly protected and esteemed species, in the mid-nineteenth century, to becoming officially classified as a major agricultural pest by the Second World War'.¹⁵ The European rabbit was first introduced to Britain as captive animals in about the twelfth century, and for several centuries their numbers remained relatively small and were primarily held in captivity for use of their meat and fur. Martin notes that the early 1800s provided Britain with 'a golden age for the increase in the numbers of wild rabbits'. This was due primarily to the increase in farmland (which provided year-round food sources) and the reduction in populations of the rabbit's natural predators. As the culture of game shooting increased, landowners 'made strenuous efforts to eliminate potential predators of game birds, such as weasels, stoats, and birds of prey'.¹⁶ By the end of the Second World War, the rabbit population in Britain was at an all-time high, and as a result, the myxoma virus was also released in a number of regions in the early 1950s. As with Australia's population, within just a few years, rabbit numbers had significantly diminished across Britain. In more recent years, also in parallel to Australia, British rabbit populations have developed substantial immunity to myxoma and other introduced viruses, and their numbers have again begun to increase.

This background on the natural, cultural and environmental history of rabbits provides insights into the varying cultural perspectives that have

---

[12] 'The Myxo Mystery: The First Virus Ever Used to Eradicate A Feral Pest', *Landline with Pip Courtney*, 8 August 2020. https://www.abc.net.au/landline/the-myxo-mystery:-the-first-virus-ever-used-to/12538292 (accessed 25 October 2021).
[13] 'How European Rabbits Took over Australia', *National Geographic*.
[14] 'Rabbits Introduced', *National Museum of Australia*.
[15] Martin, 'Case Study of a Changing Human–Animal Relationship', 84.
[16] Martin, 'Case Study of a Changing Human–Animal Relationship', 84.

emerged within both Britain and Australia. It also provides some illuminating context for how rabbits have been represented in Australian animation and how these representations compare with *Watership Down* and other British animated features.

Bunnies, bunyips and joeys: Animals in Australian animation

Rabbits have figured prominently in Western mythology; for centuries, the rabbit had been appropriated by European Christians as a symbol of purity and of the Virgin Mary (which was based on an erroneous belief that rabbits and hares were hermaphrodites and could therefore produce offspring 'without loss of virginity').[17] Echoes of this mythology continue in the narrative of the Easter Bunny, and rabbits continue to permeate our modern narratives. *Watership Down*, although ostensibly about the livelihood and struggles of wild rabbits, also serves as an allegory for human (particularly British) society. In parallel, Australians have routinely been caricatured as kangaroos (one of the most prevalent animal groups on the continent); in fact, many have found it difficult to represent Australia or Australian culture in cartoon form without resorting to native bush animals. The Australian animator Harry Julius, in addressing this issue in 1938, noted that 'this problem has always rankled with Australian cartoonists. It has never been solved. . . . When you are dealing with animals it is easy. The dressed-up kangaroo is recognizable at once – and he is exclusive.'[18]

Early Australian animated films often featured animated native animals, such as Eric Porter's *Waste Not Want Not* (1939) which was the first of his cartoons to star the character 'Willie the Wombat'; and Dick Ovenden's comic book series and accompanying short animated film about the koala *Billy Bear* (1938). In some instances, Australian animators tried exporting their animals into animated films overseas, but these often failed to succeed. Australian Pat Sullivan, creator/producer of *Felix the Cat* cartoons, upon returning from New York for a visit to his family in Australia in 1925, recounted how one of his Felix cartoons was censored in America because it featured a kangaroo with a joey hopping out of its pouch. The American censor misinterpreted the scene as depicting a smaller kangaroo rupturing

---

[17]Simon Barnes, *The History of the World in 100 Animals* (London: Simon & Schuster, 2020), 386.
[18]Harry Julius quoted in Dan Torre and Lienors Torre, *Australian Animation: An International History* (London: Palgrave, 2018), 3.

out of the stomach of a larger kangaroo.[19] Another Australian animator, Dennis Connelly, set up a small studio in London in the 1930s. Notably, his studio gave renowned British animator Joy Batchelor her start and initial training in animation. She and other British animators worked throughout the mid-1930s on Connelly's *Billy and Tilly Bluegum* series of animated short films which depicted the adventures of two Australian koalas. Initially, he had hoped to overtake Disney's extremely popular Mickey Mouse cartoons, but unfortunately for Connelly this was not to be and the studio closed down in late 1937. Joy Batchelor later recalled, '[Dennis Connelly] thought he was going to make his fortune with a couple of koala bears but he didn't. He just lost other people's money.'[20] Interestingly, Eric Porter's animated short, *Rabbit Stew* (1954), pits an Australian native animal, Willie the Wombat, against a non-native rabbit. Willie, wanting to make a rabbit stew, unsuccessfully attempts to kill the rabbit. In the end, both the rabbit and the wombat die, but Willie the Wombat does not give up and continues to pursue the rabbit, relentlessly chasing and shooting at him across Heaven. Although, on the one hand, this cartoon suggests a rather crude imitation of a *Bugs Bunny* cartoon, Porter's film also contains a greater degree of violence and vitriol than its American counterpart – clearly reflecting the cultural impacts of the rabbit plague that Australia was experiencing at the time. *Rabbit Stew* was screened widely in Australia, and it did moderately well for its distributor in the United States; however, the film also caused some confusion, with American audiences reportedly asking, 'What the heck is a wombat?'[21] As a result, Porter transformed his Australian wombat character into a North American bear named 'Bimbo' for his next animated short, *Bimbo's Auto* (1954).

It was not until the 1977 release of the animated feature *Dot and the Kangaroo* (directed by Yoram Gross) that an Australian animated film (featuring Australian animals) performed well overseas. *Dot and the Kangaroo* is not entirely animated, as the animated characters are composited primarily on live-action backgrounds. The film is based on the classic Australian children's book, *Dot and the Kangaroo*, by Ethel Pedley which was first published in 1899. The film describes a young girl named Dot and her adventures after she becomes lost in the Australian bush. Fortunately, she encounters a variety of friendly native animals, and after eating from 'the root of understanding' she is given the ability to understand and communicate with the animals. A large kangaroo then helps her to find her way back home, and on her journey, she learns a good deal about the natural world. The film contains a strong environmental

---

[19] Torre and Torre, *Australian Animation*, 42.
[20] Joy Batchelor quoted in Torre and Torre, *Australian Animation*, 59.
[21] Torre and Torre, *Australian Animation*, 67.

message and is prefaced with a quote from the book's author, Ethel Pedley: 'To the children of Australia – in the hope of enlisting their sympathies for the many beautiful and frolicsome creatures of their fair land; whose extinction, through ruthless destruction, is surely being accomplished.' This represented a decidedly conscientious perspective for 1899. *Dot and the Kangaroo* would eventually screen (either theatrically or on television) in over fifty countries. However, the take-up of the film was initially rather slow, and it took a variety of marketing tricks to achieve sales. In the United States, the distributor, Satori, rented a kangaroo suit and would hand deliver the film to all of its buyer-bookers. Gross recalled, 'The effect was terrific, because when a kangaroo walks in with a picture that no one has heard of, they'll never forget that film.'[22] As further publicity, they would photograph these kangaroo deliveries and send them out as press releases to all of the trade magazines and local newspapers.

Both *Watership Down* and the original *Dot and the Kangaroo* film utilize an Indigenous-styled animation sequence in order to articulate a 'creation myth' narrative. It is interesting to compare these two sequences, as each share similarities and exhibit some differences. In the case of *Dot and the Kangaroo* the styled artwork (painted on rock and cave walls which subsequently come alive) tells the origin story of an Australian mythical creature called a 'bunyip'. The film appropriates renditions of actual Indigenous rock-painted animal forms, and the scene follows directly after lengthy sequences depicting Indigenous ceremonial dances. The animators attempted to faithfully recreate both the choreography of the dancers and the Indigenous rock-art (and notably, the Indigenous characters are represented in a less 'cartoony' style than Dot and the other humans of the film). From today's perspective, these would be regarded as having been removed from their cultural context; however, at the time there was a strong desire by the filmmakers to articulate these in a faithful manner. In *Watership Down*, the imagery of the prologue sequence is much more removed from Australian Indigenous culture. Although in recent years, many have claimed the sequence was inspired specifically by Australian Aboriginal Art,[23] and notably, the sequence was co-designed (along with the film's original animation director, John Hubley) by artist and production designer Luciana Arrighi (who grew up in Australia). However, in *Watership Down*, the design treatment is actually quite generalized and could arguably have been inspired by the art practices of many different cultures. It merely evokes a sense of ancient narrative – emanating from a much earlier era

---

[22]Torre and Torre, *Australian Animation*, 137–8.
[23]Gerard Jones, '*Watership Down*: "Take Me with You, Stream, on Your Dark Journey"', *The Criterion Collection*, 26 February 2015. https://www.criterion.com/current/posts/3475 -watership-down-take-me-with-you-stream-on-your-dark-journey (accessed 23 August 2021).

of human history. In fact, it could be considered disingenuous to attribute these narratives and design elements to any Australian Indigenous culture. The rabbit invasion (in parallel with European settlers) had a direct and detrimental effect upon Australian Indigenous peoples, and the imposition of rabbit myths could be interpreted as a further example of cultural colonization. Furthermore, since rabbits have inhabited the Australian continent for only about 150 years, while Indigenous Australians (who make up the oldest continuous civilizations in the world) have resided on the continent for some 60,000 years, any rabbit-themed stories told by these civilizations would be deemed, in comparison, to be extremely contemporary narratives.

The initial *Dot and the Kangaroo* film was followed by eight other 'Dot' feature-length sequels. In the third instalment, *Dot and the Bunny* (Gross, 1983), Dot again goes searching for a lost baby kangaroo, but in this instance, she is accompanied by a young orphaned rabbit. The bunny repeatedly tries to adopt characteristics of native kangaroos, so as to fit in and to convince Dot that he is the joey that she is searching for. Of course, there are a few superficial similarities between the kangaroo and the European rabbit; for example, both hop with the aid of their strong back legs, and both are herbivores, eating a wide range of grasses and leaves. However, Dot is very knowledgeable about Australian native animals, and she is not at all fooled. Importantly, she is also careful not to denigrate or embarrass the rabbit. Even though the bunny is not native to the Australian bush, Dot still cares for him and has great empathy for the creature – particularly when she learns that he is both an immigrant and an orphan. Such a sentiment reflects the director Yoram Gross's own views and experiences. Nearly all of his films contain underlying themes of immigration and childhood trauma as he was born in Eastern Europe and had been greatly impacted by the Nazi occupation of Poland during the Second World War, before migrating to Australia. He recalls his childhood as being full of 'horrible days,' and that, 'In everything I make I can find my childhood, my history, my troubles.'[24] In the case of *Dot and the Bunny*, Gross reflects both his love and respect for native wildlife and also his empathy for even Australia's most invasive animal – the European rabbit. Both *Dot and the Bunny* and *Watership Down* employ rabbits in order to attract empathy for those who are considered maligned or marginalized. *Dot and the Bunny* is clearly aimed at small children, and the themes of finding acceptance and fitting-in are made accessible through the bunny character. Despite the rabbit's continuing plague-like status in Australia, it is obvious that they are not threatening animals and, like children, are quite vulnerable. Similarly, in *Watership Down*, despite the fact

---

[24] Yoram Gross quoted in Torre and Torre, *Australian Animation*, 143.

that there are a number of bad rabbit characters (Woundwort, etc.), rabbits also emerge as very sympathetic animals.

A more recent publication, and one that perhaps reflects a more modern perspective, is the 1998 children's picture book, *The Rabbits*, illustrated by Shaun Tan and written by John Marsden. This picture book uses rabbits to tell a decidedly different perspective of the arrival of white Europeans to the Australian continent. It is an allegory that describes the colonialization of Australia, with rabbits representing invading white settlers and native marsupials representing Indigenous peoples. An excerpt of the text reads:

> The rabbits spread across the country. No mountain could stop them; no desert, no river. . . . They ate our grass. They chopped down our trees and scared away our friends . . . and stole our children. Rabbits, rabbits, rabbits. Millions and millions of rabbits. Everywhere we look there are rabbits. . . . Who will save us from the rabbits?[25]

One writer describes the illustrator Shaun Tan's 'disturbing depictions of anthropomorphized, rabbitish invaders' as being 'agencies of displacement'.[26] This picture book, in parallel with the animated *Watership Down*, contains surprisingly complex and disturbing imagery and ideas. For many it was unexpected to find such things within a large format picture book; just as many audiences did not expect an animated film about bunnies to contain mature themes, and blood and violence. Another writer, Maureen Nimon, declares that

> While those well versed in children's literature recognise *The Rabbits* as an allegory best suited to the reflective, informed and mature reader in high school or beyond, the choice by author and illustrator of the picture book format and the marketing of the title in bookshops alongside titles for preschoolers confounds many. Certainly, reading *The Rabbits* is a discomforting experience.[27]

Although the book reads as an allegory of the rampant destruction of the world's oldest human civilization, its depiction of an increasingly desolate landscape also, quite demonstrably, decries 'the ecological devastation perpetrated by the rabbits'.[28]

---

[25]John Marsden and Shaun Tan, *The Rabbits* (Melbourne: Lothian Books, 1998).
[26]Dianne McGlasson, 'A Toothy Tale: Themes of Abjection in John Marsden and Shaun Tan's Picture Story Book, *The Rabbits*', *The Lion and the Unicorn* 37, no. 1 (2013): 22.
[27]Maureen Nimon quoted in Bidisha Banerjee, 'Utopian Transformations in the Contact Zone: A Posthuman, Postcolonial Reading of Shaun Tan and John Marsden's *The Rabbits*', *Global Studies of Childhood* 3, no. 4 (2013): 419.
[28]Nimon in Banerjee, 'Utopian Transformations in the Contact Zone', 419.

Reception of *Watership Down*, down under

Given Australia's rather conflicted attitudes towards rabbits, it is interesting to consider the initial reception of both the novel and the film *Watership Down*. Richard Adam's novel was somewhat slow to take off in Australia. The book was first published in the UK in 1972 but was not published in Australia until late 1974, and it took nearly a year for Australian sales to reach a relatively meagre 45,000 copies. One publishing executive of the time suggested, 'Maybe that's because they hate rabbits so much there.'[29] However, gradually, the book did become positively received in Australia. With the subsequent announcement of the film's production – and later when it became known that Australian composer Malcolm Williamson (who was by then residing full-time in London) was slated to score the music – *Watership Down* became a periodic news item. One newspaper article from 1977 noted:

> Australian composer Malcolm Williamson is writing the music for what is said to be the longest animated film ever made – $3.2 million version of Richard Adam's book *Watership Down*. 'It's rather like composing a long tone poem' Williamson said at the weekend. The film, by producer Martin Rosen, is being made in a 'very democratic' way, he said, 'I sketch the music and see the picture as it progresses in rough cut, rushes and fine cut. Martin Rosen and I cut and expand at will. It's enchanting to work in a context where the music is treated with such respect. I speak advisedly, having sometimes been treated as a mere functionary to provide musical wallpaper to a picture.' Williamson was recommended for the work by author Adams, whose daughter appeared in one of Williamson's children's operas in 1968.[30]

However, Williamson was unable to do the music for the film as he had been faced with 'a flood of unexpected commissions', which according to one article included

> the rather controversial *Jubilee Hymn* written in collaboration with the Poet Laureate, Sir John Betjamen, music for the BBC series on the House of Windsor, an opera for a cast of 17,000 children called *The Valley and the Hill*, an organ piece composed for Benjamin Britten's memorial service, a setting of a Christmas poem penned by Lady (Mary) Wilson,

---

[29] 'Rabbit Book Became a Cult – But Why?', *Papua New Guinea Post-Courier*, 6 December 1974: 19.
[30] 'Williamson Music for $3.2m Film', *Canberra Times*, 17 February 1977: 21.

a symphonic song cycle called *Les Olympiques* and music for the film, *Watership Down*.[31]

While in the midst of so many projects, it was reported that Williamson became quite ill and had to pull out of several of the projects, including *Watership Down*. In his place, British composer, Angela Morley took over scoring the film. Williamson ended up with the minor film credit of 'incidental music by Malcolm Williamson'. Only six minutes of his original score was included in the film, and even this was finalized by his replacement, Angela Morley. As was typical of the Australian press at the time, once the *Australian* composer Malcolm Williamson was no longer involved in the project, interest in *Watership Down* seemed to sharply abate.

The film was belatedly released in Australia in May 1979, during the Easter school holidays. This provided a marketing opportunity to tie in a rabbit-themed movie (presumably 'for kids') with the Easter holidays. Although some might have found this curious as it has little to do with Easter – and the one tenuous link, that of rabbits, certainly did not coincide with the cute celebratory theme that one would expect at Easter.[32] *Watership Down* received generally favourable reviews by Australian film critics. Many celebrated the fact that it was an animated film that did not look at all like the animated films of Disney. The Australian Women's Weekly noted:

> Rosen handles the film with the touch of a man who has fallen in love with the characters. . . . Woundwort is no Bugs Bunny and blood, albeit animated, flows freely in *Watership Down*. . . . *Watership Down* is drawn in a totally un-Disney style. Instead of the smooth, almost effortless artwork in Disney cartoons, the animators have opted for a stiffer and less glossy production.[33]

The *Canberra Times* proclaimed that 'It's beautiful to look at, the animation [is] simple, precise and nicely understated. This aspect of the film owes little if anything to Disney, for which let us give thanks.' But, nevertheless, concluding that it 'is ideal film fare for school holidays, including for parents'.[34] The child-friendly, but also decidedly non-Disney, Academy Award-winning stop-motion animated short *The Sand Castle* (1977) by Co Hoedeman of the National Film Board of Canada screened as the opening short to *Watership Down* in Australian cinemas.

---

[31] 'People', *The Bulletin*, January 10, 1978: 27.
[32] Interestingly, it was about this time that some began to suggest that in Australia the Easter bunny should be replaced with an Easter bilby (a small, hopping, native marsupial).
[33] Greg Flynn, 'A Trio of Cottontailed Musketeers Star in a Cartoon for Adults – Watership Down', *Australian Women's Weekly*, 14 March 1979: 27.
[34] Dougal MacDonald, 'Cinema', *The Canberra Times*, 9 May 1979: 28.

As would be expected, *Watership Down* did attract some criticism due to its more mature themes. Notably, the film was released during a challenging era when the feature animation market was reserved primarily for children and largely dominated by Disney studios. This left very little room for non-Disney or non-children's animated features. At the time, the highest profile alternative was 'adult' animated features, such as the X-rated *Fritz the Cat* Bakshi, 1972). Many therefore considered animation to be either strictly for children or strictly for adults, which further complicated *Watership Down*'s promotion. Of course, there *were* a handful of other films produced at this time, which were situated between these two extremes, such as *Yellow Submarine* (Dunning, 1968), *Fantastic Planet* (Laloux, 1973), *Allegro Non Troppo* (Bozzetto, 1976), *Wizards* (Bakshi, 1977) and *The Lord of the Rings* (Bakshi, 1978). At the time of *Watership Down*'s Australia release, a small animation studio in Melbourne was hard at work on a similarly positioned animated feature, *Grendel Grendel Grendel* (Stitt, 1981).[35] Some years later, the film's animation director, Frank Hellard, maintained how inappropriate *Watership Down* was for young children:

> *Watership Down* is a really horrifying film for young kids. It was advertised as 'not a children's film', yet it would be packed with mothers and their babies going along to it. You cannot convince people that it is not for kids, especially when it is about animated bunny rabbits. It must be a kid's film![36]

Regardless of its moments of graphic violence, *Watership Down* is a mature and serious film, punctuated with only the slightest moments of comic relief (emanating primarily from the antics of the bird character, Kehaar), which certainly sets it apart from most other animated films of this era, Australian and otherwise.

Beyond *Watership Down*

More recent British animated films like *Wallace and Gromit: The Curse of the Were-Rabbit* (Park and Box, 2005) also centre around rabbits. But in this case, the narrative takes a decidedly humorous approach to their invasive abilities. Wallace and Gromit's pest control operation, Anti-Pesto, rather than being lethal, purports to provide 'Safe, secure and humane pest control'. Their intention is to not kill the rabbit pests but, instead, to

---

[35]Dan Torre and Lienors Torre, *Grendel Grendel Grendel – Animating Beowulf* (New York: Bloomsbury, 2021).
[36]Frank Hellard, interview with Dan Torre and Lienors Torre (3 September 2004).

simply remove them and attempt a process of 'rabbit rehabilitation'. The viewer is certainly meant to empathize with the rabbits – and in a very post-human alignment, of 'becoming animal', Wallace actually becomes part rabbit and the rabbit becomes part-Wallace. Although directly referencing Frankenstein's Monster or Wolf Man scenarios of transformation, it also suggests degrees of correlation and empathy for the rabbit species, while at the same time referencing the unrelenting infestations of European rabbits in Australia (and, to a lesser degree, the UK). When Lady Tottington requests the services of Wallace and Gromit's Anti-Pesto company to rid her of her rabbit problem, Wallace is shocked when he observes that her property is completely infested with the animals. In shocked tones, he exclaims to Gromit, 'They must be breeding like ... well ... rabbits!' Of course, as noted earlier, real-life rabbit infestations are often exacerbated through human intervention; and later the character of the Vicar reflects upon this theme when he proclaims:

> By tampering with nature, forcing vegetables to swell far beyond their natural size we have wrought a terrible judgement upon ourselves. And for our sins, a hideous creature has been sent to punish us all. Repent! Repent, lest you too taste the wrath of the Were-Rabbit!

The Curse of the Were-Rabbit can be seen as an allegory (albeit a very light-hearted one) of the ongoing infestations of rabbits both in the UK and Australia.

Another recent rabbit-themed film, *Peter Rabbit* (Gluck, 2018), also takes a very light-hearted approach to rabbit infestations, as Mr McGregor and the new owner of the farm try to eradicate the pesky rabbits. *Peter Rabbit* was a co-production between the UK and Australia, and what is of particular note is that the live-action portions of the film were shot in England and the animated elements were created at Animal Logic studios in Sydney. This proved to be a feasible approach as the fabricated nature of animation allows for it to be produced in virtually any location and to represent any other location. However, some of the live-action backgrounds were actually filmed just outside of Sydney, in rural New South Wales. Such flexibility and ambiguity of production locations differed quite strongly from the production practices of *Watership Down*. As one magazine article noted at the time,

> The remarkable thing about *Watership Down* is that it is set in actual parts of England, and all the nature backgrounds have been researched in intricate detail. 'Nuthanger Farm *is* Nuthanger Farm,' says Rosen. 'Watership Down appears as it really is. The English locations are there on the screen in perfect detail.'[37]

---

[37] Mike Munn, 'The Filming of Watership Down', *Photoplay* 29, no. 12 (1978): 10.

Although the production attracted animators from all over the world, the producers of the film made a great deal of the fact that the backgrounds and settings of the film accurately represented specific locals and were therefore very authentic and very English. In comparison, *Peter Rabbit* adopts a much more mainstream and contemporary approach and, in doing so, sheds much of its British origins.

As Richard Mabey writes in his book on weeds, 'Plants become weeds when they obstruct our plans, or our tidy maps of the world. If you have no such plans or maps, they can appear as innocents, without stigma or blame.'[38] Even though rabbits have proven their ability to be 'animal-weeds', many do not regard them with any 'stigma or blame' and continue to view them with a great deal of affection. Bruce Munday sums up, 'The bunny really is something out of central casting – soft fur, big ears, big round eyes, and that cute white tail.'[39] There will always be a significant portion of the population, in Australia, Britain and elsewhere, that will not accept their 'weed' status and find it very difficult to celebrate the destruction of such pleasant animals. Most have also accepted that rabbits will always be a part of the Australian continent and that they will continue to play prominent roles in literature and, of course, animated films; as Lord Firth advises the rabbit in *Watership Down*, 'Be cunning, and full of tricks, and your people will never be destroyed.'

---

[38]Richard Mabey, *Weeds: How Vagabond Plants Gatecrashed Civilisation and Changed the Way We Think About Nature* (London: Profile Books, 2010), 1.
[39]Munday, *Those Wild Rabbits*, xiii.

PART III
Aesthetics of sound and image

CHAPTER 8

'English pastoral melodies': The traditions and connotations of Angela Morley's musical score for *Watership Down*

Paul Mazey

Angela Morley describes her score for *Watership Down* (Rosen, 1978) as being largely 'built on gentle English pastoral melodies'.[1] This chapter explores the connotations of this musical style. In particular, it considers how Morley's score and her arrangements engage with a tradition in British concert music for a style of composition that evokes the natural landscape, and it looks at how music in this idiom combines with the film's pastoral imagery to emphasize the English countryside and its associations. In addition, it explores how this melding of pastoral music and image aligns the film with an earlier tradition in British film music and how all of these elements contribute to the faithful adaptation of Richard Adams's source novel.

---

[1] Angela Morley, 'How the Music Score for the 1978 Feature Film *Watership Down* Came Together', *Angela Morley*. http://www.angelamorley.com/site/watercues.htm (accessed 4 April 2018).

At a young age, the largely self-taught Morley played clarinet and alto saxophone in dance bands. She later studied composition with Mátyás Seiber (coincidentally the composer for another animated feature, *Animal Farm* (Halas and Batchelor, 1954)) and conducting with Walter Goehr, and arranged and conducted recording sessions for popular singers, before moving into composing and arranging for radio and film. Morley became musical director for *The Goon Show* and Tony Hancock's radio and television shows, as well as writing scores for what she describes as 'not very good . . . light comedy films'.[2] Around 1960, she gave up film work 'in disgust at the quality of material being offered, and at the appalling quality of film studio recording',[3] although later in the decade she relented and composed scores for *The Looking Glass War* (Pierson, 1969), *Captain Nemo and the Underwater City* (Hill, 1969) and *When Eight Bells Toll* (Périer, 1971). From the 1970s Morley was occasionally called upon by Herbie Spencer to help with orchestrations for John Williams's film scores ('so I did some cues for *Star Wars*, for *Superman* and for *The Empire Strikes Back*'[4]). Morley was later nominated for Academy Awards for her work on *The Little Prince* (Donen, 1974) and *The Slipper and the Rose* (Forbes, 1976). In 1980 Morley moved to the United States, where she worked mainly in television, providing music for popular series including *Falcon Crest* (1981–90), *Dallas* (1978–91) and *Dynasty* (1981–9).

Morley was not the first composer the filmmakers approached to write music for *Watership Down*. The events that led to her taking on the commission are summarized by the film's screenwriter, producer and director, Martin Rosen, in an interview included on the film's DVD and Blu-ray release, and detailed by Morley herself on her website. Martin Rosen's idea was to have 'a classical overall theme' for the film, and he commissioned a score from the Australian concert composer Malcolm Williamson, who was then the Master of the Queen's Music.[5] Williamson found himself overwhelmed with work during the Queen's Silver Jubilee year in 1977 and produced only two short sketches that covered the film's prologue and main titles, a situation the filmmakers became aware of only days before the score was due to be recorded. Marcus Dods, the film's musical director, contacted Morley to ask her to orchestrate Williamson's sketches. Time was short, so she asked Larry Ashmore to orchestrate the music for the film's prologue sequence while she worked on the main title music. Once these

---

[2]Christopher Palmer, 'Angela Morley in Conversation', *Crescendo* 15, no. 3 (1976): 10.
[3]Palmer, 'Angela Morley in Conversation', 10.
[4]Angela Morley, Talk at the American Society of Music Arrangers & Composers (A.S.M.A.C.) Luncheon, Sherman Oaks, California, 19 May 1999. http://yost.com/humor/the-goon-show/angela-morley/ (accessed 20 September 2018).
[5]Martin Rosen, 'A Conversation with the Film Makers', in *Watership Down*, Blu-ray (UK: Universal Features, 2013).

were completed, Dods introduced Morley to Rosen and the film's editor Terry Rawlings. Rosen explained that Williamson's ill health would prevent him from continuing with the score, and he asked Morley to take over. She recalls, 'I was not too keen on the idea, simply because I was so unprepared: I hadn't even read the book.'[6] Rosen arranged to show her the film the next day, after which, and notwithstanding her concerns about the tight deadlines, she agreed to take on the assignment. Morley wrote the majority of the film's music and incorporated Malcolm Williamson's two pieces and Mike Batt's song 'Bright Eyes', for which she provided an instrumental interlude between Art Garfunkel's two vocal sections.

Morley's compositions, and her arrangement of Malcolm Williamson's main title and Mike Batt's song, convey a pastoral atmosphere. This is a result of both the style of the music and the way it is orchestrated. Geoffrey Chew defines the pastoral as a 'musical genre that depicts the characters and scenes of rural life or is expressive of its atmosphere'.[7] In music, the pastoral idiom came to be characterized by uncomplicated and lyrically flowing melodies with moderately slow tempi and a seemingly improvised quality. In respect of orchestration, woodwind instruments conjured 'the fluting or playing of reed pipes by classical shepherds', and flutes and oboes are frequently found in pastoral modes, 'often in pairs'.[8] Woodwind melodies predominate in the pastoral music of *Watership Down*, and Morley notes that her 'pastoral melodies and harmonies [were] played by concert, alto, bass flutes and cor anglais with French horns and harp and strings'.[9] As well as imbuing the film with a pastoral ambience, Morley's compositions and arrangements have a deeper historical significance.

The pastoral mode adopted by Morley engages with a tradition in British concert music. I have explored elsewhere the influence this pastoral tradition exerts upon British cinema of an earlier era and its importance to the movement that resulted in what has been dubbed the English Musical Renaissance.[10] The Victorian architects of the Renaissance sought to revitalize musical life in Britain by establishing a national style of composition that would liberate it from domination by European composers. The pastoral style formed a central plank in the quest of composers in the second wave of the Renaissance, the generation of Ralph Vaughan Williams and Gustav Holst, for a musical idiom that was accessible, that could lay claim to a national tradition, and that was different to Continental developments.

---

[6] Morley, 'How the Music Score for the 1978 Feature Film *Watership Down* Came Together'.
[7] Geoffrey Chew, 'Pastoral', in *The New Grove Dictionary of Music and Musicians*, ed. Stanley Sadie, Vol. 19 (London: Macmillan, 2001), 217.
[8] Chew, 'Pastoral', 223.
[9] Morley, 'How the Music Score for the 1978 Feature Film *Watership Down* Came Together'.
[10] Paul Mazey, *British Film Music: Musical Traditions in British Cinema, 1930s-1950s* (Basingstoke: Palgrave Macmillan, 2020), 49–82.

Robert Stradling notes that following the outbreak of the First World War in 1914, 'the pastoral style of Vaughan Williams and his associates became the dominant discourse of music in Britain', a situation Stradling attributes to the popular appeal of its resistance to the modernist influences emerging in contemporary European music.[11] The pastoral elements in the score for *Watership Down* evoke these historical antecedents and the connotations of pastoral concert music.

Frank Howes refers to the 'English pastoral note' as the 'gentle, undramatic, but strong and persistent musical equivalent of the English landscape'.[12] This is echoed by Eric Saylor, who summarizes the 'pastoral effect' as 'one of gentle understatement, restraint, and calm, characteristics frequently associated with the peacefulness of the English countryside'.[13] In its idealized representation of the English landscape, pastoral music brings into play the elements associated with that landscape. These include reassuring notions of timelessness and stability connected to an unchanging natural scene. At the same time, as urbanization has increased over time, the image of the countryside has shifted from being a place to work and live to being a place to visit for leisure and relaxation. In the process, it becomes a locus for the values we imagine ourselves to have lost in the wake of modernization and for a time when we imagine life to have been simpler and lived in a more harmonious relationship with nature. The nostalgia we feel for this imagined past is thus also tinged with a sense of loss. The idyllic landscape symbolizes a desirable sense of continuity with the past, and this and its other connotations are evoked by the pastoral melodies in *Watership Down*.

Angela Morley's score is built upon a number of recurring musical motifs, with four principal themes in a pastoral idiom, each of which I will consider individually. These pastoral themes recur most frequently in the film, and each is associated with the group of rabbits and the harmonious community they seek to establish. The first is the 'Main Title' theme by Malcolm Williamson, which is heard four times. Morley describes it as 'a very beautiful piece mainly for woodwind and strings . . . that exude[s] the pastoral charm of the rolling downs of southern England'.[14] It is first heard in the film's opening title sequence, where significantly it accompanies images of Watership Down. Thereafter it is always associated with Watership Down itself, and it enters the soundtrack when the location is significant.

---

[11] Robert Stradling, 'England's Glory: Sensibilities of Place in English Music, 1900–1950', in *The Place of Music*, ed. Andrew Leyshon, David Matless, and George Revill (New York: Guilford Press, 1998), 183.
[12] Frank Howes, *The English Musical Renaissance* (London: Secker & Warburg, 1966), 261.
[13] Eric Saylor, *English Pastoral Music: From Arcadia to Utopia, 1900–1955* (Urbana: University of Illinois Press, 2017), 20.
[14] Morley, 'How the Music Score for the 1978 Feature Film *Watership Down* Came Together'.

The second recurring pastoral theme opens the main body of the film, as Hazel and Fiver leave the warren to feed. Morley titles this short cue for harp and flute 'Venturing Forth', and it is heard five times in the film. This was the first piece that Morley composed for the film. She wrote it on the day she accepted the commission, and she recalls that 'I simply had to prove to myself that I could compose something before I went to bed'.[15] 'Venturing Forth' represents the calm order of the Sandleford Warren before it is unsettled by Fiver's vision of its impending destruction. The theme returns to the soundtrack in the rabbits' moments of calm when they consider their lack of does. Later in the film, it is used to good effect to reflect the tranquil scene at Watership Down before the warning is given that Woundwort has discovered the warren before the final conflict. Here, as at its first hearing, it conveys a peaceful atmosphere and its gentleness contrasts starkly with the menacing march theme on drums and brass which shatters the peace and heralds the attack.

The third motif is the 'Quest' theme, which expresses 'the determination of Hazel and his friends to find a new home'.[16] This is the most frequently recurring theme in the film, and it is heard fifteen times. It is introduced after Bigwig joins the group and the rabbits set off on their journey, its main melody played in full on lower woodwinds. Its first section is then reprised in the strings before slowing and faltering as the rabbits reach the boundary of the woods. The theme's association with the onward progress of the group is confirmed at its next hearing after they have made it through the woods and across the river. It rings out brightly as the group crosses the open countryside, through a field of grazing cows and on towards the road. The 'Quest' theme has a stable march-like rhythm that marks the onward momentum of the group, and it leaves the soundtrack when the journey is curtailed by obstacles. The theme is used consistently in this way, and it has the effect of bringing unity to the episodic structure of *Watership Down*'s narrative. In this respect, its use mirrors that of the march themes employed in British war films whose narratives focus on a journey or a mission, such as *Ice Cold in Alex* (Thompson, 1958).[17] Morley also employs it at a much slower tempo in the orchestral interlude between the two choruses of 'Bright Eyes', which 'had the effect of lengthening and heightening the drama of Hazel's near death experience'.[18] Here, in her arrangement of both pieces of music, Morley brings Art Garfunkel's vocal in over the last sustained woodwind note of the 'Quest' theme melody to move seamlessly from the latter back to the song. The orchestral interlude scores Fiver's journey towards the injured

---

[15]Morley, 'How the Music Score for the 1978 Feature Film *Watership Down* Came Together'.
[16]Morley, 'How the Music Score for the 1978 Feature Film *Watership Down* Came Together'.
[17]Mazey, *British Film Music*, 168–9.
[18]Morley, 'How the Music Score for the 1978 Feature Film *Watership Down* Came Together'.

FIGURE 8.1 *A 'rabbit's-eye-view' framed by foreground elements.*

Hazel, guided by the stylized representation of the Black Rabbit in a textured pencil effect. As the theme accompanies Hazel's 'near death experience' in this sequence, it appropriately returns at a building tempo towards the end of the film for the scene of Hazel's death, where he is escorted from his physical body by the Black Rabbit. The reprise of the 'Quest' theme here, and its association with onward momentum, conveys the sense not of an ending but of a continuing journey, and in this way it supports the quasi-religious mysticism of the rabbit mythology created by Richard Adams in his novel.

The fourth theme, heard five times, strikes a more sombre note. Titled 'Violet's Gone' and first heard after Violet is taken by the bird of prey, it is a melancholy pastoral theme on alto flute that marks the darker and more challenging parts of the rabbits' journey. As the group continue on their way, the image dissolves into an open landscape with distant trees on the horizon and a darkening sky above. The sky occupies the top two-thirds of the frame, accentuating the openness and the scale of the countryside in the manner of a landscape painting, and the camera glides towards the trees. The scene dissolves to another moving camera shot overlooking a tree-lined ploughed field. The image is framed by the undergrowth in the lower foreground and lengths of barbed-wire fencing above (Figure 8.1). Martin Rosen notes that the film is 'presented largely from the rabbits' point-of-view', and this is evident here in the low-angle framing and the slow movement into the image.[19] The threat presented by human interference is suggested by the

---

[19] Martin Rosen quoted in Iain F. McAsh, 'How Rabbits Took over a Studio in Warren Street', *Film Review*, November 1978: 53.

barbed-wire, and more explicitly by a gunshot on the soundtrack that momentarily freezes the camera movement and suggests the sudden stillness of the rabbit whose perspective we are sharing, followed by the squawk of disturbed birds. A further dissolve brings another moving camera shot as evening falls, towards a graveyard with stone crosses and the silhouetted shapes of a tree, grass and iron railings. The image, reminiscent of gothic horror iconography, suggests impending danger. The strings heard at this point give 'the distinct impression of a chiming clock', and thus emphasize the passing of time and the growing urgency for the group to find a safe place to rest overnight.[20] The sense of danger in the location is also conveyed in voice-over dialogue when Blackberry says to Hazel – 'we can't rest there – that's a man place.' The 'Violet's Gone' theme returns as the rabbits trudge through the dark landscape in the rain after being chased from the shelter of the barn by the rats and owl. The theme is heard again later in the film when ideas of death and loss are evoked. First, when Blackberry and Dandelion tell Fiver that Hazel is dead after he has been shot at the farm, and then after Woundwort makes his first kill in the warren during the final conflict. These four pastoral motifs constitute the main thematic musical material of the film, and they dominate the score.

The pastoral ambience promoted by these four musical motifs is accentuated by their juxtaposition with music cues in contrasting styles. These opposing musical styles are mostly associated with the obstacles or threats the rabbits face on their journey, from the eerie darkness and brass blasts of Fiver's vision and the trek through the wood to the edgy percussive modernism of the music that accompanies the scampering rats in the barn. An exception to this is the theme for the seagull Kehaar, voiced by Zero Mostel, the only international member of the otherwise all-British voice cast, for which Morley adopts the form of a 'Viennese novelty waltz'. For this, she sets aside 'English pastoral instrumental vocabulary in favour of a Belgian invention, the alto saxophone'.[21] Jack Curtis Dubowsky identifies the origin of the theme in 'a fragment of the opening flute motive of Debussy's "Prélude à l'après midi d'un faune"' that Morley develops 'into a majestic, soaring, romantic swing waltz'.[22] In this way, she employs a Continental source, instrument and dance rhythm to represent the 'foreign visitor from over the "big water"'.[23] Morley's incorporation of this range of musical styles has the effect of intensifying each style by its contrast with the other and of emphasizing the pastoral atmosphere that dominates the film.

---

[20]Robert Walton, Liner Notes, *Watership Down* original soundtrack, CD (UK: Vocalion, 2017).
[21]Morley, 'How the Music Score for the 1978 Feature Film *Watership Down* Came Together'.
[22]Jack Curtis Dubowsky, *Intersecting Film, Music and Queerness* (Basingstoke: Palgrave Macmillan, 2016), 125.
[23]Morley, 'How the Music Score for the 1978 Feature Film *Watership Down* Came Together'.

The film's pastoral ambience is further amplified by the combination of landscape imagery on screen and music in a pastoral idiom on the soundtrack. The seemingly natural marriage of English pastoral music and visions of the English rural landscape has been discussed by Hughes and Stradling, who note that many people 'have a mental portfolio of the English variety [of "serious" music] as comprising images of the countryside'. The connection is forged and reproduced in the promotional packaging of much English music, which carries 'seductive landscape photographs or reproductions of Palmer, Turner or Constable'.[24] Writing at the time of the film's release, the critic Julian Fox echoes these references when he describes the film as a 'celebration of the English Pastoral ethic [that] evokes all our sturdy and/or misty-eyed reflections of Constable, George Moreland and Thomas Hardy'.[25] Fox's references to landscape painting are apposite, as the watercolour backgrounds of the film's natural settings and the way that they are framed and composed frequently recall the conventions of British landscape painting.

In the case of *Watership Down*, the seemingly natural combination of pastoral music and landscape imagery is bolstered by the film's use of techniques that align it in certain respects with live-action filmmaking. The film's director Rosen confirms that the filmmakers 'approached the production as if it were a "live" feature film'. He continues:

> We closely researched the nature backgrounds, which are an integral part of the story, in intricate detail. We even did helicopter recces of the area so it would look as accurate as possible.... Watership Down appears as it really is. The English locations are there on screen in perfect detail.[26]

Added to this authenticity in the locations is a further aspect of the 'more realistic approach' taken by the filmmakers. In a reversal of the usual process whereby animators work with a pre-recorded music track, and in common with standard practice on live-action films, the music for *Watership Down* was written after the visuals were completed. This departure from standard animation practice, Rosen confirms, would allow the composers to 'take into account the effects that have been brought to the screen by the animators and nature backgrounds when writing the music score'.[27]

---

[24]Meirion Hughes and Robert Stradling, *The English Musical Renaissance, 1840–1940: Constructing a National Music*, 2nd edn (Manchester: Manchester University Press, 2001), 166.
[25]Julian Fox, 'Watership Down', *Films and Filming*, December 1978: 34.
[26]Rosen quoted in McAsh, 'How Rabbits Took over a Studio in Warren Street', 53.
[27]Martin Rosen, 'Production Notes' insert, *Watership Down* Pressbook (1978), British Film Institute Special Collections, PBS – 50833.

The film is further aligned with live-action features in its use of pastoral music in a manner that amplifies the rural landscape. This is found both in the way *Watership Down* introduces its combination of pastoral music and rural imagery and in the filming techniques it employs to emphasize its landscape settings. In common with other British films in which the location plays a significant role, one that exceeds its background position, pastoral music is introduced in conjunction with landscape imagery in the main title sequence.[28] Following the film's prologue, its on-screen titles appear in white against watercolour background images of Watership Down itself and are accompanied on the soundtrack by Malcolm Williamson's pastoral 'Main Title' theme. The rural landscapes are emphasized not only by the music but also by the way they are filmed. P. Adams Sitney identifies three filming techniques that emphasize landscape on screen: the long shot, the panoramic sweep and the moving camera.[29] The long shot reflects and evokes the traditions of landscape painting and is the least specific to cinema of the three techniques. The pan shot reproduces the point-of-view of the spectator scanning the landscape and provides a sense of 'the landscape extending in all directions beyond the edge of the screen'.[30] Similarly, the moving camera creates an impression of travelling through the landscape, and the use of both the filmic pan and the moving camera 'contribute[s] to the illusion of the camera's presence in the field of vision'.[31] To take the example of the main title sequence, this is made up of a series of long shots. Each shot slowly dissolves into the next and in each the camera pulls back to take in a wider view, which emphasizes the scale of the landscape all around. The first shot opens at the top of the down. Blades of grass swaying in the foreground of the shot act as a *repoussoir* element to indicate depth and to guide the eye into the image in the convention of landscape painting and still photography (Figure 8.2). The camera descends the down and pulls back to reveal the pylon in the valley before it dissolves to a more distant view of the scene, and then to the view from the hill opposite, always pulling back to reveal a wider scene in a way that accentuates the expanse of the landscape. The sequence introduces the down and reverses the last part of the journey the rabbits will make to reach it. The leisurely movement of the camera aligns with the slow tempo of the 'Main Title' theme to promote a gentle ambience and a contemplative experience for the spectator.

In addition to camera techniques that emphasize visually the presence of landscape, Sitney notes that spoken dialogue may be used to draw the

---

[28]Mazey, *British Film Music*, 56–7.
[29]P. Adams Sitney, 'Landscape in the Cinema: The Rhythms of the World and the Camera', in *Landscape, Natural Beauty and the Arts*, ed. Salim Kemal and Ivan Gaskell (Cambridge: Cambridge University Press, 1993), 107–8.
[30]Sitney, 'Landscape in the Cinema', 107.
[31]Sitney, 'Landscape in the Cinema', 107.

FIGURE 8.2 *Grasses act as a 'repoussoir' element.*

spectator's attention to what is depicted on screen.[32] Each time one character exhorts another to look at something, the instruction is equally issued to, and acted upon by, the spectator. This occurs explicitly when Fiver describes his vision of Watership Down to the other rabbits as it comes into view, in a sequence accompanied on the soundtrack by Malcolm Williamson's 'Main Title' theme. While the screen is filled with a long shot of the down from the hill opposite, which moves in to a slightly closer view, we hear Fiver in voice-over – 'Look! Look! That's the place for us . . . high lonely hills where the wind and sound carry . . . '. The shot pulls back to reveal a wider view, and the rabbits are visible in the bottom left-hand corner of the screen (Figure 8.3). The image dissolves to a shot that travels through tall grasses at ground level to a view of the landscape beyond – a rabbit's-eye-view shot – as Fiver's narration continues – 'and the ground's as dry as straw in a barn. That's where we ought to be. That's where we have to get to.' A further dissolve brings a slow pan across the open landscape beneath a sunset sky with grasses silhouetted in the foreground of the image, before a final dissolve to the rabbits sheltering underneath a cart as the music draws to a close and the screen fades to black. The pastoral ambience created by the music and watercolour imagery is amplified not only by Fiver's excited voice-over and his instruction to look but also by the use of wide shots, panning shots and shots of the camera moving through the undergrowth.

A similar combination of elements is employed in the sequence where the rabbits climb the down. The sequence begins as they reach the open

---

[32]Sitney, 'Landscape in the Cinema', 110.

FIGURE 8.3 *Long shot of Watership Down.*

countryside and head towards the down, accompanied by a gentle statement of the 'Quest' theme as the camera pans across the flat ground to keep the rabbits in the frame. As they pause to look up at the hill, the image provides an upward tilting point-of-view shot from their perspective and the music builds to mark their mounting excitement. As the rabbits ascend the hill, shot from ground level with thistles and grasses in the foreground, the 'Quest' theme gains in tempo and becomes increasingly triumphal until, at the top, Dandelion cries 'Come and look. You can see the whole world.' His words usher a full-blooded statement of the 'Main Title' theme onto the soundtrack as the image cuts to an extended pan across the fields below, before the sequence ends with a shot of the rabbits from behind, enjoying the view across the landscape (Figure 8.4). Again, the dialogue encourages the spectator to observe the landscape, which is emphasized by the pan shot and accompanied by uplifting music that promotes a celebratory feel.

The pastoral emphasis of Morley's score constructs an English atmosphere, and in doing so it acts as a marker of fidelity in the film's adaptation of Richard Adams's novel. Rosen has spoken of Adams's 'enormous love for the English countryside' and how he has brought this into his book.[33] In its idealization of the natural landscape, Adams's work is essentially pastoral in nature, and this is reflected and compounded in the film's use of landscape imagery combined with music in a pastoral idiom to bring it to life. In interviews, Rosen promotes the film's fidelity to the novel as a selling point

---

[33]Rosen, '*Watership Down* Pressbook'.

FIGURE 8.4 *The scale of the landscape is emphasized.*

for *Watership Down*. He had not always envisaged the story 'in cartoon form' and expresses his desire to guard against 'the "cute" and "cuddly" connotations that can so easily be given to any story involving animals', as this 'would be totally opposed to the essence of Richard Adams's book'.[34] In aiming to retain the spirit of Adams's story, Rosen notes that he made the film in England with a largely British cast, whose distinctive and often familiar voices prove useful in differentiating between the characters. 'The animals', he notes, 'speak with standard English accents, while the humans have a soft Berkshire-Hampshire burr.'[35] A further voice that acts as a potent marker of Englishness is that of the presenter who announces the BBC Home Service on the radio heard at the farm. The station had been replaced by BBC Radio 4 in 1967, and this reference therefore promotes a nostalgic view of national identity and suggests that the narrative is set at an earlier time than that of the novel's publication. Levels of authenticity extend to other parts of the soundtrack. Terry Rawlings, the film's editor and sound editor, spent time at Watership Down to record the ambient sounds used in the film. He explains that, as the location had been visually reproduced so accurately in the film, he 'wanted to know what this area sounded like'.[36] In this way, the whole soundscape of the film, its dialogue and its sound effects, as well as its music, evokes an atmosphere of Englishness and as such is faithful to Adams's novel.

---

[34]Rosen quoted in McAsh, 'How Rabbits Took over a Studio in Warren Street', 53.
[35]Rosen quoted in McAsh, 'How Rabbits Took over a Studio in Warren Street', 53.
[36]Terry Rawlings in 'A Conversation with the Film Makers', in *Watership Down*, Blu-ray (UK: Universal Features, 2013).

The filmmakers' aim for fidelity in adapting its source novel is evident in the way that each of the film's elements contributes to this overall effect. In terms of the score, a similar impulse can be found not only in Morley's compositions but in her musical arrangements, which play a key role in creating the pastoral ambience that infuses the film. The way the score of *Watership Down* engages with the pastoral tradition in British music is a measure of Morley's experience not only as a composer but also as an orchestrator and an arranger. Christopher Palmer observes that, in spite of its importance, the role of the arranger is one that is often overlooked.[37] Morley has described each musical instrument as being 'rather like an actor – it has a certain role that it plays in music' and how arranging music requires you 'to have all that in your mind, of the roles that these instruments like to play'.[38] John Wilson, the conductor and musicologist who has made recordings of her film and television music and her arrangements of song standards, highlights Morley's particular feeling for woodwind sonorities. In her arrangements, Wilson finds 'flute-type figurations happening in other instruments . . . woodwind figurations that flit right through the orchestra'.[39] Given the role woodwinds play in pastoral music, Morley's affinity for this family of instruments places her in an ideal position to convey the film's deeply pastoral atmosphere. John Wilson feels that *Watership Down* 'couldn't have been written by anyone else':

> It has that slightly wistful melancholy to it, a pastoral sweetness – and always, beautiful woodwind writing. If Angela had one signature, it was her woodwind writing – those flowing, wonderful flute fantasias.[40]

Morley embraces a pastoral idiom in her score and in the additional music written by Malcolm Williamson and Mike Batt that she incorporates and arranges into a coherent whole on the soundtrack. Her pastoral musical themes combine with the film's pastoral imagery to amplify the presence of the natural landscape on screen. This seemingly natural audio-visual blending of pastoral elements, bolstered by filming techniques that further emphasize the landscape, accentuates the cultural associations of the English countryside and constructs an atmosphere of Englishness. Morley's score acts as a significant element of fidelity in the film's adaptation of

---

[37] Christopher Palmer, 'Bringing *The Slipper and the Rose* to Life', *Crescendo* 15, no. 2 (1976): 11.
[38] Morley, A.S.M.A.C. Talk.
[39] John Wilson, 'Musical Variations: The Life of Angela Morley', *Seriously . . .*, BBC Radio 4, 23 February 2016. https://www.bbc.co.uk/programmes/p03kr6bs (accessed 1 May 2018).
[40] John Wilson quoted in Jon Burlingame, 'Angela Morley Obituary', *Film Music Society*, 19 January 2009. http://www.filmmusicsociety.org/news_events/features/2009/011909.html?isArchive=011909 (accessed 1 May 2018).

Richard Adams's novel by compounding its pastoral nature, and in doing so it supports Martin Rosen's stated desire to remain true to the spirit of its literary source. Moreover, by engaging with a culturally significant historical mode of musical expression, Angela Morley evokes both the connotations of the natural landscape and those of the earlier era of British music. Her musical sensibility endows *Watership Down* with the paradoxical qualities of being simultaneously both nostalgic and timeless.

CHAPTER 9

'I know now. A terrible thing is coming':

Watership Down, music and/as horror

Leanne Weston

Since its release in 1978, *Watership Down* has maintained a significant presence in popular and visual cultures. On screen, DVD and Blu-ray releases, YouTube clips, repeat television broadcasts and special cinema screenings have stimulated ongoing interest in the film. Off-screen, the film features consistently in discussions on social media, or as subject matter for publications including *The Guardian*, *NME* and *The Gloss*, all contributing to its continued visibility and cultural longevity. Integral to the film's endurance is music, which forms a central part of the spectatorial experience. Music is entwined in the memories of its multi-generational audience, illustrated by the numerous trailers, reviews and remix videos on YouTube, building an interactive dialogue between the text and the audience through a process of reappreciation and remediation. Such processes open the film up to wider viewership, extending beyond Richard Adams's source novel and the film's subsequent home viewing releases.

Discussion around the cultural memory and understanding of *Watership Down*, particularly regarding its music's affective potential and emotional resonances, can be divided into two distinct forms of remembrance, which shape how the film continues to be narrativized and memorialized. The first form, typified by the nostalgic leanings of Art Garfunkel's song 'Bright Eyes', is typically expressed in sentimental terms of 'cuteness' and 'sweetness' and remains the film's central musical association. However, a second form has also emerged, indicating a shift in the film's cultural associations. This is characterized by Angela Morley's score[1] and centres on 'scariness', 'horror', and the associated trauma that stems from the film's depiction of violence and death. Such readings have come to dominate contemporary readings of *Watership Down* and provide the focus of the analysis that follows.

This chapter explores the film's relationship both *to* and *with* horror, how this is complicated by shifting cultural associations between sound and image, and the affective and emotional implications of these shifts. By exploring how music and affect operate in *Watership Down*, this work responds to the lack of discussion on music and affect in film, a neglect that has continued beyond the affective turn.

I begin by examining the relationship between the film *and* horror to locate the common interpretations of *Watership Down* as 'scary' and 'traumatic' in direct opposition to its status as an animated film 'for children'. While much of this discourse relates to the film's depiction of graphic violence, I argue that the horror evoked by and within *Watership Down* is not solely related to its subject matter or visceral animation style but can also be read or *heard* within its score. Following this, I consider how the film can be read *as* horror, drawing on theories of film music to examine the role Angela Morley's score fulfils in the cultural construction and classification of the film as horror. Next, I analyse the text, specifically how its underutilized subtitle track can be used to map out the relationship between sound and image, revealing where the film's emotional and affective potential may be derived. Finally, I move beyond the text, focussing on remix videos dedicated to the film. These reappropriated sounds and images generate potential new meanings and interpretations due to their inter-textual complexity. Through the process of remixing, the film's perceived 'scariness' is rendered in both positive and negative terms. By applying such a reading, or rather, a *listening* to *Watership Down*, we can also begin to reconsider how film and music work together to generate meaning and create affective resonance, outside the boundaries of film genre and style.

---

[1] I wish to briefly acknowledge the significance of Malcolm Williamson in the film's soundscape as the composer of initial sketches, the opening title and Frith prologue. Following Williamson's departure, Morley took over and composed the rest of the score, including character pieces for each rabbit. Morley's compositions form the basis of my analysis.

Watership Down and horror

Within the last decade, discussion surrounding *Watership Down* has increasingly turned towards its relationship with horror, which underpins how the film and elements of its mise en scène, and in particular its score, can be interpreted, revealing the origins of the film as horror. Discussion of the film's depiction of violence, treatment of death and the impact of both upon the audience has influenced numerous articles and Twitter threads. This popular discourse is characterized by two interrelated features, where *Watership Down* is consistently discussed in association with trauma: it is either part of curated lists that detail 'terrifying' or 'scary' children's films, such as those by Charlotte Shane for *The Gloss*[2] and Jess Denham for *The Independent*,[3] or in Twitter threads, where it is framed as a traumatic formative experience, which easily leads to the use of the film form as 'evidence' for such a reading. Exemplary of this is a February 2020 discussion started by the prompt 'What Film Traumatised You as a Kid?',[4] in which *Watership Down* features alongside a GIF of Fiver in the bloody field to illustrate the choice.[5] Responses to the prompt fell into three main categories, derived from their affective and emotive resonances and/or a clear relationship to the uncanny: films categorized intentionally as horror, such as *Jeepers Creepers* (Salva, 2001) and *The Exorcist* (Friedkin, 1973); films that unintentionally read as horror including *Pinocchio* (Luske and Sharpsteen, 1940) and *The Wizard of Oz* (Fleming, 1939); and finally, films exemplary of an emergent subgenre that Catherine Lester describes as children's horror,[6] reflected in multiple references to *Coraline* (Selick, 2009). In this schema, *Watership Down* falls somewhere between films that are intentionally categorized as horror due to their content, and those which are unintentionally read as such due to the fear response they provoke in the audience. The subtleties of this distinction can be read, or rather heard,

---

[2]Charlotte Shane, 'Terrifying Children's Movies: *Watership Down*', *The Gloss*, 22 February 2013. https://web.archive.org/web/20160624200533/http://www.thegloss.com/odds-and-ends/terrifying-childrens-movies-watership-down/ (accessed 29 January 2021).
[3]Jess Denham, '11 Unintentionally Terrifying Children's Movies', *The Independent*, 30 October 2015. http://www.independent.co.uk/arts-entertainment/films/news/halloween-2015-unintentionally-terrifying-childrens-movies-from-dumbo-to-watership-down-a6715426.html (accessed 29 January 2021).
[4]Ashley Bower, 'Oh This Is a Good One. I'll Start: Jumanji', *Twitter*, 18 February 2020. https://twitter.com/loudandfearless/status/1229902686876684288 (accessed 29 January 2021).
[5]Jennifer Hayden, '@loudandfearless Watership Down', *Twitter*, 19 February 2020. https://twitter.com/scout_finch/status/1230005450747371521 (accessed 29 January 2021).
[6]Catherine Lester, 'The Children's Horror Film: Characterizing an "Impossible" Subgenre', *The Velvet Light Trap* 78 (2016): 22–37.

in the film's score, warranting further analysis of how it contributes to the film's production of meaning.

Phil Hoad's 2014 article on the film for *The Guardian*'s 'The Film That Frightened Me the Most' series is exemplary of contemporary moves to explicitly position *Watership Down* as horror.[7] Its appearance in the series is intriguing yet anomalous. Of the ten films featured, *Psycho* (Hitchcock, 1960), *Eden Lake* (Watkins, 2008) and *The Shining* (Kubrick, 1980) among them, *Watership Down* is the only animated film *and* the only film that is not traditionally categorized as horror or rated as such.[8] Under Rick Altman's model of genre, entrants in *The Guardian* article series may, at first glance, appear to fall under the semantic approach, where genre depends on the building blocks of 'common traits, attitudes, characters, shots, locations' and so on.[9] However, their actual appearance in the list, as Hoad's reflections illustrate, is also exemplary of the syntactic approach, where genre is considered in terms of the 'constitutive relationships' or, the structures *around* genre's established building blocks.[10] Hoad's discussion is indicative of the dual syntactic/semantic approach Altman ultimately advocated to allow for crossover, or interplay between the two approaches, acknowledging the complexity and the 'slipperiness' of genre classification. In the case of *Watership Down*, understanding its relationship to genre, meaning and how this relates to spectatorial experience requires further qualification. Jason Mittell's work on genre as a cultural category provides a useful entry point. Writing on television genres, he argues that genre categories are inter-textual cultural products, and genres themselves develop within 'interrelated sites of audience, industrial and cultural practices'.[11] Mittell's model of genre is more flexible, taking account of the fluidity and sense of exchange between the internal elements of a text (the form and content of it) and the external ones (marketing and fan paratexts, scholarly and popular criticism). The most significant aspect of this model is the more nuanced approach to genre as a cultural construction, and he would later note, 'Even though texts certainly bear marks that are typical of genres, these textual conventions are not what define the genre. Genres exist only through the creation, circulation, and consumption of texts within cultural

---

[7] Phil Hoad, '*Watership Down*: The Film That Frightened Me the Most', *The Guardian*, 30 October 2014. https://www.theguardian.com/film/filmblog/2014/oct/30/watership-down-the-film-that-frightened-me-the-most (accessed 29 January 2021).
[8] The film's age classification in the UK is a continued source of debate, as discussed in the Introduction of this book.
[9] Rick Altman, 'A Semantic/Syntactic Approach to Film Genre', *Cinema Journal* 23, no. 3 (1984): 10.
[10] Altman, 'A Semantic/Syntactic Approach to Film Genre', 10.
[11] Jason Mittell, 'A Cultural Approach to Television Genre Theory', *Cinema Journal* 40, no. 3 (2001): 18.

contexts.'[12] Following Mittell, it is entirely possible for a film not constructed as horror by the sum of its 'textual conventions' to ultimately be perceived as such through wider cultural practices of circulation and consumption, allowing for a greater multiplicity of meanings, impacting upon readings and subsequent meanings conferred upon the film through these extra-textual discursive cultural processes.

The pertinence of Mittell's work to the perception of *Watership Down* as horror stems from his acknowledgement of the cultural life of genres, and by extension, the text itself. The film's complex surrounding discourse(s) illustrates that its legacy and reputation *may* carry greater significance in terms of genre classification than actual textual features, demonstrated by its numerous remix videos, as I will explore later. Nevertheless, this must be contextualized by attention to its textual features, which equally and actively contribute to film's status as horror. As the BBFC's archive case study describes, the film contains 'violence and threat'.[13] Though further qualified as mild, that 'younger or more sensitive viewers have found some scenes upsetting or worrying' is acknowledged.[14] These observations illustrate that despite necessary qualification, the base elements for its horror categorization – blood, violence and gore – are already present and, when combined with Morley's score, amplify its affective conditions to enable its reading as horror. When examining the film's relationship to genre, its textual and cultural qualities must be taken into account on the understanding that genre categories can be conferred as well as read. The horror label and the fear evoked are something both personal and collective. The film's scariness can remain textually located while simultaneously being culturally conferred, where films can become horror solely by reputation, a clear constituent of *Watership Down*'s legacy.

The BBFC's acknowledgement of *Watership Down*'s effect upon child audiences is especially important when considering the film's relationship to horror and the specific context of the child spectator's affective engagement, distinct from an adult reflecting back upon their experience. For Hoad, the horror of the film is based around the affective power of 'the child's belief that whatever you see is real'. Hoad highlights the blurring boundaries between fiction and reality, noting they are 'most porous when it comes to filmed images'.[15] These qualifications are valuable ones, and while they contribute to *Watership Down*'s relationship to, and perception as, horror, they also complicate what that relationship might be, and how it is expressed.

---

[12]Jason Mittell, *Genre and Television: From Cop Shows to Cartoons in American Culture* (London: Routledge, 2004), 11.
[13]'Watership Down', *British Board of Film Classification*. https://www.bbfc.co.uk/education/case-studies/watership-down (accessed 29 January 2021).
[14]'Watership Down', *British Board of Film Classification*.
[15]Hoad, '*Watership Down*'.

The film's score has a very particular role in establishing the film's horror potential. Scoring is an element that Mittell omits from analysis and is often excluded from discussions of 'textual conventions', but, as I will now go on to explore, it is an equally important aspect of textuality and the production of meaning. Morley's score is a central component in reading *Watership Down* as horror and understanding its emotive and expressive potential, capacities that are increased by its status as animation. Rebecca Coyle argues that 'sound is a central component of animation that initiates, assists and extends its critical expressive tools'. She continues, 'sound enables animation film to leap out of the screen and engage the viewer's imagination'.[16] By outlining the connections between sound, animation, imagination and audience engagement, Coyle illustrates where the horror in *Watership Down* may originate, and the reasoning for its enduring associations with horror and trauma beyond just its images of blood and gore.

For the audience, this horror is seen and felt but, most importantly, *heard* throughout Morley's score, contributing to how the film's narrative, characterization and representation are experienced. George Burt describes how film music holds its own power, revealing the film's 'inner life', which cannot be articulated through other means, to 'deepen the effect of a scene or bring an aspect of its story into sharper focus'.[17] Burt's observations hold particular relevance to *Watership Down* and how its score reflects the changing emotions of the characters, adding expressive emphasis to the on-screen action. This is particularly evident during moments of threat or violence, such as when Violet is killed by a hawk or, later, when Bigwig becomes caught in a snare. Danger is signalled by rising strings on the soundtrack, amplifying the emotions being experienced, so that the score becomes the sonic manifestation of terror.

Watership Down as horror

The function of *Watership Down*'s score is twofold: a facilitator of engagement and a transmitter of affect that can be used to read the film as horror. However, the relationship between sound and image within *Watership Down* requires further qualification beyond notions of engagement and affective transmission. Guido Heldt defines horror as an effect-led genre, a description that is applicable to the audience's experience of and extreme reactions to *Watership Down*. However, the emotional affective resonance of the film is not solely limited to the sonic relationship between horror and

---

[16]Rebecca Coyle, ed., *Drawn to Sound: Animation Film Music and Sonicity* (London: Equinox Publishing, 2010), 1.
[17]George Burt, *The Art of Film Music* (Boston: Northeastern University Press, 1994), 4.

affect, but it is also concerned with how those elements work together to cumulatively *create* that affect relationship. Neil Lerner argues that for the audience, music within horror can sometimes be just as disturbing as its images, saying, 'they cover not their eyes, but their ears.'[18]

Lerner's assessment carries significance both in terms of the film's narrative, and characterization and identification, particularly regarding Fiver. His status as a seer, haunted by dark premonitions of the colony's future, marks him out as different, leaving him ostracized, ridiculed and isolated. Fiver's anxiety and dread are replicated within the score and reflected back at the audience, particularly during moments of high dramatic tension, when the rabbits are in peril. The score intensifies the nightmarish qualities of Fiver's visions, allowing the audience to emotionally align and identify with the character. As Murray Smith persuasively argues, how and if we identify with a character is more complex than the term implies. Fiction narratives elicit levels of *'imaginative engagement* with characters, distinct types of responses normally conflated under the term "identification"', comprised of recognition, alignment and allegiance, that when taken together culminate to produce what he defines as a 'structure of sympathy'.[19] Smith's model usefully incorporates space for affective responses and, in particular, empathy to acknowledge the role it plays in the larger process of identification. Though typically applied to live-action narratives, I wish to focus on two elements of Smith's model, alignment and allegiance, in relation to *Watership Down* to consider how the score functions to amplify the affective responses they invoke. Throughout the film, we are invited to engage with Fiver, to the 'degree to which we are spatially attached, and given subjective access' to him.[20] Equally, our allegiance remains with Fiver in 'moral and emotional terms', in a manner that is distinct from other characters in the narrative.[21]

With the exception of Hazel, the other members of the warren treat Fiver as an object of ridicule, viewing him as cowardly and fearful, without knowing the true reason for his anxiety. Our alignment with and allegiance to him are increased by the subjective access afforded to us, namely the privilege of seeing but, most importantly, *hearing* his visions when no one else within the narrative can. Does this mean that the fearful responses prompted by *Watership Down* and its relationship to horror are solely based on spectatorial alignment with Fiver's fear? For Smith, the structure of sympathy is acentral but draws on related forms of empathic imagining

---

[18]Neil Lerner, ed., *Music in the Horror Film: Listening to Fear*, (London: Routledge, 2009), ix.
[19]Murray Smith, 'Altered States: Character and Emotional Response in the Cinema', *Cinema Journal* 33, no. 4 (1994): 35; emphasis added.
[20]Murray Smith, 'Engaging Characters: Further Reflections', in *Characters in Fictional Worlds*, ed. Jens Eder, Fotis Jannidis, and Ralf Schneider (Berlin: De Gruyter, 2010), 234.
[21]Smith, 'Engaging Characters', 234.

– including affective mimicry and autonomic reactions, such as the startle reflex that occurs in response to loud sounds.[22] While affective mimicry does exist, and the score in particular creates the conditions for this to occur, the affective responses characters evoke are more than mimetic. Emotional response occurs in a context that is appropriate to judgements of the character and the on-screen action.[23] We may be scared because Fiver is, but the film also generates the sensation of being scared in and of itself.

Through the composition and instrumentation of the score, Fiver is positioned as the film's emotional centre, with Hazel as its moral one. Both rabbits are given distinct musical identities reflective of their character and affective state. Hazel's musical identity is largely linked to the score's lighter, pastoral, picturesque overtones, while Fiver's remains darker, centred around his fear, reflecting the film's horror undertones. This follows Stan Link's observations regarding the subjectivity of the horror soundtrack, which 'frequently positions the viewer as victim'.[24] Morley's string-heavy score carries with it melodic and compositional echoes of Bernard Herrman, cuing the adult listener into the horrors that lie beyond the bloody fields central to Fiver's visions. Each time the strings rise on the soundtrack, they act as an affective cue that reminds us of their initial appearance, signalling the origin of Fiver's fears. Its meaning and affective resonance are complicated and enriched through consistent repetition, exemplary of Claudia Gorbman's assertion that leitmotifs, while appearing to hold fixed meanings, can 'evolve and contribute to the dynamic flow of the narrative carrying its meaning into a new realm of signification', in this instance, signifying fear and horror, expressing sonically what the film cannot show visually.[25]

Joe Tompkins describes horror music as having an 'assaultive character' by design, characterizing the deeply influential string orchestration of *Psycho* as 'aggressive' – the sonic manifestation of Norman Bates's murderous intent.[26] These aggressive qualities are also applicable to *Watership Down*, and General Woundwort's malevolence, achieved in several ways throughout Morley's composition of the character. By employing several musical techniques, including changes to volume and timbre, dissonance – 'unusual combinations of notes'[27] – and the use of stinger chords, Woundwort is

---

[22]Smith, 'Altered States', 39.
[23]Smith, 'Altered States', 42–3.
[24]Stan Link, 'Horror and Science Fiction', in *The Cambridge Companion to Film Music*, ed. Mervyn Cooke and Fiona Ford (Cambridge: Cambridge University Press, 2016), 204.
[25]Claudia Gorbman, *Unheard Melodies: Narrative Film Music* (London: British Film Institute, 1987), 3.
[26]Joe Tompkins, 'Mellifluous Terror: The Discourse of Music and Horror Films', in *A Companion to the Horror Film*, ed. Harry M. Benshoff (Chichester: Wiley Blackwell, 2014), 189.
[27]Tompkins, 'Mellifluous Terror', 190.

sonically defined as threatening and villainous. To borrow from Tompkins, the 'assaultive character' lent to the score occurs when Woundwort is physically present or simply nearby, signalled at several significant points in the narrative. Initially, through a change in tone (and mood) when the rabbits first enter the Efrafa Warren, later when Hyzenthlay is forced to reveal the expedition plans to Woundwort, and finally, during his fight with Bigwig. The use of stinger chords maintains an overall presence within the film indicative of its relationship to horror. Tompkins defines these as 'sudden musical blasts that coincide with moments of shock and revelation'.[28] Both qualities are present in the film's opening moments – a loud fanfare 'blast' preceding the origin narrative of Frith and El-ahrairah. While not an explicit expression of horror in itself, this fanfare is indicative of the space created by the narrative to confront horror, danger, trauma and grief within relatively safe boundaries.

Mapping the soundscape

In thinking through the dynamics of sound and image, and the emotional and affective potential of Morley's score, particular patterns emerge that strengthen the film's relationship to and with horror. How might we begin to assess the soundscape of the film to consider its affects more critically? The subtitle track of *Watership Down*'s 2013 Blu-ray offered an elegant solution, enabling me to plot the score's presence within the film and the meaning it generates to create a musical and affective map based upon it. Subtitles remain undervalued within film studies, with their usefulness largely pertaining to disability studies and accessibility. However, they have an equally significant function as an analytical tool for considering the effects of interpretation and meaning on a film text. By their nature, subtitle tracks involve the adaptation, translation and reinterpretation of sound and other sonic material into its written equivalent. During this complex process, the subtitler engages in an act of critical categorization and interpretation, resulting in a rich discursive resource that confers meaning on the sounds in the film. In describing what is *heard*, the subtitle track also tells us how to react to what is being *seen*. The subtitle track is both a mediator between sound and image and an intermediary between the text and the audience that anticipates and directs affective response. In other words, the subtitle track also tells us how we should feel.

Alongside indicative captions for diegetic sounds – birdsong, dogs barking, twigs snapping, and so on – the subtitle track contains seventy

---

[28]Tompkins, 'Mellifluous Terror', 190.

separate captions relating to the music being played, categorizing the score's sound using over twenty different adjectival descriptions. Some relate to its musical attributes, detailing the music's pacing and/or tone, describing it as 'fast-paced', 'soft' or 'slow'. Others describe the music's style, reiterating particular musical identities for characters and/or character groups, such as the 'military-style' description used for the Owsla officers. The majority of the captions relate specifically to the mood being *conveyed* by the music, making them a useful indicator of the role played by the score in maintaining the film's relationship to horror and generating negative affect.

The most frequently used caption is 'dramatic', either on its own or in conjunction with descriptions relating to pace or tone. However, there are notable exceptions to this, including words like 'eerie', 'unnerving' and, most interestingly, 'sinister'. This descriptor appears several times throughout the film: when the rabbits first leave the warren and navigate the woodland in the dark, during the attack on Violet, and the mere sight of Woundwort's henchman Campion. In describing the mood of the scene and the intent of the unfolding action, the captions direct the audience's emotional and affective response, as well as illustrate how the film's moments of horror are constructed. The subtitle track makes visible how *Watership Down*'s associations with horror and trauma have become so entrenched, making concrete links between the film, the audience, emotion and affect, which are directly expressed through its score.

The complexity and strength of these relationships mirror the emotional underpinnings that characterize, as Annabel J. Cohen argues, our experience of both film *and* music. In defining music as an emotive source, Cohen suggests that '[t]he emotional associations generated by music attach themselves automatically to the visual focus of attention or the implied topic'.[29] This attachment not only underlines how the film's relationship to music has become so entrenched within *Watership Down*'s identity but also how it contributes to the ways in which the film and its meanings are discussed and represented within popular and visual cultures, ultimately shaping how its legacy and cultural longevity are maintained.

Remixing musical meaning

As I mentioned earlier, YouTube holds a particular position in *Watership Down*'s cultural longevity. Alongside trailers and reviews, the site features numerous remix videos, which reappropriate the film's footage and edit it

---

[29] Annabel J. Cohen, 'Music as a Source of Emotion in Film', in *Music and Emotion: Theory and Research*, ed. Patrik N. Juslin and John A. Sloboda (Oxford: Oxford University Press, 2001), 250.

to different pieces of music. These textual re-encounters complicate how the film is read and understood. In what remains of this chapter, I will analyse how these videos articulate how the interaction between sound and image operates, the affective power of music and the impact of recontextualizing the familiar.

Described by Eduardo Navas as 'a cultural glue',[30] remix videos contribute to *Watership Down*'s received cultural meanings and generate new ones. These remediated forms complicate how the film can be read, and its associated emotional and affective resonances. Furthermore, they consolidate *Watership Down*'s relationship *to* and *with* horror, trauma and violence, albeit in a compressed and often excessive manner that is sonically and visually distinct from the original. These remix videos draw upon numerous genres of music to express the concerns, experiences and memories of their makers.

Reconstructed to enhance their existing meaning, these composite videos intensify qualities already present in the film, reflected most obviously in common music selections across videos. The most frequently used piece is Clint Mansell's theme from *Requiem for a Dream* (Aronofksy, 2000), reappropriated as the soundtrack to Fiver's premonitions.[31] Their editing patterns are predicated upon the tensions between moments of conjunction and disjunction between sound and image. Other videos amplify these tensions to make links between violence and warfare, using Frank Klepacki's 'Hell March', originally composed for the videogame *Command and Conquer: Red Alert 2* (2000).[32] Not all music selections are made for their thematic or narrative appropriateness, however. Some remixes further emphasize the disjunction between sound and image through an unexpected choice, such as the use of thrash metal band Slayer's 'Angel of Death' (Hanneman, 1986) over numerous scenes from the film.[33] Focussing once more on violence and gore, the remix begins with an impactful remediation of sound and image. An excerpt of the film's opening sequence during the rabbit massacre is edited to the opening chords of the track, intensifying the violent and vicious nature of the attack itself. The result on-screen is both powerful and amusing, given the juxtaposition between death metal and animation and the dissonance this causes, particularly when the thrash metal playing style sometimes coincides with the gnashing teeth of the rabbit predators, further amplifying the darker undertones of the film's narrative.

---

[30]Eduardo Navas, *Remix Theory: The Aesthetics of Sampling* (Wien: Springer, 2012), 4.
[31]schaloddelschen, *Watership Down - Requiem For A Dream*, 2008, https://www.youtube.com/watch?v=lv0OP7OmcKw (accessed 29 January 2021).
[32]benoitforchamp, *Watership Down Violence*, 2009, https://www.youtube.com/watch?v=aPBck3xcUJc (accessed 29 January 2021).
[33]kaltag7, *Watership Brutality*, 2007, https://www.youtube.com/watch?v=gfAtBLgRPSE (accessed 29 January 2021).

Of the many remix videos on the platform, one set to Marilyn Manson's cover version of the Eurythmics' 'Sweet Dreams (Are Made of This)' offers a particularly effective and affective representation of the film's relationship to horror.[34] This double remediation of song and film are edited together to focus on the film's nightmarish qualities and, implicitly, the emotional impact of these events. Beginning with the hyperrealist close-up on a rabbit's face from early in the film, we then enter into its 'mind's eye', witnessing multiple instances of violence, including Captain Holly's wounding during the human destruction of the Sandelford Warren. The inherently horrific and traumatic nature of these moments is further intensified through the song's reinterpretation from nu wave to industrial metal – signified through its loud, heavy instrumentation and the deep, gravel-like vocals of their eponymous frontman. The editing of the remix often matches sonically what is shown visually, and the video is at its most effective and affective during the excerpts that show the diggers clawing the ground, signalling the beginnings of Sandleford's destruction. Both the cover song and the recontextualization of footage add a new layer of signification to the film, making clearer its connections to horror. The remix video illustrates how extra-textual content contributes to and complicates the cultural categorization of genre, while also offering an indication as to why this reading has become such a significant part of the film's contemporary legacy.

It is important to acknowledge that *Watership Down* remix videos amplify visual and thematic elements that are *already present* within the narrative. Like the subtitle track, they offer an interpretation of its meaning and, in turn, present new ways to read the film. Though new ways of seeing and reading are constituent parts of the underlying functions of the remix video and the cultural work it performs, this video displays a particular awareness of its role in challenging how *Watership Down* is read and understood, reflected in the video's title. Stylized in all caps, its Spanish-language title, 'DESPUES DE ESTO NO VOLVERAS A VER A LOS CONEJOS CON TERNURA', roughly translates to 'After This You Will Not See the Rabbits with Tenderness Again'. This is exactly what the remix does, opening up the film to wider interpretation, moving away from sweetness and sentimentality and allowing it to be something else.

Music plays a central role in this reinterpretation, and the remix video has a particular extra-textual role to play in this discourse. Remix videos exemplify the significant power of what Kathryn Kalinak calls 'the collective resonance of musical associations', present in the inter-

---

[34]Victor Arroyo Vic, *DESPUES DE ESTO NO VOLVERAS A VER A LOS CONEJOS CON TERNURA*, 2016, https://www.youtube.com/watch?v=YIM0Y2prySk (accessed 29 January 2021).

textual construction of the remix.³⁵ Music, she suggests, performs a dual function, being an 'articulator of screen expressions and initiator of spectator response [that] binds the spectator to the screen by resonating affect between them'.³⁶ Comment threads on remix videos reinforce the affective bonds between spectator and screen. They not only illustrate the impact of received meanings but also perpetuate the film's reputation for scariness, consolidating its position as a site of childhood trauma. However, the comment threads these videos generate are also based around subjective judgements of taste, which complicate *Watership Down*'s reading as horror and the affective response such a reading elicits. Offering insight into the fears of the viewer, they emphasize the blurring that occurs between pleasure and displeasure, with some commenters noting their enjoyment of the fear it provokes. It is significant that most comments focus on the original film, and rarely the remix video itself, which is used as a jumping off point to talk about commenters' respective experiences and attitudes. The inter-textual complexity of these videos and the generative comment threads dedicated to them allow for new meanings to emerge. In this new, remediated context, *Watership Down*'s scariness and, by implication, its relationship to horror is embraced, perceived as both a positive and negative trait, facilitated through the deconstruction and subsequent reconstruction of sound and image through remixing.

Conclusion

In *Watership Down*, sound and image work both for and against common perceptions surrounding the film and its legacy. Sound brings what Michel Chion calls 'added value' enriching the filmic image on informative, expressive and, I suggest, affective levels, illustrating both *how* and *why* the film has endured.³⁷

Through close reading and mapping of Angela Morley's score, its mood and meaning, I have revealed a specific relationship that *Watership Down* has with horror and trauma that is in direct opposition to its popular status as a children's animated film, challenging perceptions of the film as sweet and sentimental. The film's relationship *to* and *with* horror is directly expressed through music and is maintained through a collective cultural process that

---

³⁵Kathryn Kalinak, *Settling the Score: Music and the Classical Hollywood Film* (Madison: University of Wisconsin Press, 1992), 87.
³⁶Kalinak, *Settling the Score*, 87.
³⁷Michel Chion, *Audio-Vision: Sound on Screen*, ed. and trans. Claudia Gorbman (New York: Columbia University Press, 1994), 5.

begins within the text itself and continues outside it through extra-textual materials including articles, subtitle tracks and remix videos.

By making correlations between music as valuable *and* music as memorable, we can begin to consider the role it occupies in the construction and generation of meaning, how this complicates the relationships between sound and image, and why a film's cultural associations, and emotional and affective resonances can change over time. In doing so, we can also recognize how the entrenched received meanings that surround a film are formed and evoked, allowing us to be more open about new ways of reading, seeing *and* hearing them.

CHAPTER 10

Pastel dreams and crimson nightmares:

Colour, aesthetics and *Watership Down*

Carolyn Rickards

At a first glance, *Watership Down* (Rosen, 1978) would appear to represent a typical fantasy animation with the world of Richard Adams's adaptation populated with an array of sentient animals. The rabbits featured in the film converse and engage with each other as their lives are transformed by unknown forces, prompting them to embark on a perilous quest to a promised land. However, on closer examination, the film provides a much more nuanced approach with notable shifts between episodes of fantasy and realism. This can be seen in the frequent use of hallucinations, visions and apparitions, which moves the action from the 'real' world experienced by the rabbits towards the uncanny and fantastic. The following chapter argues that this artistic movement is foremost determined by the animated colour palette which is explicitly employed to register this shifting aesthetic throughout the film. It explores how colour operates in the interplay between fantasy and realism and considers how colour can be used for subjective, emotive and symbolic effect in the context of an animated feature film.

To understand how moments of fantasy and realism are distinguished in *Watership Down*, we need to interrogate the theoretical basis for such claims. The film ostensibly adheres to recognized features associated with animated fantasy production. As Christopher Holliday and Alexander Sergeant outline in their writing on the topic, fantasy and animation are considered 'natural bedfellows within contemporary film culture', citing Disney as a leading figure in the propagation of animated fantasy features.[1] Many films produced by the studio showcase talking animals that interact with each other, occasionally unbeknownst to human characters, and operating within 'fictional worlds that we believe in, all the while knowing them to be fantastic'.[2] This trope can be found in Disney fare from *Dumbo* (Sharpsteen, 1941) and *Bambi* (Hand et al., 1942) through to *The Lion King* (Allers and Minkoff, 1994) and *Zootropolis* (Howard and Moore, 2016). However, as Sergeant and Holliday argue, by claiming such films exist within the distinct and defined category of 'animated fantasy', this approach fails to consider latent and 'broader sets of intertwining aesthetic concerns'.[3] This can certainly be evidenced in a film such as *Watership Down* which operates on different levels of aesthetic impulses. As James Walters notes, the film 'is designated as a fictional "reality" [where] the fantasy of talking animals is subdued as it takes place in a more realistic context'.[4] Walters describes how we can see this from the opening prologue which depicts a creation myth that explains how the animals of the world, including El-ahrairah, the prince of rabbits, were formed by the powerful sun god Frith. This fantasized creation sequence then shifts into the opening frames of the film where the abstract image of Frith morphs into a 'realistic portrait of a real sun, low hanging in a hazy sky'.[5] In contrast to the prologue with its stylized figures presented against a stark white background, this 'real' world is based on an actual location: the South Downs in Hampshire. The camera sweeps through this landscape with detailed animation replicating the colours, shades and sounds of the natural environment as birds sing in the trees and bees buzz in the meadows. It is only within this more realized setting that we are then introduced to the principal rabbit characters.

The creation myth featured in the prologue is a fantasized space that provides both contrast and connection to the real world. It forms the basis not only for the belief system of the rabbits but also for the reveries experienced by some of the central characters. We witness an example of this in the opening moments of the film when the sensitive youngster, Fiver,

---

[1]Christopher Holliday and Alexander Sergeant, eds. 'Introduction: Approaching Fantasy/Animation', in *Fantasy/Animation: Connections Between Media, Mediums and Genres* (London: Routledge, 2018), 7, 10.
[2]Donald Crafton, *Shadow of a Mouse: Performance, Belief and World-Making in Animation* (Berkeley: University of California Press, 2013), 16.
[3]Holliday and Sergeant, *Fantasy / Animation*, 7.
[4]James Walters, *Fantasy Film: A Critical Introduction* (Oxford: Berg, 2011), 124.
[5]Walters, *Fantasy Film*, 124.

encounters human footprints and a smouldering cigarette butt discarded beside an ominous wooden sign. As Fiver warns his brother, Hazel, that a 'terrible thing is coming', the serene setting suddenly transforms into a surreal nightmare. The meadow before him begins to turn red with blood while the trees morph into black abstract formations. The contorted shapes eventually swirl into a pattern around the sun, evoking Frith as announced in the prologue. Fiver believes his disturbing vision is a warning sign, and sensing that danger might soon be on the horizon, it provides the impetus for the rabbits to leave their warren and seek a new home. As Paul Wells observes, animation lends itself to fantasy because it has the capacity to depict and reveal 'the conditions of consciousness – dream, memory, processes of thought, solipsism, the *un*conscious, rationale beyond reason'.[6] In *Watership Down*, this is played out in the visions experienced by Fiver as we are allowed intimate access to his subconscious. The fantasy associated with such moments is demarcated as different yet still connected to the reality portrayed elsewhere thus 'binding together fantasy and coherence within its fictional world'.[7] It is this highly layered approach that underscores the various levels of aesthetic impulses evident in the film.

This chapter explores how this shifting aesthetic movement between fantasy and realism operates in relation to colour. *Watership Down* can be compared with similar British animated films such as *Animal Farm* (Halas and Batchelor, 1954), *The Plague Dogs* (Rosen, 1982) and *The Snowman* (Jackson, 1982) which 'in obvious contrast to Disney [project] muted colour palettes'.[8] This can be seen in the emphasis on realism in the artistic designs with earthy browns and greens used to depict the natural environment of pastures, hedgerows and woodlands while human structures such as farmhouses, churches, roads and electricity pylons are shaded in muted browns and greys. However, this is not to suggest that *Watership Down* displays an absence of notable colour. Instead, there are moments of vibrant and intense colour, from the impressionist watercolours seen in the sweeping shots of open countryside through to the more extreme, expressionistic colour used for hallucinatory dream sequences featured in the film. As Steve Neale notes, colour aligns with cinematic fantasy and spectacle because it can be used 'creatively in those genres whose rules of verisimilitude are not tied to conventions of realism [and] in genres designed to provide the eye with visual pleasure'.[9] Animation offers a unique mode for deconstructing

---

[6]Paul Wells, 'Wonderlands, Slumberlands and Plunderlands', in *Fantasy/Animation: Connections Between Media, Mediums and Genres*, ed. Christopher Holliday and Alexander Sergeant (London: Routledge, 2018), 29–30.
[7]Walters, *Fantasy Film*, 124.
[8]Noel Brown, *British Children's Cinema: From the Thief of Bagdad to Wallace and Gromit* (London: I. B. Tauris, 2017), 198.
[9]Steve Neale, *Cinema Technology: Image, Sound, Colour* (London: Macmillan, 1985), 146.

these generic conventions, providing a rhetorical space where colour can be coded with enhanced meaning and symbolism. *Watership Down* features many moments where colour is employed for this purpose with expressive and symbolic colour used to convey heightened states of visual spectacle and fantasy. This chapter thus seeks to explore the different ways colour presents itself in *Watership Down* and considers how it influences and effects the balance between fantasy and realism engendered by the diegetic world of the film.

Arcadian landscapes and the threat of colour

Colour plays a significant role in representing the different locations featured in *Watership Down*, particularly the natural environment experienced by the rabbits. Greens and browns associated with nature are evoked in the emphatically realist depiction of fields, meadows, hills and woodlands that the rabbits inhabit and travel through on their journey. This agrarian landscape is peppered with occasional country roads, rustic farmhouses and bucolic churches. The film places strong emphasis on the spectacle of the English countryside, providing 'visually splendid manifestations of an essentially pastoral national identity'.[10] This is particularly evident in our first glimpse of the eponymous Watership Down. As the music soars and the camera sweeps over field and coppice, we are entitled to a wide frame shot of the hillside standing proud in the distance.[11] In this scene, the animation adopts a more impressionistic style as the detail becomes obscured with the earth and sky forming pastel shades that appear to merge together. Fiver exclaims to the other rabbits: 'that's the place for us. That's where we ought to be. That's where we have to go.' The hillside thus functions as both an actual and spiritual site; it is a location that commands fantasized appeal for the rabbits because it appears to exist beyond the ordinary or every day. This notion of a romanticized landscape resonates with John Urry's definition of the 'place myth' ideal where 'places are chosen to be gazed upon because there is an anticipation, especially through day-dreaming and fantasy, of intense pleasures, either on a different scale or involving different senses from those customarily encountered'.[12] Urry applies this term to describe rural landscapes such as the English Lake District, a place that

---

[10]Andrew Higson, 'Re-presenting the National Past: Nostalgia and Pastiche in the Heritage Film', in *Fires Were Started: British Cinema and Thatcherism*, ed. Lester Friedman (London: UCL Press, [1993] 2006), 93.
[11]See Chapter 8 for more on the role of music in the film's representation of the countryside and for illustrations that complement the following analysis.
[12]John Urry, *Consuming Places* (London: Routledge, 1995), 132.

has been romanticized over time in art, poetry and literature. The South Downs landscape seen in *Watership Down* evokes a similar 'place myth' ideal, inspiring countless writers and artists such as Alfred Lord Tennyson, Rudyard Kipling and William Blake who wrote *Jerusalem*, a poem that celebrates 'England's pleasant pastures' and 'mountains green', while residing in the Sussex village of Felpham.[13] This nostalgic evocation of the English countryside features at length in *Watership Down*, with the hillside itself providing a landmark to be 'gazed upon' due to its prominent position within the landscape.

This is emphasized in a later scene where the rabbits eventually reach and climb the steep hillside of Watership Down. The view from the top of the hill revels in the spectacular, with a panning shot of the countryside far below swathed in pastoral colour. As one of the rabbits exclaims: 'you can see the whole world!' This is a bucolic vista that evokes a potent sense of Blakeian majesty. As the rabbits exclaim: 'oh Frith on the hills! He made it all for us!' This comment underscores the mythical and quasi-religious quality of the landscape by connecting back to the creation sequence featured in the prologue. Watership Down not only provides a safe new home for the rabbits, far removed from the threat of badgers, foxes and human encroachment, but also signifies a promised land and their manifest destiny. As Hazel sagely proclaims: 'Frith may have made it, but Fiver found it.' However, this idyllic scene is also compromised by the addition of roads and electricity pylons glinting in the distance. The presence of such man-made structures highlights a central theme of the film which concerns the danger to the natural world associated with human intervention. Although the countryside featured in the film provides visual spectacle and romanticized appeal, it is consistently portrayed as threatened by the impact of human activity. This makes the scene when the rabbits finally reach the top of Watership Down all the more poignant because it underscores their deep, spiritual connection to the world around them. There is an obvious contrast between humans who, in the pursuit of advanced industrialization, have seemingly lost their primitive connection to the natural environment, with the rabbits who continue to comprehend their world based on ancient lore and mythology. The pastel colours used in such moments emphasize this by evoking a sense of nostalgia for an agrarian past increasingly at risk.

In the natural environment of *Watership Down*, more extreme and vivid colour is associated with danger. Although the rabbits confront many obstacles throughout their journey, human activity poses the most serious threat, and this is often represented through colour contrast with the natural world. For example, when the rabbits encounter and cross a country road,

---

[13]'Writers and the Downs', *South Downs National Park*. https://www.southdowns.gov.uk/discover/heritage/writers-and-the-downs/ (accessed 22 May 2020).

they are forced to deal with the motorcar or 'hrududu'. As the brawny rabbit, Bigwig, explains to the others that the 'hrududu' fail to pose a major concern, a bright red sports car speeds past almost killing him outright. And in a later scene, when the rabbits are fleeing from the authoritarian Efrafa Warren, lauded over by the vicious General Woundwort, two of his guards are killed by an oncoming train which glistens red as it streams across the countryside. This chromatic association with peril and danger connects with David Batchelor's argument that colour has historically been considered as a threat in Western culture. He describes how colour represents an exotic otherness, a 'dangerous' force, a 'loss of consciousness [and] a kind of blindness' which provokes a sense of 'delirium' and 'madness'.[14] There are many moments in *Watership Down* where colour evokes such sentiment, most evocatively witnessed in the destruction of the natural habitat. An early example of this can be seen when, shortly after leaving their home, the rabbits meet the elusive Cowslip who invites them to take shelter from a passing storm. In contrast to the rabbits' original home with its earthy browns, Cowslip's Warren is much more colourful with the underground burrows partly constructed from man-made bricks and shaded in yellow, orange and purple tones. The use of unnatural colour immediately indicates something strange not only about the warren itself but also about Cowslip and the other rabbits who subside there. As the rabbits eat a plentiful supply of fresh carrots, Fiver begins to suspect Cowslip's hospitality: 'there is something unnatural, evil and twisted about this place. It feels like mist. Like being deceived and losing our way.' This description about 'losing our way' and experiencing a sensation similar to 'mist' connects with Batchelor's comments on how colour can operate as a 'kind of blindness'. The vibrant colour found in Cowslip's Warren is not the actual colour the rabbits would have witnessed given its natural, underground setting but instead serves as a symbolic warning of imminent threat and danger. The garish hues are visually coded as 'unnatural' and 'evil' with the ground itself appearing tainted and poisoned. This concern is later realized once the rabbits decide to leave the warren and Bigwig is caught in a snare trap hidden outside in the undergrowth.

Excessive colour as subjective fantasy

Excessive colour in *Watership Down* is thus predominantly utilized to signal human impact on the natural world. This danger is most prominently explored through the subjective view of Fiver who appears

---

[14]David Batchelor, *Chromophobia* (London: Reaktion Books Ltd., 2000), 51.

to have psychic abilities. It is his initial vision of the red field that prompts the rabbits to leave their home in search of new territory, and his sense of foreboding alerts everyone to the concealed dangers of Cowslip's Warren. In analysing *Watership Down*, Walters connects these 'psychic episodes and motifs of death' with the 1970s British horror film *Don't Look Now* (Roeg, 1973).[15] In the film adaptation of Daphne du Maurier's short story, Donald Sutherland and Julie Christie play John and Laura Baxter, a married couple mourning the sudden death of their young daughter, Christine. In the haunting opening scenes of *Don't Look Now*, we witness the death of Christine who falls into a garden pond while playing outside the family home. At the same time inside the house, John knocks over a glass of water that spills on to a photograph he is studying of a Venetian church with a red cloaked figure seated facing away from the camera in the foreground. As the red ink and water combine, it causes a spiral effect on the photographic image, providing a sudden eruption of colour. As Andrew Patch notes, 'it is the presence of red, its autonomous subversion of both form and temporality, that brings John into a state of delirium.'[16] It is this moment in the film that appears to trigger John's latent psychic abilities, leading to a devastating exploration of grief and loss. The colour red continues to haunt John as he later wanders through the narrow waterways of a wintery Venice in search for something (or someone) that might provide answers to his daughter's untimely demise. *Don't Look Now* thus shares with *Watership Down* not only an interest with death and the supernatural but also a visual preoccupation with the colour red. For example, in Fiver's early vision, the formation of red on the field appears to be cast from the setting sun which provides a seemingly innocent and insignificant occurrence in a similar vein to the spilled ink on the photographic image in *Don't Look Now*. However, the red glow cast across the meadow from the sunset adopts more sinister overtones as Fiver witnesses the transformation of this into a swirling pattern of blood that envelops the entire scene. In the same way that John subconsciously associates the red spiral pattern as a sign of imminent danger from the opening sequence, Fiver believes the encroaching red is a warning sign. As this swirling red pattern turns skyward towards the beams of the evening sun, there is also a suggestion that Fiver has received a psychic message from Frith to leave the warren immediately or face perilous consequences. It is this subconscious premonition of death that initiates the start of Fiver's and John's journeys in both a literal and metaphorical sense.

---

[15] Walters, *Fantasy Film*, 124.
[16] Andrew Patch, 'Beneath the Surface: Nicolas Roeg's *Don't Look Now*', in *Don't Look Now: British Cinema in the 1970s*, ed. Paul Newland (Bristol: Intellect, 2010), 187.

Extreme colour is therefore used in *Watership Down* to emphasize when the rabbits experience a 'loss of consciousness, a kind of blindness',[17] acting as visual 'hyperbole' to 'express the full depth of a heightened and extreme circumstance'.[18] Laure Brost applies this term to discuss films which employ exaggerated colour to convey the inexpressible – often linked to intense thoughts, feelings and emotions experienced by characters. In relation to the colour red, we can point to filmic examples such as *Black Narcissus* (Powell and Pressburger, 1947) whereby Sister Ruth's (Kathleen Byron) rejection by Mr Dean (David Farrar) is registered through a saturation of red that descends across the screen, 'colouring everything in the frame with the association of anger and jealousy'.[19] In *Bigger Than Life* (Ray, 1956), James Mason's family man succumbs to mental torment due to a combination of intense pain and cortisone treatment which is visually articulated by a red mist that permeates the image. We find a similar effect in *Watership Down* with the red field acting as a signifier for the heightened sense of fear experienced by Fiver against a threat so terrible that it cannot be conveyed in words alone. Fiver himself fails to determine exactly what this danger consists of other than stating: 'something very bad is going to happen.' It is this saturation of colour that works to provide a sense of overwhelming fear and danger. Fiver's red field vision also evokes the artwork of Edvard Munch's most striking piece, *The Scream* (1893), which features a distorted man facing outward with his hands to his face in a silent scream as the sky above swirls in a sea of burnished orange and red. In describing his conception for the piece, Munch later recalled how the setting sunlight turned the sky a blood red as he sensed a 'scream passing through nature; it seemed to me that I heard the scream. I painted this picture, painted the clouds as actual blood. The colour shrieked.'[20] The swirling hues of the sunset that seemingly turn to blood during Fiver's vision are highly reminiscent of Munch's work, conveying a sense of a literal 'scream passing through nature'. This sentiment strongly connects with the narrative themes, and it is the disconnect between the natural colour of the real world and excessive colour of the nightmare that makes this sequence so alarming.

Fiver's psychic vision is later realized when the rabbits are reacquainted with Captain Holly who initially tried to stop them leaving their home warren. Holly reappears midway through the film, acting severely

---

[17] Batchelor, *Chromophobia*, 51.
[18] Laure Brost, 'On Seeing Red: The Figurative Movement of Film Colour', in *Questions of Colour in Cinema: From Paintbrush to Pixel*, ed. Wendy Everett (Bern: Peter Lang, 2007), 131.
[19] Sarah Street, *Colour Films in Britain: The Negotiation of Innovation 1900–1955* (London: Palgrave Macmillan, 2012), 181.
[20] Edvard Munch, 22 January 1892, quoted in Zuzanna Stanska, 'The Mysterious Road From Edvard Munch's *The Scream*', *Daily Art Magazine*, December 2016.

traumatized from his recent experiences. What follows constitutes one of the most disturbing moments of the film. In a flashback from Holly's perspective, he recounts how humans arrived one day and destroyed their warren. However, rather than showing the actual physical act of destruction from a realist perspective, with men using chainsaws and diggers to purge the land, the animation here adopts a surrealist tone. There are haunting images of upturned trees and earth that appear in quick succession across the screen. We see harrowing shots of dying rabbits, pallid grey with bloodshot eyes from a lack of oxygen, driven deep into the ground as their homes are destroyed. The congested warrens evoke the bleak imagery of British artist Henry Moore's 'Shelter Sketch' series depicting scenes inside the London Underground during bombing raids of the Second World War which were described at the time as 'a terrifying vista of recumbent shapes, pale as all underground life tends to be pale; regimented, as only fear can regiment'.[21] A giant black claw scrapes across a bright green background to reveal a crimson layer underneath the surface. In contrast to other violent scenes in the film which adopt a more realist approach, such as the snaring of Bigwig and the death of Violet by a swooping hawk, this sequence shows no actual blood or physical injury but instead provides a figurative depiction of the event that was initially foretold in Fiver's vision. However, unlike Fiver's apparition, this does not play out as an hallucination but as a re-imagining of the events that occurred. There is an element of fantasy in such scenes which include images that Holly could not have witnessed directly for himself, such as the horrific close-ups of suffocating rabbits crushed to their deaths, but remain a vivid part of his recollected story. This sequence thus functions in the following ways. Foremost, it serves as a traumatic memory for Holly who, while realizing the actions as an attack on their home, is not aware of the reasons for the wanton destruction (as viewers we understand from an earlier cue on an advertising board that humans are developing the land to build a new housing estate). Second, it provides evocative visual imagery that underscores the harrowing impact of this action, serving as 'hyperbole' where excessive colour conveys a traumatic sense of 'delirium' and 'madness'. As Holly laments during his recollection: 'everything turned mad, warrens, earth, roots, all pushed into the air.' The image of the black claw scraping against the green background to reveal red earth underneath is a surreal re-imagining of the actual destruction that occurred, registering as a heightened response to the event. The excessive colour witnessed in this sequence is again used to convey a sense of the unnatural with man's destructive force causing a visual disconnect from the natural world.

---

[21] Anon., catalogue description, Tate Art Gallery, 1941. https://www.tate.org.uk/art/artworks/moore-tube-shelter-perspective-n05709 (accessed 3 June 2020).

The absence of colour and symbolic meaning

Colour thus operates on multiple levels during *Watership Down* by functioning as a way to differentiate between moments of heightened reality and vivid fantasy. The opening prologue stands out in this respect due to its employment of colour within a simple, stylized animated aesthetic which depicts how the world was created by Frith. The style of animation in this sequence evokes ancient indigenous rock painting and artwork with simplified brown trees and animals depicted against a stark white background. In this creation myth, with its analogous links to Genesis and the Garden of Eden, all the animals are initially created equal; however, the rabbits eventually start to dominate by eating all the food available in the forest. Frith chastises the rabbit prince, El-ahrairah, for his supreme arrogance in leading his people and, as a punishment for his actions, turns the other animals into ferocious beasts with claws and teeth. The brown fur of the cat, fox and badger become tinged with bright blues and reds, making them appear more menacing. When the rabbits are inevitably killed by the newly created predators, their carcasses appear ochre red on the forest floor. In line with other moments in the film, there is a strong correlation between colour, danger and death. This chromatic motif recurs throughout *Watership Down*, from Fiver's premonition through to Holly's nightmarish flashback. Occasionally, this is presented in more subtle forms, for example, when depicting Efrafa, where the rabbits that populate this warren are enslaved to General Woundwort's brutal regime. The first shot of Efrafa conveys a sombre atmosphere with gnarled tree roots and dusty burrows set against a dark and stormy sky. The warren is animated in muted greys to give a sense of authoritarian dystopia as we see lines of rabbits ordered into rank and file. They are immediately differentiated from the other rabbits in the film by their dark grey fur and striking blue eyes which are always posed as stern or fearful. This evokes the colour schemes seen in later dystopic science fiction films such as *1984* (Radford, 1984) and *Brazil* (Gilliam, 1985) whereby grey is used to signify oppressive and totalitarian societies where freedom and individuality have become obsolete. Grey is imbued with similar meanings in the representation of Efrafa to underscore the Orwellian horror associated with Woundwort's ruthless empire. It also serves as a chromatic inference that the unfortunate rabbits living there are perhaps closer to the finality of death.

The connection between colour and death can also be seen later in the film when Hazel is shot and wounded by a gun pellet after attempting to escape from a farmhouse. While the other rabbits presume Hazel has been killed, Fiver remains adamant his brother is still alive. As he looks out across the hillside, Fiver sees a ghostly vision of the Black Rabbit, a messenger of Frith and a prophetic symbol of death. He then decides to leave the warren to search for Hazel. As Fiver runs down the hillside following the Black Rabbit, the music fades seamlessly into the haunting strains of 'Bright Eyes', a piece created for, and now synonymous with, the film, composed by Mike Batt and performed by Art Garfunkel. The animation here adopts a dreamlike quality with flashbacks to the moment Fiver witnessed his initial vision of the red field. Such imagery would suggest a personal conflict of grief and guilt for leading his friends to a place he believed was safe. Interspersed with these impressionistic flashbacks, we see spectral images of Fiver and Hazel playing with each other and depicted in alternating blue, green and red colours. This is the film's only use of multicoloured animation, and it works in this sequence more as a musical interlude as opposed to a strict diegetic passage.[22] However, similar to the visions, hallucinations and flashbacks employed elsewhere, the meanings conveyed in such images (including love, loyalty and kinship) fuel the broader narrative as Fiver continues his desperate search. Despite his firm belief that Hazel is still alive, the continued presence of the Black Rabbit suggests that his brother's demise may only be moments away. Black is used sparingly in the film and typically only appears during more abstract scenes such as the distorted trees Fiver witnesses during his initial vision. As Tom Gunning argues, black 'marshals powerful connotations (death, evil, mystery, nothingness) [and] can swallow or overwhelm other colours in darkness, asserting control over visibility itself'.[23] It is notable that the film starts with a black screen before the creation myth prologue, suggesting a void or 'nothingness' prior to the emergence of the almighty Frith, and the ending provides a reverse of this transition by slowly fading to black after the final death takes place. As discussed, the Black Rabbit represents the ultimate avatar associated with death, and it is a figure that instils fear and awe in the rabbits. As Bigwig articulates: 'we go by the will of the Black Rabbit. When he calls, you have to go.' These words resonate towards the end of the film as we see a now aged Hazel living peacefully with his fellow rabbits on the hilltop when the Black Rabbit appears once more and invites Hazel to embrace eternal sleep. It constitutes a poignant and moving scene, but the re-appearance of the Black Rabbit is also a cautionary reminder that the Arcadian idyll epitomized by Watership Down is 'only temporary, for the warren has

---

[22]*Bright Eyes* was rearranged as a pop single with footage from the film featuring in the accompanying music video and released by Columbia Records in 1979.
[23]Tom Gunning, 'Where Do Colours go at Night?', in *Colour and the Moving Image: History, Theory, Aesthetics, Archive*, ed. Simon Brown, Sarah Street, and Liz Watkins (London: Routledge, 2013), 88.

already become overcrowded [and] the noise of the cars and buses below will eventually force the rabbits to move once again'.[24]

Watership Down utilizes both a varied animation style and shifting colour palette to depict the world inhabited by the rabbits. This is a world that is multi-layered with a belief system and societal order that strikes parallels with our own, and Adams's narrative allows access to both the conscious and subconscious thoughts of its characters. It is in the realization of this world from authorial page to animated screen whereby colour becomes the primary arbitrator of meaning. Colour is utilized not only as a formal, stylistic convention that is associated with animated filmmaking but also as a visual mechanism that creates intimate comprehension and understanding of the rabbit universe. The film includes detailed imagery of the flora and fauna associated with the South Downs countryside with the fields, coppices and hedgerows that comprise this environment shaded in naturalistic greens and browns. The presence of vivid colour such as the sudden eruption of crimson blood following an attack or the shimmer of a bright red motorcar is intended to be unsettling, often associated with natural predators or human activity that pose visceral threats to the rabbits. However, colour in *Watership Down* not only depicts the 'real' world of the natural environment but is also used specifically to convey meaning. This is expressed in numerous ways such as the pastel tones used to depict the first glimpse of the hillside sanctuary where the rabbits find a new home – a mythical 'place' sanctioned by Frith himself – or the lurid colours in Cowslip's Warren which immediately evoke an implicit warning of impending danger. The colours shift from the realistic tones associated with the natural and human world to become more abstract and symbolic. Colour is used in such moments to signify and emphasize various meanings attached to the various locations experienced by the rabbits on their journey.

As discussed throughout this chapter, *Watership Down* is an animated fantasy film which invests in multiple 'aesthetic concerns'.[25] It constantly moves from the 'real' world to the fictionalized and (re)imagined, and it is in the film's more fantastical moments where we find the colour palette at its most luminous, expressive and surreal. This is most evident in the visions experienced by Fiver and in the articulation of Holly's traumatic flashback where colour again assumes the role of primary arbitrator of meaning. In both examples, the characters cannot fully express in words a comprehension of their experience or the intensity of their emotions, and colour provides the visual mode by which to convey their troubled psyches.

---

[24]John Pennington, 'From Peter Rabbit to *Watership Down*: There and Back Again to the Arcadian Ideal', *Journal of the Fantastic in the Arts* 3, no. 2 (10) (1991): 76.
[25]Holliday and Sergeant, *Fantasy/Animation*, 7.

As these visions and hallucinations are presented as fantasy, this allows for the creative scope to experiment with various artistic techniques and chromatic motifs. The result is a complex, multi-layered animation that reflects Adams's complex, multi-layered story. In contrast to the prevailing notion that *Watership Down* adheres to a muted colour scheme throughout, it is clear from this analysis that the film instead employs expansive and varied colour that serves to inform and emphasize its shifting aesthetic. It also provides a vital means of navigating and understanding the dreams, nightmares and beliefs of its fictionalized rabbits.

CHAPTER 11

Prince with a thousand faces:

Shifting art styles and the depiction of violence in *Watership Down*

Sam Summers

Decades after its release, *Watership Down* (Rosen, 1978) remains notorious for its violence, with television screenings of the film in particular continuing to cause a stir in news outlets and on social media.[1] Certain scenes and images have become ubiquitous in these contexts: Bigwig trapped in the snare; the battle with the Efrafans in the warren's tunnels; a crazed, blood-soaked Woundwort leaping through the air. Curiously, though, the film's most brutal act of violence is omitted from this canon, seemingly passing

---

[1] Amy Duncan, 'Channel 5 Showed *Watership Down* on Easter Sunday (Again) and it's Scarred Viewers for Life (Again)', *Metro*, 16 April 2017. https://metro.co.uk/2017/04/16/channel-5-showed-watership-down-on-easter-sunday-and-its-scarred-viewers-for-life-6578101 (accessed 27 July 2020); Ed Power, 'A Piercing Screen: How *Watership Down* Terrified an Entire Generation', *Independent*, 19 October 2018. https://www.independent.co.uk/arts-entertainment/films/features/watership-down-film-bright-eyes-rabbits-disease-martin-rosen-richard-adams-disney-a8590226.html (accessed 27 July 2020); Henry Barnes, 'Bunny Fury Boils over after Channel 5 Screens *Watership Down* on Easter Sunday', *The Guardian*, 20 March 2016. https://www.theguardian.com/film/2016/mar/29/parents-furious-after-channel-5-screens-watership-down-on-easter-sunday (accessed 27 July 2020).

most viewers by. It occurs in the film's first two minutes, in its opening prelude sequence: the massacre of the children of El-ahrairah, the world's first clan of rabbits, at the hands of a pack of predators. Fifteen rabbits are slain on-screen, their bodies left to linger lifeless on the ground. The scene racks up a body count far higher than the film's climactic battle, and yet it is rarely if ever cited among *Watership Down*'s most traumatic moments. The reason, of course, is that the film's entire opening prelude sequence is highly stylized. The aetiological tale of the sun god Frith's creation of the world and the origin of the rabbit species is rendered against a minimal background comprised of faint watercolour hills floating in a spacious white void. Its animal characters are simplified, flat and elastic, falling stylistically somewhere between cave paintings and Looney Tunes cartoons. The rabbits' deaths are similarly devoid of detail: in rapid succession across a single static shot, we see them bitten or clawed by cats, dogs and hawks. The blows instantly transform their bobbing, grey bodies to lifeless and red, symbolizing blood without depicting it, until fifteen such scarlet abstractions litter the screen (see Figure 1.2 in Chapter 1). This is how violence is introduced into the world *Watership Down*, and while the sequence is not necessarily innocuous – its striking simplicity and stark detachment are in their own way potentially shocking – it lacks the visceral horror associated with the more realistic depictions of gore found later in the film.

The film wastes no time in transitioning its audience from the stylized, abstracted past into a much more recognizable present, through a match cut which fades from the pulsating symbol of Frith, bright-orange and suspended against the white void, to a pale yellow sun illuminating a naturalistic countryside scene. A montage of tracking shots takes us through this lusciously detailed environment, establishing its depth and scope in contrast to the flatness and fixed perspectives of the prelude. Suddenly and sharply the film cuts to an extreme close-up of a rabbit's eye, vividly detailed down to its reflective sheen and each individual hair surrounding it. The rabbit, Hazel, blinks as the 'camera' pulls back to reveal the rest of his face, startlingly lifelike in its design and its movements. The image lasts for mere seconds before fading to a longer shot of Hazel emerging from a bush, this time in a simplified form, his meticulously painted hairs replaced with solid fields of brown and beige. This is the Hazel we will follow for the remainder of *Watership Down*; we will never see him, or any of the film's characters, depicted in such detail again. Indeed, it would have been prohibitively difficult and expensive to maintain this level of almost-photorealistic fidelity for the duration of a ninety-minute film involving tens of animal characters engaging in fast-paced action. But the existence of this shot and its use as our introduction to *Watership Down*'s setting is significant, particularly following the abstracted introductory sequence, as it grounds the action of the film proper in a version of our own lived reality, establishing stakes for the violent acts to come that were absent in

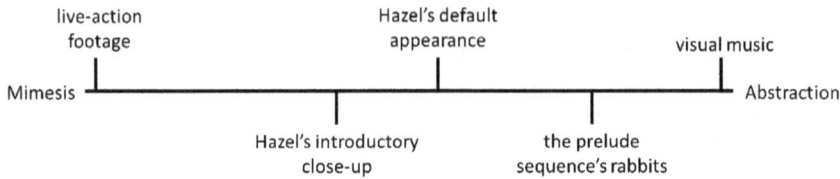

FIGURE 11.1 *An illustration of Furniss's continuum of animation styles.*

the prelude's massacre. More broadly, by switching in a short space of time from the flat, cartoonish rabbits of the opening to the hyper-detailed Hazel and finally to a realistically proportioned but relatively simplified middle ground, the film exhibits its most pronounced example of a technique it shall utilize throughout its runtime. In each of its scenes of graphic violence, *Watership Down* makes use of its status as a work of animation to closely control the effects of its violent acts by subtly shifting its art style, in a more nuanced variation of the prelude's use of abstracted animated imagery to temper its horrific potential. Through a close analysis of several such scenes, this chapter seeks to elucidate how and why this is the case.

Analysing animated violence

First, we must establish the terminology we will be using to discuss the film's animation styles and look at existing accounts of the impact of stylistic differences on the reception of animated violence. In the case of the former, it is useful to begin with Maureen Furniss's conception of a 'continuum' designed to measure different forms of animation against live-action media in terms of their fidelity to reality.[2] One end of her spectrum is labelled 'mimesis', towards which falls unaltered live-action cinematography, and the other is labelled 'abstraction', occupied by non-representative styles of animation such as visual music. Somewhere right of centre, towards the 'abstraction' side, lands Disney's *Snow White and the Seven Dwarfs* (Hand et al., 1937), which 'has a relatively naturalistic look' but whose 'characters and landscapes can be described as caricatures, or abstractions of reality, to some extent'.[3] This description can also be applied to the default designs of *Watership Down*, outside of its stylized introduction and Hazel's initial photorealistic close-up. As such, a version of Furniss's continuum comparing the film's animation styles might resemble Figure 11.1. Further, as we shall see, the visual style which I have termed the film's 'default' is

---

[2]Maureen Furniss, *Art in Motion: Animation Aesthetics* (London: John Libbey, 2007), 5–6.
[3]Furniss, *Art in Motion*, 6.

not rigidly defined, instead subtly oscillating between more mimetic and abstracted variations on the look demonstrated by Hazel in his first full-body appearance. These transitions are particularly apparent in the violent scenes we will be looking at here.

While the film's predominant visual style cycles between slight variations on a default mode of representation, as a whole it can be broadly classified as 'hyperrealist'. This is the term used by Paul Wells to describe the aesthetic codified in Disney's *Snow White*, an aesthetic which dominated Western hand-drawn animated features for the duration of their lifespan as a major commercial art form, with *Watership Down* being no exception. Wells characterizes hyperrealism as a mode in which 'the characters, objects and environment . . . are subject to the conventional physical laws of the "real" world'[4] and 'the construction, movement and behavioural tendencies of "the body" . . . will correspond to the orthodox physical aspects of human beings and creatures in the "real" world'.[5] This is clearly what we see adhered to in the main body of *Watership Down*, as opposed to the skewed proportions and elastic movements seen in its opening sequence. This bodily and physical consistency is key to the film's realism, compensating for the simplified, streamlined forms afforded to the rabbits following Hazel's more photorealistic introduction and maintaining the inference that *Watership Down*'s characters exist in a world of consequences mirroring our own. Hazel might never again literally resemble a rabbit so much as he does in that initial shot, but his body *behaves* like that of a rabbit and is subject to more or less the same physical laws, emphasizing the movie's stakes. While visually the creatures' representations may subtly shift towards mimesis or abstraction, this physical fidelity remains in place. The bodily damage enacted upon the rabbits in these moments of violence is not in question, but the medium through which it is conveyed has the potential to affect its reception.

Although it seems intuitive that this would be the case, historically the majority of studies regarding violence in animation have omitted any acknowledgement of the specificities of the medium, and the myriad divergent ways in which its unique properties and idioms allow for violence to be represented on-screen. Instead, they typically focus on the effects of violent scenes in children's cartoons on young viewers' behaviour, without distinguishing between the effects (behavioural or otherwise) of viewing abstracted and mimetic animated violence, or any of the multiple variations in between. And yet, both industry professionals and overseers have cited the differences between certain visual styles of animated violence as being tied to its reception (again, invariably couched in the context of potential

---

[4]Paul Wells, *Understanding Animation* (London: Routledge, 1998), 25.
[5]Wells, *Understanding Animation*, 25–6.

negative effects on children's behaviour). In the late 1960s, growing concerns around violence in Saturday morning cartoons, specifically centred on the action-adventure, thriller and superhero genres, led to the US networks moving away from this kind of animated programming in favour of 'comic' cartoons.[6] These genres were disproportionally targeted despite the fact that, according to David Perlmutter, 'a closer look at the program narratives of this time shows that violence was actually used, if at all, as a last resort'.[7] This speaks to a perception that what violence did take place in the likes of *Birdman* (1967–9) and *Space Ghost* (1966–8), with their relatively realistic proportions, designs and physics, was somehow more visceral or harmful than that found in contemporaneous comic cartoons like *Dastardly and Muttley* (1969–71) and *Scooby Doo* (1969–70). This is a position seemingly shared by Bill Hanna who, with Hanna-Barbera Productions, was responsible for all of the above. 'I am glad we are moving from the realistic adventure cartoon that was filled with real violence,' he is quoted as saying in 1968, as this shift was taking place. 'There is nothing wrong with the unreal fantasy type violence. For instance, in *Tom and Jerry* the harder the cat gets hit, the funnier it is, but it is for comedy not violence.'[8] Hanna, then, emphasizes the significance of the shows' respective tonal qualities, which are derived in part from their divergent visual styles. This reflects orthodox assumptions made by earlier animators regarding realism and audience identification: Michael Barrier suggests that Disney animators' adoption of a hyperreal aesthetic for their early features was due in part to concerns that 'pursuing caricature could diminish audience acceptance of their characters'.[9] If realistic animation encourages or facilitates this kind of identification more so than cartoonal aesthetics, it stands to reason that violence depicted in more mimetic visual styles is liable to have a more tangible horrific effect.

This basic assumption – that violence animated in different styles with different levels of adherence to realist principles can engender different effects and responses – forms the basis of several studies that do account for the specificities of animation, and the divergent forms of representation of which it is capable, when considering its potential effects on children's behaviour. Richard Haynes's 1978 survey looks at children's perceptions of what he terms 'comic' and 'authentic' violence. In light of the debate around

---

[6]Richard B. Haynes, 'Children's Perceptions of "comic" and "authentic" cartoon violence', *Journal of Broadcasting and Electronic Media* 22, no. 1 (1978): 63.
[7]David Perlmutter, *America Toons In: A History of Television Animation* (Jefferson: McFarland, 2014), 123.
[8]Bill Hanna quoted in 'Hanna-Barbera—Go to Adventure or Comic?', *New York Times Magazine*, 23 November 1969, cited in Haynes, 'Children's Perceptions of "comic" and "authentic" cartoon violence', 63.
[9]Michael Barrier, *Hollywood Cartoons: American Animation in its Golden Age* (Oxford: Oxford University Press, 1999), 268.

whether comic cartoons are less 'harmful' than action-adventure series, Haynes screened examples of each to groups of ten-to-twelve-year-olds and found that 'violent content in comic cartoon programs is, at the very least, recognized as violent by children'.[10] What's more, contrary to the common assumption, 'the findings also point to the possibility that comic violence is seen as more violent, possibly more feared by the child viewer, and less acceptable than violence occurring in authentic type cartoon programs'.[11] However, Haynes's survey primarily measures 'perception of violence' and 'acceptability of violence', so the fact that the comic cartoon scored higher on the former count and lower on the latter can likely be attributed to the fact that acts of violence in such programmes tend to be foregrounded and exaggerated for humorous effect. The study tells us that violence is perceived, but not *how* it is perceived. To that point, another 1978 study conducted by Lagerspetz, Wahlroo and Wendelin, while including live-action footage alongside different kinds of animation, found that 'the strongest emotional reactions occurred to the clips depicting the most realistic violence. Such scenes invoked the greatest expressions of fear and worry, tenseness and anger [while] cartoon violence elicited joy.'[12] Similarly, Gunter and Furman's 1984 survey reported that 'in more realistic settings, viewers exhibit greater sensitivity to other features, such as the form of the violence and its consequences for victims when judging the seriousness of violent incidents'.[13] Gunter, Harrison and Wykes summarize that 'an important element that should be considered when assessing the likely impact of screen violence on children is the degree of identification a viewer has with the victim or aggressor', and that 'the degree of identification is related to the amount of realism portrayed in the violent scene'.[14] This is in keeping with the effects of hyperrealism as posited by the animation scholars cited earlier, while also directly and empirically linking the audience's investment and belief in the fictional world with their perception of violent acts specifically.

Returning to *Watership Down*, it is noteworthy that the initial BBFC report on the film does account for the effect of realism on the perception of violence, but its conclusions reveal a simplified conception of the animated medium in this regard. The report, which handed the film a U rating, suggests that *Watership Down*'s animation alone is enough to 'remove the realistic gory horror in the occasional scenes of violence and bloodshed'.[15] The

---

[10]Haynes, 'Children's Perceptions of "comic" and "authentic" Cartoon Violence', 69.
[11]Haynes, 'Children's Perceptions of "comic" and "authentic" Cartoon Violence', 69.
[12]Barrie Gunter, Jackie Harrison, and Maggie Wykes, *Violence on Television: Distribution, Form, Context and Themes* (New York: Routledge, 2003), 9.
[13]Gunter, Harrison, and Wykes, *Violence on Television*, 162.
[14]Gunter, Harrison, and Wykes, *Violence on Television*, 162.
[15]'Watership Down', *British Board of Film Classification*, 15 February 1978. https://darkroom.bbfc.co.uk/original/1b0cb7188e02ac62c6cdcce5f2d1b928:2199e5760ab7c37b5b037fd

wording here is telling; animation is said to 'remove' the horror, not temper or neutralize it, and yet by acknowledging it the report suggests that there *was* horror there to be removed. This presents *Watership Down*'s violence as a paradox, whereby horror both exists in the text and does not by virtue of its mediation through the seemingly monolithic prism of 'Animation'. In fact, the film displays a far more nuanced utilization of these three pertinent properties: violence (as an action), gore (as a visual property of violence here associated with realistic detail) and horror (as an effect). Putting aside arguments of whether or not it is suitable for children – which too often preoccupy any discussion of violence in both animation in general and in *Watership Down* in particular, stemming from a reductive pigeonholing of the medium as children's entertainment – the remainder of this chapter will focus on how and why the film modulates its *horror* by controlling the *goriness* of its *violence* through a shifting gradation of animated realism.

Animating violence in *Watership Down* (1978)

The first scene in which this takes place is the one in which Bigwig is trapped in a farmer's snare. The sequence is built around escalating tension and relief, in which the film's use of shifting levels of mimesis and gore to elicit varying degrees of horror plays a significant role. The snaring in question occurs off-screen, with the audience first made aware through a sharp cut to a close-up of Bigwig's writhing head which shortly zooms out to reveal the full scene. Bigwig's friends attempt to save him by digging up the snare's peg, conveyed in a series of medium shots which retain the rabbits' default, streamlined designs – realistically proportioned but lacking in excessive detail. As the tension builds – accompanied by suspenseful, up-tempo strings – their efforts are intercut with a succession of extremely brief close-ups of Bigwig's face, mirroring the first but escalating in graphic detail. Four such shots occur throughout the process, each one drawing closer to his face. The first depicts thin streaks of blood, coloured a solid maroon and standing stark against his grey features (Figure 11.2). From its positioning it has clearly streamed from his nose and mouth, but it appears still in the image. In addition there is nebulous white detailing against the black of his open mouth, giving the impression of rising foam.

The second and third shots are similar to one another, both building on the details afforded to the viewer by the first. As we get closer to Bigwig, rather than the static abstracted streaks of the previous image, we see the blood in motion as it gushes from his mouth and nostrils and gradually

---

ee3a35735/watership-down-report.pdf (accessed 13 April 2021).

FIGURES 11.2 AND 11.3 *Successive shots of Bigwig's face build in proximity and gory detail.*

covers his face. While initially solid and self-contained, the blood's mass here interacts with his other features, coating portions of his nose and teeth, thereby suggesting depth. Its colouration is also more detailed, mixing a higher tone of pink with the existing maroon, while flecks of white give the blood a reflective quality as well as producing frothy bubbles of foam. Finally, a single fly circles the bleeding rabbit, emphasizing the detail and proximity of the framing and imparting an unsettling, foreboding quality. The last of these shots takes us closer still, showing what seem to be Bigwig's death throes as the snare is released too late (Figure 11.3). We are now close enough to make out the blades of grass in the foreground, previously rendered in broad watercolour strokes but now individually drawn on a separate plane position in front of Bigwig's face. The gushing and foaming have ceased with the release of the snare, but the rabbit is still covered in blood, which ripples as he moves his head. We see more clearly than before how it cakes his nose and teeth, and the patterns it forms around his mouth are more specific and intricate. His hair is also more clearly visible; it is delineated by thick, zigzagging black lines against his body's solid grey colouration which, while not approaching the photorealistic detail of Hazel's first close-up, stands out next to the faint impressions of fur seen in previous shots. Lastly, the flies have multiplied, with three now hovering around the writhing rabbit, underlining the image's graphic morbidity. With Bigwig apparently dead, the music fades and the scene's tension releases; we revert to a medium shot as the rabbits mournfully surround his body, which is now rendered in the same streamlined fashion as the other characters', devoid of the gory detail that had cast it as grotesque.

Here we have a prime example of the film's use of subtly shifting variations of hyperrealism to utilize the horror of the violent image to a specific end, in this case escalating tension and stakes and encouraging empathy with the ensnared rabbit. For the majority of the scene the 'camera' is focussed on the other characters attempting to free Bigwig by digging up the snare's peg, consistently depicted in the default streamlined style. The quick cuts to Bigwig build in proximity and detail commensurately with the growing intensity of the situation, along with the rabbits' progressively panicked efforts to save their friend, and the increasing levels of danger and pain suffered by the character. Moving, for instance, from the static, abstracted streaks of blood in the initial shot to the more mimetic, visceral cocktail of blood and foam in the second and third emphasizes the urgency of the threat, mobilizing the horrific qualities of the animated gore to instil revulsion and a desperate desire to see Bigwig saved.

The shifting levels of detail and mimesis in *Watership Down* are situational, then, utilized to create specific effects depending on the context of the violence being enacted and the presiding tone of the scene in question. This becomes clear when the snare scene is contrasted to other bloody events depicted in the film. Take, for example, the scene later in the film where Hazel, having been shot, has his wound treated by Kehaar the seagull, who removes the buckshot with his beak. This is, in a sense, analogous to the snare sequence: a rabbit has suffered a bloody injury, and another character must help them through it. Where it differs is in terms of context and tone; whereas Bigwig's rescue is a matter of urgency with a character's life at stake, in Hazel's case the threat has long passed. He has already escaped from the farmers who shot him, and his wound is clearly not life-threatening, so the scene in which Kehaar tends to him is far more relaxed in tone. There is no race against time here, and no suspenseful music to create tension – no music at all, in fact. The seagull's improvised surgery is not even the focus of the scene; its primary purpose is to facilitate a conversation between Kehaar and Hazel in which the rabbit learns about the Efrafa Warren. With these contextual differences in mind, comparing the depiction of Hazel's wound in this scene to that of Bigwig's strangulation clearly shows that *Watership Down* modulates the level of realistic gore according to the tonal, narrative and aesthetic needs of a given scene. We see several close shots of the wound, the closest being roughly the same distance from the 'camera' as the second shot of Bigwig in the snare, in which the foam first became visible along with the gushing motion of the blood. However, the wound is not presented in anywhere near this level of detail. It is fixed in shape and solid in colour, rendered as a large jagged blotch of crimson. Within it we can see a handful of pellets, shown simply as small black dots. The lack of detail is such that their positioning is inconsistent from frame to frame: as Kehaar removes each pellet it reappears, sometimes in the same spot but just as often elsewhere. This attests to the fact that the detail of the image does not simply correlate with the object's proximity to the 'camera' – as a work of animation, *Watership Down* is unconstrained by what its lens is and isn't able to capture. From a similar vantage point, the audience is able to see much more clearly the appearance and behaviour of the gore in the snare scene. Because tension, horror and empathy – the core functions of the graphic gore in that instance – are not overriding concerns in this case, such detail is not necessary. Instead, Hazel's wound is abstracted so as not to distract from the verbal exposition being delivered.

Empathy, and which characters are and are not apportioned it, is central to the depiction of violence in one of the film's most notoriously brutal set pieces. The scene in question is the film's climax, in which Woundwort attacks Hazel's warren with a group of Efrafan soldiers. The battle is fought on two fronts: Woundwort himself confronts Blackavar and Bigwig in the warren's tunnels, while his soldiers contend with a vicious dog above ground. What is noteworthy here are the distinct ways in which these two conflicts – equally violent in terms of the actions taking place – are visually depicted. Woundwort's attack involves extremely graphic gore. On entering the warren he immediately kills Blackavar with a bite to the throat, an action which appears on-screen only briefly, but is depicted in enough bloody detail that a strip of flesh is distinctly visible as it is torn from the victim's body between Woundwort's teeth. The next shot lingers on Blackavar's discarded corpse, intricately detailed and gushing with blood. Woundwort's subsequent clash with Bigwig continues in this vein, opening with a close-up of the villain's claws entering his enemy's flesh and moving through a series of shots visualizing scratches and bites as the battle unfolds (Figure 11.4). Even at breaks in the action, we see blood and foam dripping from Woundwort's jaws as he speaks. Meanwhile, the violence wrought by the dog upon the Efrafan soldiers is visualized altogether differently. Arriving at the warren, the creature darts towards its prey and grabs two

FIGURES 11.4 AND 11.5 *The two parallel fight scenes differ markedly in terms of graphic detail.*

rabbits by the stomach in turn, swinging them around in its jaws before flinging them through the air. As it does so, the animation style once again subtly shifts, adopting a more cartoonal technique (Figure 11.5). The visualization of both the dog and the rabbits is notably more abstracted, lacking in detail but also physically distorted. The animators adopt squash-and-stretch principles to convey the speed with which the rabbits are being mauled, allowing their bodies to visibly shrink and elongate. Motion lines are also used, albeit briefly and almost imperceptibly, as the dog snaps its jaws, and the rabbits are anthropomorphized to a greater-than-usual extent, exaggerating their screaming expressions.

Essentially the same actions are being depicted in these two portions of the scene – teeth and claws entering flesh, rabbits being killed and maimed – so it is worth focussing on the effects of their drastically different representations. There are technical explanations behind this disparity, of course. It is far easier to animate the fast-paced action of the dog attack if the characters' models are simplified, while the most mimetic shot of the Woundwort fight, that of Blackavar's corpse, is a mostly static image requiring no animation beyond the flow of blood. But this nonetheless has the added effect of encouraging or discouraging empathy, linked to the 'degree of identification' with the characters that Gunter finds is 'related to the amount of realism portrayed in the violent scene'.[16] The fact that the violence inflicted upon Blackavar and Bigwig in this sequence is far gorier and more detailed than that inflicted upon the Efrafans correlates with the degree of empathy audiences are expected to experience for the characters based on their roles in the scene and in the story. The deaths of the heroic characters are treated as horrific because audiences are expected to mourn and fear for them. The dog's attack on the soldiers, meanwhile, is more than anything a celebratory, cathartic moment. Though the dog itself is depicted as a frightening creature, at this point in the story it has been freed by Hazel for the purpose of chasing off the Efrarans besieging the warren. Its attack is soundtracked by triumphant brass, presenting it primarily as a victory for the protagonists rather than a tragic loss for the villains. The abstracted realization of the violent acts themselves is consistent with this approach, avoiding drawing attention to the gory details of the characters' wounds and thereby discouraging any empathetic response to their suffering that might distract from the sequence's function: to illustrate the turning of the tide in the heroes' favour. The outlier here is Woundwort, who despite being the story's ultimate villain is here the subject of several memorable close-ups showing him covered in viscera in roughly the same level of detail afforded to similar shots of Bigwig. In addition to the fact that much of the blood dripping from his face is not his own, the villain's grotesque appearance, guttural roars and the unnatural, canted angles of these shots instead ensure that the gore here serves to amplify the horror of Woundwort as a figure and the threat he represents.

If the different visual depictions of violence in *Watership Down* as discussed earlier were roughly plotted on the mimesis-abstraction continuum, it might resemble Figure 11.6. It is clear from the preceding analysis that the positioning of these portrayals on this spectrum is tied to the degree of identification the film encourages with its on-screen characters at any given time, which in turn can be deployed to heighten or lessen the levels of horror or empathy engendered by the images. Note, though,

---

[16] Gunter, Harrison, and Wykes, *Violence on Television*, 162.

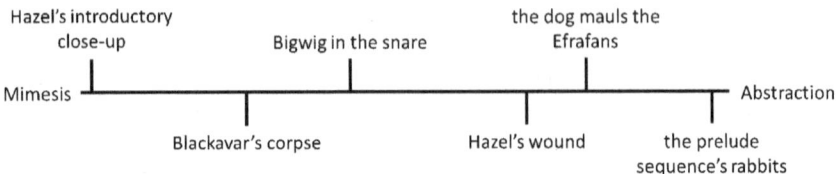

FIGURE 11.6 *Watership Down's styles plotted on Furniss's continuum.*

that I have shortened the continuum as proposed by Furniss, taking as its two extremities the most mimetic and abstracted images found in the film itself. Both of these images – the abstracted depictions of the rabbits in the prelude sequence and the mimetic introductory shot of Hazel – occur in the film's opening moments, and these extremes are not reached again by any of the images that follow. In this way *Watership Down* establishes early on the basis for its own conception of realism, presenting its audience with a hypothesis of the limits of the representative playing field on which it will take place. This is important for guiding viewers' interpretations of these violent images in terms of their realistic qualities relative to the other forms of imagery in the film. As Paul Ward writes, 'what is deemed to be "realistic" in particular circumstances . . . is often judged against other, more established forms of textual production.'[17] Broadly speaking, this means that animation, for example, is perceived as unrealistic relative to live-action cinema, while abstracted animation is perceived as unrealistic relative to more mimetic animation. Through its use of subtly shifting art styles throughout and, most notably, in the more drastic switches seen in its opening minutes, *Watership Down* seizes control of these parameters. The almost-photorealistic introductory shot of Hazel functions as a benchmark representing 'reality' against which its varying representations of violence can be measured, ultimately serving as a model example for the potential of shifting animated art styles to modulate the horrific and empathetic effects of animated violence and gore.

Computerized violence in *Watership Down* (2018)

As an epilogue of sorts to this discussion, it is worth taking some time to look at the ways in which the original *Watership Down* feature film's notorious violence is translated to the 3D computer-animated television adaptation

---

[17]Paul Ward, 'Videogames as Remediated Animation', in *Screenplay: Cinema/Videogames/Interfaces*, ed. Geoff King and Tanya Krzywinska (London: Wallflower Press, 2002), 125.

of the same name released in 2018. The character models featured in the series are realistically posed and proportioned and boast detailed layers of fur. Although the show's budgetary limitations keep it from approaching the levels of realism displayed in the likes of *The Lion King* (Favreau, 2019), the show's aesthetic clearly aspires towards mimesis, and by most metrics it comes closer than anything seen in the original film, with the possible exception of Hazel's introductory close-up. It is noteworthy, then, that the 2018 series shies away from indulging in anything like the levels of graphic violence found in the original film, despite the fact that it could theoretically leverage its mimetic potential to depict far more realistic images of gore in the pursuit of horrifying its audience. Indeed, the show's executive producer, Rory Aitken, stated that 'visually [the remake] won't be as brutal and scarring' as the original, in order to 'bring [the story] to a wider family audience'.[18] Given the shift to a more realistic aesthetic, however, the cautious approach to depicting violence in the series also speaks to the unique properties of the computer-animated medium itself and its attendant potential for mimetic representation.

Bloody violence is rare in 3D computer-animation, owing in part to the overwhelming majority of works created in the medium being targeted squarely towards children. Aside from this, though, there is an extent to which the specific qualities of the medium – dealing as it does with three-dimensional bodies imbued with a convincing sense of volume absent from conventional hand-drawn animation – discourage filmmakers from using it to depict acts of graphic violence. As Christopher Holliday argues, 'as a consequence of this bodily sturdiness, computer-animated films have sidestepped animation's lengthy tradition in cartoons of dismemberment and the sensationalism of suffering bodies.'[19] Not only can computers replicate lifelike textures, then, but they can create a lifelike illusion of mass generally devoid of the elasticity exhibited to some degree by much hand-drawn animation. This has historically seen computer-animated films visibly work to counteract any potentially uncanny effects arising from depicting graphic violence being enacted upon believably three-dimensional animated bodies. One example of this is *Beowulf* (Zemeckis, 2007), a motion-capture fantasy action film featuring lifelike human characters which generally relegates actual on-screen violence to discrete, darkly lit shots. Another is *Where the Dead Go To Die* (ScreamerClauz, 2012), a low-budget independent horror film which is designed to disturb and yet nonetheless

---

[18]Hannah Furness, 'BBC Remake Watership Down with Less Violence to Avoid "scarring" children', *The Telegraph*, 27 April 2016. https://www.telegraph.co.uk/news/2016/04/27/bbc-remake-watership-down-with-less-violence-to-avoid-scarring-c (accessed 27 July 2020).
[19]Christopher Holliday, *The Computer Animated Film: Industry, Style and Genre* (Edinburgh: Edinburgh University Press, 2018), 187.

adopts a stylized form of representation utilizing thick, black outlines around its characters' features, resulting in a conspicuously artificial comic book aesthetic. The *Watership Down* remake hews closer to the *Beowulf* approach: any violation of the characters' bodies typically occurs off-screen or in shadow. Instead, we see only the results of the violence, such as cuts and scars, or blood faintly smeared into the rabbits' fur. This is how Bigwig and Woundwort are depicted after their battle, although we don't clearly see their wounds being inflicted. Meanwhile, blood and foam are entirely absent from the scene involving Bigwig in the snare, save for a small amount of blood gathered around Fiver's mouth after he chews through the wooden peg, and the climactic dog attack is similarly devoid of on-screen violence.

Using the 2018 series as a point of comparison provides us with one final piece of evidence attesting to the effectiveness of the 1978 film's shifting art styles as a tool for conveying animated violence and for manipulating its effects. In more ways than one, the animators of the series prioritize visual consistency, ostensibly resulting in a more believable, lifelike setting for the story. Like many three-dimensional computer-animated characters, the rabbits here retain a consistent volume, avoiding the squash-and-stretch techniques commonly used to accentuate motion or to facilitate violence in hand-drawn animation. The series also retains a consistent visual style: outside of its fantasy sequences, which here employ a shadow-puppet aesthetic, each shot of the rabbits exhibits the same level of detail, occupying an identical position on the mimesis-abstraction continuum. What little violence and gore we do see, then, is consistently represented, with an innocuous bloodstain around Fiver's mouth given no more or less attention, fidelity or stylization than the blood adorning Bigwig's coat following his battle. This commitment to visual and aesthetic consistency means that, with the stated goal of appealing to a family audience, the series' producers had little choice but to obscure the violence, rather than modulate the level of abstraction with which it is depicted. The feature film, meanwhile, operates under no such constraints. While maintaining a broadly hyperreal aesthetic for most of its runtime, *Watership Down* the film is elastic in every way in which the show is consistent. Its characters' bodies are, albeit most often quite subtly, elastic, which in turn facilitates an aesthetic elasticity. This is what allows the filmmakers to shift between art styles, entering into a bespoke visual mode for each act of violence, tailored to the narrative and tonal requirements of the scene. Anchored in a version of reality by the implications of Hazel's initial close-up, the film is free to explore the representative potential of its medium in a way in which the computer-animated remake is not. Christened by Frith as the 'Prince With A Thousand Enemies', the rabbit in *Watership Down* is drawn with as many faces, a thousand incremental deviations which together provide the film's notorious violence with its mythical power.

PART IV
Affective and ethical encounters with the rabbit

CHAPTER 12

Drawing blood:
The forms and ethics of animated violence in *Watership Down*

Joshua Schulze

In spite of its numerous qualities, discussions of *Watership Down* (Rosen, 1978) tend to focus on its scenes of graphic violence. Often characterized as traumatizing for its bloody realism and injury detail, the film's cultural legacy is inextricable from the impact of such scenes on child viewers. The vitriol inscribed in complaints against the film's violence attests to the general lack of similar displays in popular animated films. In this respect, *Watership Down* automatically offers a useful case study for thinking about the ethics of animated violence. However, that the film offers radically different kinds and styles of violence in its short runtime – from the mythical, folkloric prologue sequence to the on-screen deaths of several main characters – provides room for reflection on the very process and production of cel animation. In particular, where the ethics of enacting violence against animals in a live-action film might be considered less ambiguous, the situation in animation is not as clear and defined. Focussing on the opening sequence, it is the objective of this chapter to elucidate what *Watership Down* brings to the discussion of animated violence and to the ethics of 'drawing blood'.

Part of the reason for the fuzziness of these ethics is the (still) peripheral place of animation within film studies at large. The relationship between the animated image and indexicality, for instance, has only recently undergone critical revision. Before discussing the nature of the violence in *Watership Down*, I begin this chapter by considering what is at stake in speaking about animated violence as opposed to live-action violence, particularly as it pertains to animals. In doing so, I argue that the materiality of cel animation should be amplified in order to think about drawing as an ethical process, rather than as the production of a final, complete product. The opening of *Watership Down*, in its overtly artificial, *drawn* nature, effectively dramatizes its own materiality; to assess how it functions in relation to the rest of the film, I then employ the critical concept of the diagram to describe the prologue as a formal abstraction, which in its 'graphic' violence provides another layer of diagramming in between the act of prototypical storyboarding and the realistic animation style that governs the narrative. Discussing the diagram in relation to animation both reiterates the materiality of the medium while offering a new way of thinking about the ethics of drawing as a process. Finally, I analyse how these ethics inform readings of the prologue as a genesis sequence devoted to establishing the ontology of the rabbit. I argue that the film sensitively walks the tightrope of anthropomorphism and animated violence in ecologically significant ways, which in turn can inform our broader understanding of animation as a medium.

No rabbits were harmed: Materiality and the index of cel animation

In *La Règle du Jeu* (Renoir, 1939), the audience are made to witness the merciless slaughtering of a group of rabbits by the main cast of characters. The photographic nature of live-action cinema imbues such a scene with discomfort and disgust: we understand perfectly well, in other words, that real rabbits died during filming. Structurally, this event plays a critical role in the film's overall tone, in the ways that it brings the audience's ethical attitudes towards the material into play. In his book on the film, V. F. Perkins takes note of this, writing:

> Organising his story round this event, [Renoir] made it impossible for the film to cast off the shadow of massacre and reclaim lightness of heart. He was disingenuous in his claim not to have understood that audiences might find the movie upsetting. He ends the sequence by holding on the image of a rabbit, its flight halted by a bullet, its death throes piteously extended. It feels like a close-up and the seconds feel very long. With such images, which must be witnessed with pain and disgust, Renoir imposes

a gulf between the attitudes of his characters and the feelings he elicits from us.[1]

Here, Perkins attributes the unflinching gaze of the camera and the unbroken stretch of time allotted to the rabbit's death as principal reasons for the displeasure it causes. At the same time, he acknowledges what such a moment does to the film on a structural level, which becomes unable to shake the memory of death. Indeed, the complicated ethics plaguing the image are undoubtedly bound to the notion of indexicality, which Perkins continues to wrestle with:

Real animals die real deaths but are placed in a fictional world on screen. There they serve as objects, metaphors, markers of themes. In their victimhood they offer a more extreme reflection than any human actor of the camera's work in seizing the life of the world and turning it over as material for an artist (or an industry) to work with.[2]

In other words, the audience's knowledge that real rabbits were sacrificed does not necessarily dampen but, rather, intensifies their semiotic function in the context of the film.

This understanding is common in writing on animals in film, which often emphasizes the ways in which they facilitate symbolism at the expense of their own subjectivity. Akira Mizuta Lippit, for example, argues that animals are frequently denied subjecthood, rendering identification 'impossible' between humans and non-humans.[3] These representational practices contribute to the production of what Giorgio Agamben calls 'the anthropological machine', which describes the ways animals have been utilized to construct the figure of human as distinctive.[4] For Agamben, the commonalities between humans and animals only emphasize their ontological difference. As a consequence of this distinction, according to Nicole Shukin, 'animals suffer the double binds of representation: they are either excluded from the symbolic order on the grounds of species difference, or anthropomorphically rendered within it'.[5] Jonathan Burt describes the on-screen animal as 'burdened with multiple metaphorical significances, giving it an ambiguous status that derives from what might be described as a kind of semantic overload',

---

[1] V. F. Perkins, *La Règle du Jeu* (London: BFI, 2012), 97.
[2] Perkins, *La Règle du Jeu*, 99.
[3] Akira Mizuta Lippit, *Electric Animal: Toward a Rhetoric of Wildlife* (Minneapolis: University of Minnesota Press, 2000), 181.
[4] Giorgio Agamben, *The Open: Man and Animal*. Trans. Kevin Attell (Stanford: Stanford University Press, 2004), 29.
[5] Nicole Shukin, *Animal Capital: Rendering Life in Biopolitical Times* (Minneapolis: University of Minnesota Press, 2009), 129.

echoing Shukin in his claim that 'the animal image is a form of rupture in the field of representation'.[6] However, Burt's argument awards a taxonomical sense of exceptionalism to animal images which risks eliding the capacity for individual instances to generate more nuanced depictions.

Paul Wells, on the other hand, proposes four possible categories of filmic representations of animals: the pure animal, the critical human, the aspirational human or the hybrid 'humanimal'.[7] Importantly, Wells suggests that animation is the best-suited means for evoking the pure animal, given its ability to operate as 'a discourse about animals, and animal identity'.[8] Wells later stresses the significance of the animator's practice in striking a spiritual affinity with the subject, which manages – for the most part – to avoid the projection of solely human attributes.[9] If this were to be true, would an animated version of the rabbit scene in *La Règle du Jeu* invoke a different type of ethical response? Would the knowledge that no rabbits were harmed in the making of the film affect its textual meaning?

The popular response and cultural legacy of *Watership Down* would suggest otherwise, as many contributions to this anthology demonstrate. The images of animated rabbits twitching and writhing to their bloody death seem not to have been softened by the knowledge that they exhibit no indexical equivalent, in spite of the hyper-realistic drawing style that characterizes the main body of the film. From a purely ethical perspective, this has the potential to yield a dangerous amount of power to animation filmmakers; one might argue that the degree of violence, in theory, is limited only by the boundaries of the imagination (or desired age rating) and is thus freed from the responsibility that normally comes with using real-life subjects. Yet, crucially, Wells also identifies animation's 'intrinsic respect' for non-human characters.[10] In a similar way, Sean Cubitt elaborates on such a sentiment and writes at length about the sense of affinity facilitated by the very act of drawing, which

> embraces both the continuity with animals and, in its deployment of space and time as raw materials, it leaps towards godhead. So drawing risks eliminating the human as a distinct zone between creator and creature. Which in turn may suggest why animators like animals: because in drawing them we pass strangely close to the divine, while at the same time flirting with animality through the kind of identification that you

---

[6]Jonathan Burt, *Animals in Film* (London: Reaktion Books, 2002), 11.
[7]Paul Wells, *The Animated Bestiary: Animals, Cartoons, and Culture* (New Brunswick: Rutgers University Press, 2008), 52.
[8]Wells, *The Animated Bestiary*, 11.
[9]Wells, *The Animated Bestiary*, 105.
[10]Wells, *The Animated Bestiary*, 11.

feel when drawing, perhaps some remnant of that identification with prey animals we can imagine among the cave painters.¹¹

Cubitt's recognition of the spatiotemporal materiality of drawing (and thus cel animation) can help us rethink the medium's relationship to indexicality and to complicate the ethically problematic understanding that anything goes – that 'no rabbits were harmed' – when there is a pen in place of a camera. This is because, as Hannah Frank demonstrates, it is commonly forgotten in film studies that cel animation *does* in fact involve a camera. Animation is not without an index; the films are photographic records of their own production and of the painstakingly drawn cels themselves. As Frank points out, '[t]he basic, undeniable fact that cel animation *was* a photographic process is almost always treated as an orthogonal concern, if it is acknowledged at all.'¹² Writing about how paying attention to the materiality of animation can complicate long-held beliefs about cinema's realism arising from its photographic qualities, Frank continues: 'While graphic in origin, these worlds are only visible to us because their constitutive elements (glass, cels, ink, paint, paper) have been photographed.'¹³ In that respect, while there is no immediate indexical relationship between an animated rabbit and a real one in the same way as in *La Règle du Jeu*, the final film of *Watership Down* instead serves as an indexical document of the labour and of the almost-divine (to use Cubitt's term) relationship between animator and subject. By putting this renewed emphasis on the materiality of cel animation into dialogue with Cubitt's ethics of drawing through a reading of *Watership Down*, we can thus begin to rethink animated violence against animals altogether.

Graphic violence: The prologue as diagram

If, as Cubitt argues, the act of drawing carries with it the potential for affinity between artist and subject, then the process of cel animation provides a number of instances that make it possible. Storyboarding, for example, becomes a generative means by which the animators begin to labour over the formal properties of their subject, cumulatively growing closer to its structures and idiosyncrasies. While storyboarding is used in the pre-production stages of both live-action cinema and in animation, it takes on a particular role in the latter. In their critical history of the subject, Chris

---

¹¹Sean Cubitt, *Eco Media* (Amsterdam: Rodopi Press, 2005), 30.
¹²Hannah Frank, *Frame by Frame: A Materialist Aesthetics of Animated Cartoons* (Oakland: University of California Press, 2019), 45; emphasis in original.
¹³Frank, *Frame by Frame*, 46.

Pallant and Steven Price describe live-action filmmaking as 'subtractive' and animation as 'additive', alluding to the differing levels of importance attributed to the editing process. As the authors argue: 'Contrastingly, the process of animation typically sees the same pre-agreed narrative building blocks remade over and over, with increasing refinement on each pass, until what remains is the complete material artefact – the final film.'[14] In other words, storyboarding in animation is fundamentally prototypical.

In terms of how this relates to *Watership Down*, for one thing, the aesthetically striking opening sequence is notable for its stylistic difference to the rest of the film. Given that it is comparatively simplistic, and that it works to set up and establish the rabbit world that follows, in its own way it is a storyboard and a prototype. Speaking to Pallant and Price's emphasis on the collaborative nature of storyboarding (particularly as it relates to below-the-line personnel), *Watership Down*'s prologue involved a team of animators that reportedly had little involvement in proceedings beyond the production of the short sequence. According to American animator Michael Sporn, the Aboriginal-inspired concept art was based on artwork by Luciana Arrighi, an Australian production designer, under the direction of former Disney animator John Hubley.[15] When Martin Rosen took over directing the film, the team is said to have changed, along with the realistic drawing style that characterizes the remainder of the film.

These historical footnotes pose interesting implications for my discussion; while I am not trying to make claims about the intended meanings motivating the prologue's animation style, I argue instead that paying attention to the materiality of cel animation production provides new ways of thinking through the ethics of animated violence. The stripped-down, minimalistic style of *Watership Down*'s opening sequence calls attention to the materiality of its production in its functioning as a kind of diegetic storyboard; the explicitly sketched nature of the subjects foregrounds their artifice in a manner that informs how the audience understands the rest of the film. Making us expressly aware that the prologue is constructed has the curious effect of communicating in microcosm, and in prototype, the (violent) logic that governs the overall narrative. In this respect, the prologue operates diagrammatically and thus offers a reflexive consideration of animation

---

[14]Chris Pallant and Steven Price, *Storyboarding: A Critical History* (London: Palgrave Macmillan, 2015), 53.
[15]Sporn had no part in *Watership Down* but worked with Hubley for a number of years, and he made these claims in a blog post in order to correct some enduring myths surrounding the film's production. In the post, he uses his knowledge of Hubley's drawing style to attest to the authorial fingerprints left on the film's opening sequence. See Michael Sporn, 'Watership Down Down Down', *Michael Sporn Animation*, 10 February 2007. http://www.michaelspornanimation.com/splog/?p=949 (accessed 23 June 2020).

ethics altogether. Turning to critical writing on the diagram can further help us to unpack how the prologue functions.

Understood as a type of schema, often graphic or drawn, that conveys an idea in straightforward, simplistic terms, the diagram has recently been taken up within various disciplines that employ representational modes of analysis, such as aesthetics, art theory and art history, to name a few.[16] Perhaps the most influential meditation on the topic emerges from Gilles Deleuze and Félix Guattari, who consider the diagram as not representational but rather generative: 'The diagrammatic or abstract machine does not function to represent, even something real, but rather constructs a real that is yet to come, a new type of reality.'[17] Similarly, Jakub Zdebik charts the common ground between this definition and that of C. S. Peirce: 'In the diagram, as explained by Peirce, there is an abstracting function that makes the diagram a productive mechanism of thought instead of simply something with which to represent reality . . . [t]he diagram is an image of something to come rather than something that is already there.'[18] Already, it should be apparent in what ways such an idea might be useful for thinking about the medium of animation, in turning the act of storyboarding into something generative in itself, rather than as a representational means for the final product.[19] This would begin to account for the prized valuation of animation storyboards and original cels that Pallant and Price discuss in their history of Walt Disney's cunning preservation (and subsequent auctioning) of such materials.

In the case of *Watership Down*, the eclectic opening images of crudely drawn rabbits dying so suddenly and unflinchingly, with their superficial anatomies turning blood red to demarcate their expiration, give new meaning to the term 'graphic violence'. The formal organization of the massacre is built around a binary code in which the mobile, brown-coloured rabbits signify their being alive, while red and still signify their being dead. Such brutality is evident also in the caption of a storyboard of the event, which reads: 'animals just kill, one after another' (Figure 12.1).[20] From a thematic perspective, the strictly graphic depiction of violence necessarily conveys the unflinching nature of the film world that the rabbits inhabit, priming the

---

[16]See Kamini Vellodi, 'Diagram: Deleuze's Augmentation of a Topical Notion', *Word & Image* 34, no. 4 (2018): 299–309.

[17]Gilles Deleuze and Félix Guattari, *A Thousand Plateaus: Capitalism and Schizophrenia*. Trans. Brian Massumi (London: Continuum, [1980] 1987), 157.

[18]Jakub Zdebik, *Deleuze and the Diagram: Aesthetic Trends in Visual Organization* (London: Continuum, 2012), 16.

[19]To my knowledge, the only other attempt to discuss the diagram in relation to animation is in Livia Monnet, '"Such is the Contrivance of the Cinematograph": Dur(anim)ation, Modernity, and Edo Culture in Tabaimo's Animated Installations', in *Cinema Anime*, ed. Steven T. Brown (New York: Palgrave Macmillan, 2006), 202.

[20]'Storyboard Comparisons', in *Watership Down*, Blu-ray (UK: Universal Features, 2013).

FIGURE 12.1 Watership Down *storyboard illustrating the prologue's rabbit massacre*.

audience for the casting off of characters that follows. Yet where the latter instances are rendered more sympathetic and sentimental by their realism, and accompanying components such as the score and the notable impact on other characters, the violence in the prologue is shocking precisely in its coldly straightforward, graphic display.

In her provocative discussion of the diagram and violence in *The Human Centipede* (Six, 2009), Eugenie Brinkema moves away from the Deleuzian conception of the diagram as a non-structuring device and instead demonstrates the intrinsic formal violence that they can invoke. For Brinkema, *The Human Centipede*'s shock value emerges from its use of diagramming to dramatize the finitude of sequencing, through the fixed figuration of subjects. Speaking specifically about the scene in which Dr Heiter (Dieter Laser) exhibits to his victims a series of medical diagrams that demonstrate the process of attaching their bodies to each other that he is about to begin, Brinkema writes: 'The diagram is what poses the formality of the problem of *escape* from the sequence that it is.'[21] She continues: 'The diagram is. Nothing prior, nothing after, nothing outside: It attests solely to its arrangement of elements.'[22] Brinkema here touches on the diagram's

---

[21] Eugenie Brinkema, 'Violence and the Diagram; Or, *The Human Centipede*', *Qui Parle: Critical Humanities and Social Sciences* 24, no. 2 (2016): 87, emphasis in original.
[22] Brinkema, 'Violence and the Diagram', 93.

matter-of-factness, arguing that its crude capacity to formalize its subjects is an act of violence far more severe than the more realistic depictions that follow it.

The opening of *Watership Down* works as a kind of stepping stone that demonstrates the process of animating violence both sensitively and realistically. By beginning with such graphic matter-of-factness, the film narrativizes the process of drawing, which, in Cubitt's terms, fosters a shared affinity and respect between drawer and subject that only increases over time (and few would argue with the fact that animation takes plenty of time). Rather than simply presenting the violence inflicted on the film's characters under the illusion of realism by leaping into the diegesis, *Watership Down* invokes the concept of the diagram to reiterate the material process of drawing blood, which the film itself, to paraphrase Frank, provides photographic evidence of. As a consequence, the comparative realism of the violence that occurs later on becomes unshakeable from the crude images in the prologue and is carefully situated within the narrative so as to avoid being graphic in the same way.

For instance, in the scene where Bigwig is caught in a snare, it begins with his initial scream occurring off-screen. The film allows us no access to his suffering until his fellow rabbits know about it. We cut from his scream to an agonizing close-up of Bigwig's pain-inflicted face, before the image pulls back to reveal him accompanied by the other characters. The illusion of movement facilitated by the realistic animation style creates a sort of twitching effect when Bigwig's body writhes in pain, although the level of horror is subdued (or rather re-contextualized) by its meaning to the other rabbits. For them, it becomes a problem they must collectively overcome by helping to untie him before he dies. In that way, the horrifying images of blood spilling from Bigwig's mouth as he struggles to stay conscious are sensationalized only to the degree that they imbue the moment with temporal tension. Yet, importantly, that we experience this violence entirely from the perspective of the rabbits, and not under the eerie, omniscient narration from the opening sequence, sets the precedent for the film's treatment of violence as the narrative progresses. Later, when Hazel is shot by the farmer, the film immediately cuts away almost as soon as the bullet hits him. This is because he is alone at this moment, and allotting time and visual attention to his pain would, as the film understands things, be unethical. Instead, it is through Fiver's vision that the others learn of Hazel's injury and find him in time to spare his life.

Arriving at such moments of heightened injury detail, after the opening sequence calls attention to its own materiality and artifice, provokes a certain level of reflexive spectatorship. The life like twitches and death throes differ so greatly from the simplistic, binary representations of violence in the prologue that they work to dramatize the animation process as developmental, one that moves from storyboard to moving figure, and from diagram to thing – a journey that is fundamental to the ethics of animating violence. It mobilizes the act of drawing, in Cubitt's terms, to characterize animation as a pursuit that fundamentally respects the animal subjects. The next question would be to consider what implications this sensibility poses for the general practice of anthropomorphism, especially as it relates to animated violence.

The sins and virtues of anthropomorphism: The prologue as genesis

The opening sequence in a sense already poses a type of barrier between the audience and the characters. In concurrence with formulations of the diagram that emphasize its non-representational qualities, the diagrammatic nature of the prologue essentially de-anthropomorphizes the rabbits: they are reduced entirely to shapes – forms with a likeness of a rabbit – and we broadly understand them as such. In his account of the diagram in the work of painter Francis Bacon, Deleuze describes 'a violence that is involved only with color and line: the violence of a sensation (and not of a representation)'.[23] Ethically, presenting us first with this strictly formal image of the rabbit, attuning us to the structures of its existence in the world, *before* introducing us to the other main characters who speak and govern the narrative, does some work in avoiding the kinds of anthropomorphic projection and identification that animation regularly facilitates. By calling attention to the process of its own production, and to animation itself, the film begins by asking less that we identify with the rabbits, but instead that we try to understand them. In this section, I will consider what the discussion up to this point can offer to conceptions of anthropomorphism, specifically with regard to the idea that the prologue of *Watership Down* functions as a kind of genesis for rabbits.

In her book *Vibrant Matter*, a key text in the new material turn, Jane Bennett posits a certain kind of anthropomorphism as one of many 'everyday tactics' that can be implemented to cultivate a deeper understanding of what she terms 'the shared minerality of things'.[24] Arguing against the assumption that anthropomorphism reinforces an exclusively anthropocentric way of perceiving the world, Bennett instead considers the practice capable of stimulating a greater understanding of our relationship with non-human

---

[23] Gilles Deleuze, *Francis Bacon: The Logic of Sensation*. Trans. Daniel W. Smith (London: Continuum, [1980] 2003), x.
[24] Jane Bennett, *Vibrant Matter: A Political Ecology of Things* (Durham: Duke University Press, 2010), 119, 13.

matter. She writes: 'Maybe it is worth running the risks associated with anthropomorphizing (superstition, the divinization of nature, romanticism) because it, oddly enough, works against anthropocentrism: a chord is struck between person and thing.'[25] In other words, and contrary to Agamben, Bennett's anthropomorphism helps to counteract the kind of anthropocentricism that refuses to acknowledge what humans and non-human entities have in common. Although her categorization of the non-human extends far beyond animals alone, Bennett's argument has interesting implications for the study of animal representation in animation.

Relating to anthropomorphism's capacity to generate affinity, Malcolm Miles believes that the recognition of the self can act as a means through which we can rescue our relationship with the environment from impending disaster:

> Seeing the world as mere object implies its exploitation; seeing it, or feeling it, as a mirror of the self, which is more or less an ecological position, may imply a sense of caring and living in relation to rather than exerting power over worlds.[26]

Yet, there is a sense of narcissism underscoring the notion that we, as humans, can only care for something that looks or acts like us – that mirrors the self. In other words, it is clear that practices of anthropomorphism are constantly in danger of fluctuating between Wells's four categories of the pure animal, the critical human, the aspirational human and the hybrid 'humanimal'. In a way, the idea that animation facilitates a better understanding of animality in its pure form without only projecting something human relates to Bennett's emphasis on the importance of a 'more refined sensitivity to the outside-that-is-inside-too'.[27] Her theorization of inter-species subjectivity builds on some of the ground covered in Donald Griffin's writing on animal consciousness. In *Animal Minds*, Griffin argues against the long-held assumption that animal consciousness is inherently anthropomorphic because it projects human thought processes onto animals. Griffin claims that, as a consequence, such thinking has led us to disregard the notion that animals can think in any capacity.[28] To consider how this might factor into the practice of drawing animals, I will now return to *Watership Down*'s opening sequence to assess how anthropomorphism is wrestled with and put into practice.

---

[25]Bennett, *Vibrant Matter*, 120.
[26]Malcolm Miles, *Eco-Aesthetics: Art, Literature and Architecture in a Period of Climate Change* (London: Bloomsbury, 2014), 59–60.
[27]Bennett, *Vibrant Matter*, 120.
[28]Donald R. Griffin, *Animal Minds* (Chicago: University of Chicago Press, 1992), 24.

The voice-over narration and the mythical, even animistic, animation style come together to convey a leporine genesis that frames the existence of the entire species, which is to say that *Watership Down* exhibits an effort to convey the very ontology of the rabbit itself. The film suggests that in order to comprehend the existence of rabbits, we need to go back to the beginning of time and reframe the entire world as they have always lived and perceived it. Accordingly, the opening sequence seeks to account for rabbit life, driven by fear and victimhood, by making rabbits the protagonists of their own creation story. The opening sequence thus informs the events of the film in a way that retains an emphasis on rabbits in order to avoid human projection, which is aided by the simplistic, diagrammatic presentation of their beginnings. In other words, when the audience first encounters Fiver's apocalyptic visions, ordinarily they might project human understandings of neurotic behaviour and identify with such paranoia as a human trait, whereas in the context provided by the film's opening, the visions are understood as an extreme expression of the constant fear of extinction shared by all rabbits. This is just one example of how the film's singular use of anthropomorphism walks the tightrope described by Griffin of acknowledging animal consciousness without necessarily projecting human understandings of cognition.

At the same time, it is important to notice the similarities between the rabbit genesis in *Watership Down* and the Christian story of creation, as well as the anthropocentric pitfalls of attempting to depict one at all, regardless of the animation style. First, the film in some respects takes Bennett's sense of affinity to an extreme, in that we witness a genesis as experienced by rabbits, but one that does not deny the existence of a human one. The Christian genesis gives humankind, which arrives last on the scene, an elevated status as the species made in God's own image. Yet, rabbits spring into existence some time along the way, and so the film purports to explain that their coming into being occurred without human witness or input. Rabbits experienced the same story of creation, in other words, only *differently*; the film thus encourages an affinity in the recognition that rabbits and humans share a spatial-temporal co-existence, one which is echoed and imbued into the very act of drawing, as described by Cubitt. The process of drawing animals is in itself a recognition that we exist in the same time and space. To that end, the extent to which we read the opening sequence as a genesis is necessarily complicated by its always-evident materiality and awareness of the animation process.

In addition, the differences between the rabbit genesis and the Christian one further complicate things: unlike in the latter, Frith does not give El-ahrairah (the rabbit prince) rules or guidance on how to live that he violates (as in Eve's Original Sin, using freewill to act against God's commands), and instead his punishment comes off as somewhat irrational, as if the rabbit existence could only ever have been a certain way – as reiterated by the sequence's graphic, matter-of-fact animation style. This disparity would also indicate, as explicated in the Christian genesis story, that humans are separate from animals in their capacity for moral choice (among many other traits). Beyond that, creation myths are a tenet of virtually every human civilization, dating back to ancient times. Are the valiant efforts to comprehend the ontology of rabbits compromised by the use of something so characteristically human? In other words, does this line of thinking lead us back down the same path of anthropocentrism and of human exceptionalism?

While it may be tempting (in an era of post-humanist thought) to decry such a conclusion as regressive, let us consider again what Bennett takes to be the principal virtue of anthropomorphism: the possibility that 'a chord is struck between person and thing'.[29] The human figure, in any instance of *anthro*pomorphism, inevitably remains – after all, who is telling this story? Who is drawing this rabbit genesis? Anthropomorphism, in this light, possesses the capacity to facilitate an affinity between the human and rabbit that acknowledges a shared minerality, but *not* a shared consciousness, to avoid the mistakes warned against by Griffin. Humans, who are burdened with moral choice, have enacted the greatest impact on animals and the environment of any species, straying over time from the recognition that they share the planet with other life. What *Watership Down* offers, even in the least radical reading imaginable, through its use of anthropomorphism to convey the existence of a species without the involvement of humans (and yet rendered and constructed entirely *by* them), is a reminder that rabbits were here before us, and that we share the world with them.

Documenting the process of drawing them, and taking us back to their beginning, even if it means that we recognize them as resembling a human civilization (rather than what they 'ontologically' are: a warren of rabbits), is at least one way in which the Bennettian chord might be struck. In addition, animating violence against them in a way that takes into account the materiality of the process is perhaps a better way of provoking a reconsideration of how that violence corresponds with the real world. If animation possesses an intrinsic respect for animals, and drawing cel after cel fosters a sense of divine affinity, *Watership Down* and its eclectic prologue ensure that this is made explicit, and that the animated violence is never lost in the illusion of movement – it is presented, instead, as a material process of colour and line.

---

[29]Bennett, *Vibrant Matter*, 120.

CHAPTER 13

'Won't somebody *please* think of the bunnies?':

Watership Down, rabbit horror and 'suitability' for children

Catherine Lester

Peter Hutchings once made an offhand remark that 'rabbits are just not that frightening'.[1] While this might ordinarily be a reasonable thing to say, it becomes questionable in the context of this collection dedicated to *Watership Down* (Rosen, 1978). *Watership Down* is widely regarded as having 'traumatised an entire generation',[2] features regularly in curated lists of the scariest children's films[3] and inspires user-generated memes that humorously juxtapose images of the film's rabbit violence with its perceived status as children's entertainment (Figure 13.1). One example

---

[1] Peter Hutchings, *The Horror Film* (New York: Routledge, 2004), 128.
[2] Ed Power, 'A Piercing Screen: How Watership Down Terrified an Entire Generation', *Independent*, 20 October 2018. https://www.independent.co.uk/arts-entertainment/films/features/watership-down-film-bright-eyes-rabbits-disease-martin-rosen-richard-adams-disney-a8590226.html (accessed 5 October 2021).
[3] For example, David Erlich, '12 Scariest Moments in Kids' Films', *Rolling Stone*, 19 October 2015. https://www.rollingstone.com/movies/movie-lists/12-scariest-moments-in-kids-films-160092/ (accessed 5 October 2021).

FIGURE 13.1 *User-generated memes that affirm* Watership Down's *popular status as a 'traumatizing' children's film.*

from 2018 places the caption 'HAPPY 40TH ANNIVERSARY TO THE MOST TERRIFYING CHILDREN'S FILM EVER' next to an image of the formidable villain, General Woundwort, with his claws outstretched, teeth bared and dripping with blood.[4] Another shows a stock photo of a man lying on a psychiatrist's couch and the therapist sitting in the foreground, taking notes. A caption conveying the dialogue of the therapist reads, 'So where do you think your childhood trauma came from?' Below the photo, in response, is a series of some of the bloodiest images from the film.[5] In this light, Hutchings appears to be mistaken with regard to the scariness of

---

[4] 'Remember Kids', *Imgur*, 23 October 2018. https://imgur.com/t/watershipdown/LznEd46 (accessed 20 August 2021).
[5] 'watership down, It even has scenes where rabbits are gassed', *Reddit*, 15 May 2021. https://www.reddit.com/r/memes/comments/ncy1m7/watership_down_it_even_has_scenes_where_rabbits/ (accessed 20 August 2021).

rabbits. This chapter takes this tension between perceptions of rabbits as 'frightening' and 'not frightening' as its focus, especially regarding questions about *Watership Down*'s suitability for child audiences.

In its original context, Hutchings's comment refers to the so-bad-it's-good cult film *Night of the Lepus* (Claxton, 1972), in which accidental humour arises from unconvincing representations of giant, carnivorous rabbits. Hutchings was not alone in holding the opinion that it is difficult to find anything scary about rabbits. Time and again, the idea that a rabbit can be frightening or dangerous is presented as a joke: the killer rabbit in *Monty Python and the Holy Grail* (Gilliam and Jones, 1975); the demon Anya being afraid of bunnies in *Buffy the Vampire Slayer* (1997–2003); *Wallace & Gromit: The Curse of the Were-Rabbit* (Park and Box, 2005); comedy-horror film *The Beaster Bunny* (Snygg Brothers, 2014); and the ridicule faced by former US president Jimmy Carter when he claimed to have been pursued by a vicious swamp rabbit.

It is obvious why the killer rabbit is a popular comedic trope. Such representations deliberately clash with, and play upon, the dominant cultural image of rabbits as the epitome of cuteness, joy and whimsy. These qualities underpin the rabbit's association with childhood and children's culture, whether the Velveteen Rabbit, Br'er Rabbit, the White Rabbit that leads Alice into Wonderland, Disney's Thumper, the Easter Bunny or Beatrix Potter's Flopsy, Mopsy, Cottontail and Peter. In most cases, rabbit characters in children's stories are substitutes for human children,[6] but this is also common in adult-targeted texts like *The Favourite* (Lanthimos, 2018), *Fatal Attraction* (Lyne, 1987), *Celia* (Turner, 1989) and *The Night of the Hunter* (Laughton, 1955). Here, rabbits are props who are endangered or killed for dramatic effect – a foreboding of what might befall the human children in the narrative.[7] Sometimes, as in *Harvey* (Koster, 1950) or *Kumiko, the Treasure Hunter* (Zellner, 2014), rabbits are representative of the human adult protagonists' wholesome view of the world characterized by childish naiveté.

If these representations indicate that rabbits are too cute to be seriously scary, what are we to make of *Watership Down* and its popular status as a traumatizing children's film? It is *because* of dominant perceptions of the rabbit as cute, passive and equated with childish, innocent vulnerability that results in strong reactions when a fictional rabbit transgresses this narrow definition. In the case of *Watership Down*, this is exacerbated by animation –

---

[6]Susan E. Davis and Margo Demello, *Stories Rabbits Tell: A Natural and Cultural History of a Misunderstood Creature* (New York: Lantern Books, 2003), 173.
[7]In the extreme cases of *La Caza* (Saura, 1966) and *La Règle du Jeu* (Renoir, 1939), which both contain scenes in which rabbits are hunted, this violent treatment of cinematic rabbits extended to their real-life 'actors', who were killed in service of the films' production.

a medium with strong associations with children's entertainment, especially the child-safe connotations of Disney – and the film's U certificate from the BBFC, which identified it as suitable for most children. The perception of *Watership Down* as a children's film, combined with the long-standing cultural associations between rabbits and children, makes for a perfect storm of anxiety among adult observers. An instructive case study is the backlash to Channel 5's televising of the film on the afternoon of Easter Sunday in 2016, and again in 2017. On both occasions, British news outlets reported on angered reactions posted to social media websites, namely Twitter. One emblematic tweet asked 'Who the hell thought it a good idea to put Watership Down on Easter Sunday? "Hey kids let's watch dead Easter bunnies!"'[8] Similar uses of the term 'bunny' over 'rabbit' is a pattern in *Watership Down*-related reporting: 'bunny slaughter',[9] 'bloodied bunnies',[10] 'Bunny bloodbath',[11] 'bloody bunny saga',[12] 'Bunnies *die*'.[13] Aside from the satisfying alliteration that 'bunny' allows, the use of this term acts as shorthand for the expected childishness, vulnerability and cuteness of the species and heightens the incongruity of its proximity to bloody violence and death. In so doing, rabbits and children are folded into one convenient target of worry. The rabbit characters are positioned as innocent victims of cruelty (as indicated by the 'dead Easter bunnies' tweet); but they are simultaneously framed as the perpetrators of this cruelty, either as a result of acts of violence directed towards other rabbits in the film or figurative

---

[8] Quoted in Jess Denham, 'Watership Down: Parents "horrified" as Channel 5 Airs "traumatising" Film on Easter Sunday', *Independent*, 28 March 2016. https://www.independent.co.uk/arts-entertainment/films/news/watership-down-parents-left-horrified-1978-animated-film-traumatises-children-easter-sunday-a6956061.html (accessed 5 October 2021).

[9] Siobhan Palmer, 'Watership Down Bunny Slaughter: How Much Less Brutal Is This New Series? We Crunched the Numbers', *inews*, 23 December 2018. https://inews.co.uk/culture/television/watership-down-new-bbc-netflix-series-original-film-how-many-rabbits-die-brutal-death-237580 (accessed 5 October 2021).

[10] Henry Barnes, 'Bunny Fury Boils over after Channel 5 Screens Watership Down on Easter Sunday', *The Guardian*, 29 March 2016. https://www.theguardian.com/film/2016/mar/29/parents-furious-after-channel-5-screens-watership-down-on-easter-sunday (accessed 5 October 2021).

[11] 'Bunny Bloodbath on Easter Sunday Sparks Outrage as Parents Slam "sick" Channel 5 for Airing Watership Down', *Daily Record*, 16 April 2017. https://www.dailyrecord.co.uk/entertainment/tv-radio/bunny-bloodbath-easter-sunday-sparks-10238663 (accessed 5 October 2021).

[12] Henry Barnes, 'Watership Down too Violent for Tots? Probably, but Parents Should Take Control of the Remote', *The Guardian*, 31 March 2016. https://www.theguardian.com/film/filmblog/2016/mar/31/watership-down-bbfc-ratings-easter-sunday-comment (accessed 5 October 2021).

[13] Jordan Bassett, 'Channel 5 Aired "Watership Down" On Easter Sunday – So Here Are The Scariest Children's Films of All Time', *NME*, 29 March 2016. https://www.nme.com/blogs/nme-blogs/watership-down-9864 (accessed 22 October 2021).

acts of violence directed towards a hypothetical child viewer who will be irreversibly traumatized by their viewing experience (like the man in the 'therapist' meme). The frequent use of the aforementioned picture of General Woundwort as the headline image in this rhetoric seems especially pertinent. The still is taken from his climactic fight with a dog, but its journalistic and mimetic use recontextualizes Woundwort as if leaping out of the frame to assault an imagined child audience. In this light, *Watership Down*'s rabbits become transgressive, unruly figures whose representation defies normative and simplistic conceptions of rabbits, children and the idea of what children's media is 'supposed' to look like.

To return to the Channel 5 broadcasts, it remains unclear whether or not any children were actually disturbed or harmed from watching *Watership Down*, or whether the viewer responses highlighted in reporting were representative of the viewpoint of the general population. Discussing the broadcasts in a 2018 retrospective of the film, Ed Power alleged that '[parents] and their children were assailed by an hour and a half of death and cruelty', a claim that elides the fact that the film contains a great deal of levity and hope that balances the film's distressing aspects.[14] More importantly, this assertion of the experience of children and adult guardians lacks evidence. (No formal complaints are logged in the reports of regulatory body Ofcom within one month of either the 2016 or 2017 Easter Sunday broadcasts; however, these reports only log broadcasts that received 10 or more complaints each.) Additionally, the social media responses were more varied than the headlines implied. For example, the broadcast inspired many fond remembrances from adult viewers, as well as those from commentators who found the ill-advised broadcasting decision to be amusing.[15] However, it is telling that the reporting foregrounded the more critical and reactionary responses. The focus on social media also meant that the voices of actual, present-day children were absent, and that the conversation was dominated by adults voicing concern not for any specific children but an abstracted *idea* of children. This is a recurring pattern in historical moral panics concerning children and their access to the media, as seen most clearly in the early 1980s 'video nasties' debate, where an imagined, idealized concept of childhood is used as a rhetorical device to usher in conservative political reforms that have little to do with protecting real children.[16]

---

[14]Power, 'A Piercing Screen'.
[15]For responses tweeted on the day of the 2016 broadcast, see https://twitter.com/search?q =watership%20down%20until%3A2016-03-28%20since%3A2016-03-27&src=typed _query (accessed 5 October 2021).
[16]For background and analysis on video nasties and similar moral panics, see Martin Barker and Julian Petley, eds. *Ill Effects: The Media/Violence Debate*, 2nd edn (London: Routledge, 2001) and Kate Egan, *Trash or Treasure?: Censorship and the Changing Meanings of the Video Nasties* (Manchester: Manchester University Press, 2007).

In the case of *Watership Down*, the likelihood is that *some* children were emotionally affected while watching it on Easter Sunday, just as there are adults who recall being distressed upon seeing it as a child in the cinema, on VHS, or on television through earlier broadcasts.[17] The fact is that *Watership Down* is regularly made accessible to children, and it is intended to provoke a strong emotional response. However, more damaging than *Watership Down*'s supposed effect on children is the idea that this experience is inherently negative, that children will be irreparably harmed from watching it, and that they must therefore be shielded from it. *Watership Down* – or rather, the way its reputation is continually framed as one of childhood trauma and harm – is thus representative of broader anxieties concerning the relationship between children and horror media.

In this chapter I am interested in the way that rabbits become the locus for these anxieties in contemporary reception of *Watership Down*. As explained earlier, concern about *Watership Down*'s rabbits becomes inseparable from concern about the imagined child audience. I will argue that this equation oversimplifies a number of issues: child audiences and their relationship with the media, especially that which is horrific in nature; the film *Watership Down* and children's horror cinema more broadly; and rabbits, both within and without the film. Like children, the rabbits in *Watership Down* and in reality are far more complex, varied and sophisticated beings than typically acknowledged.

From cute objects to horrific subjects: Rabbits and children in horror cinema

First I will outline the similarities between the cultural constructions of rabbits and children, especially within horror cinema, in order to position *Watership Down* as a progressive departure from dominant patterns of representation. The cultural association between rabbits and children stems largely from the former's status as a prey animal, meaning that the two groups share a status as marginalized and vulnerable in a dangerous world dominated by bigger, more authoritative beings. That rabbits are a paragon of cuteness also contributes to this association, as cuteness is equated with youth and childishness.[18] Exemplar of this is that Thumper the rabbit

---

[17]Long before the Channel 5 Easter Sunday controversies the film already had a history of being televised in Britain during the Christmas holidays, including one broadcast by BBC Two at 9.30 am on 25 December 1990.
[18]Gary Cross, *The Cute and the Cool: Wondrous Innocence and Modern American Children's Culture* (Oxford: Oxford University Press, 2004).

from *Bambi* (Hand et al., 1942) topped a 2020 YouGov poll of 'America's Cutest Character'.[19] Thumper exudes endearing qualities designed to evoke the sympathy and protective instinct that babies evoke in adults: a gap-toothed smile, mild-lisp, big eyes and a tendency towards harmless mischief. Animated rabbits like Thumper, the rabbit in *Over the Moon* (Keane, 2020), and even Bugs Bunny are further 'cutified' through anatomically incorrect embellishments like pads (known colloquially as 'toebeans') on the soles of their paws – a body part that animals like cats do have, but real rabbits do not. Animated rabbits are thus subjected to a 'human gaze' that represents animals in terms of their aesthetic value to human characters/spectators, similar to the way that children and women in film are subjected to a restrictive 'adult gaze' or 'male gaze', respectively.[20]

Rabbits and children are further linked by their contradictory positions within culture and society. Susan E. Davis and Margo DeMello explain that 'Real rabbits have traditionally served as both childhood pet and family meal, as both highly prized show animal and hunted pest . . . imaginary rabbits have been portrayed as both innocent and sexual, clever and stupid, timid and brave'.[21] This extends to the rabbit's surprisingly frequent occurrence in horrific contexts, to the extent that Ernest Mathijs and Jamie Sexton identify rabbits as a 'key component' of cult cinema.[22] For every rabbit in popular culture that is too cute to be intimidating, another is presented and received as genuinely disturbing, such as in *Akira* (Otomo, 1988), *Alice* (Svankmajer, 1988), *Sexy Beast* (Glazer, 2000), *Donnie Darko* (Kelly, 2001),[23] *Bill and Ted's Bogus Journey* (Hewitt, 1991), Joe Dante's segment of *The Twilight Zone: The Movie* (1983), David Lynch's surreal sitcom *Rabbits* (2002), short films like *Rabbit* (Wrake, 2005) and *Stalk* (Hodgkinson, 2005), and rabbits as uncanny background extras in *Us* (Peele, 2019). On the latter, director Jordan Peele explained that this arose from his own fear of rabbits, reasoning that

> Rabbits are cute and lovable and fluffy, and yet if you really get up close and look at their eyes, it's like *Jaws*. . . . If you'd put a rabbit brain in

---

[19] Mark White and Linley Sanders, 'Who is America's Cutest Character?', *YouGov*, 10 April 2020. https://today.yougov.com/topics/entertainment/articles-reports/2020/04/09/americas-cutest-character-poll (accessed 5 October 2021).
[20] Randy Malamud, 'Animals on Film: The Ethics of the Human Gaze', *Spring* 83 (2010): 7–8.
[21] Davis and DeMello, *Stories Rabbits Tell*, 130.
[22] Ernest Mathijs and Jamie Sexton, *Cult Cinema: An Introduction* (Malden: John Wiley and Sons Limited, 2011), 228.
[23] According to director Richard Kelly, *Donnie Darko*'s Frank was directly inspired by *Watership Down* and not – as one might naturally assume – the imaginary rabbit in *Harvey*. Devan Coggan, 'The Behind-the-Scenes Story of *Donnie Darko*'s Creepy Bunny Suit', *Entertainment Weekly*, 31 March 2017. https://ew.com/movies/2017/03/31/donnie-darko-bunny-suit-frank-untold-stories/ (accessed 5 October 2021).

a human body, you would have Michael Myers. They do not have any sympathy, empathy, they would rip your head off if they could. They scare me.[24]

This might seem an overreaction, but mistrust of rabbits has roots in folkloric associations between rabbits, evil and witchcraft, and they are known to exhibit violent behaviour to assert dominance or in self-defence.[25] These qualities remain mostly unknown by the general public, however, as rabbits are less popular as pets and as subjects of academic research than other domestic animals.[26] If rabbits are indeed mysterious, marginalized and misunderstood creatures, this goes some way to explaining their contradictory representations in popular culture and especially their representations as strange and uncanny in cult and horror cinema.

Despite this apparent kinship between rabbits and horror, unsettling representations of rabbits in the genre nevertheless comply with a restrictive human gaze. Randy Malamud highlights the two-dimensional representation of filmic animals as either 'angels' (like dogs, horses and other 'cute' or 'useful' creatures) or 'monstrous others' (like sharks, rats and spiders).[27] Rabbits occupy both sides of this binary, where in children's films they almost exclusively remain on the cute/good side, but in adult-addressed films rabbits are equally as likely to be horrific villains who need to be destroyed as helpless victims who suffer tragic deaths. This is the most instructive link that rabbits have with children, who also have a history of being represented in reductive, oppositional ways in the horror genre.

Children, like rabbits, occupy a conflicted sociocultural position, often described in one breath as 'little angels' and 'little monsters, devils or beasts' in the next.[28] This tension between veneration and suspicion plays out in extreme ways in horror cinema. In his seminal work on the American horror film, Robin Wood identifies children as 'others' to the dominant adult culture, whose representations as evil or unruly threaten the social order

---

[24]Jordan Peele in Ben Travis and Chris Hewitt, 'Us: 15 Spoiler Facts From Jordan Peele', *Empire Online*, 29 March 2019. https://www.empireonline.com/movies/features/15-spoiler-facts-jordan-peele-us/ (accessed 5 October 2021).
[25]Davis and DeMello, *Stories Rabbits Tell*, 152. Martin Rosen learned about rabbits' violent tendencies first-hand from a misbehaving rabbit extra on the set of *Women in Love* (Russell 1969) long before he embarked on directing *Watership Down*. Glenys Roberts, 'The Rabbits of Warren Street', *The Times*, 19 October 1978: 11.
[26]Jeffrey Moussaieff Masson, 'Foreword', in Davis and DeMello, *Stories Rabbits Tell*, xiv.
[27]Malamud, 'Animals on Film', 7.
[28]Cary Bazalgette and David Buckingham, eds. 'Introduction: The Invisible Audience', in *In Front of the Children: Screen Entertainment and Young Audiences* (London: British Film Institute, 1995), 1.

which defines children as vulnerable, innocent and subservient to adults.[29] Child characters from *The Bad Seed* (LeRoy, 1956) to *The Omen* (Donner, 1976) and beyond thus exploit the paedophobic anxieties of adult society. On the other end of the spectrum, films like *The Sixth Sense* (Shyamalan, 1999) initially play into the evil child trope before revealing the children to be persecuted victims who are saved by, and serve the narrative of, an adult protagonist, thus reaffirming the adult–child social hierarchy.

Dominic Lennard identifies a particular type of child antagonist called the 'looking child', as seen in *Village of the Damned* (Rilla, 1960) or the young Michael Myers in *Halloween* (Carpenter, 1978). Lennard argues that these children are disturbing because their active employment of the gaze is an 'upheaval of the comforting passivity the adult expects'.[30] In this context, it is apt that Peele likened the gaze of rabbits to that of Michael Myers, constructing both as unreadable and mysterious, and therefore unpredictable, uncontrollable and threatening. This unknowability ascribes an uncanny quality to children and rabbits, in that one of the things that makes them frightening in the context of horror is the ease with which they could slip from angel to demon, passive victim to active villain, and where a sweet smile could easily transform into a maniacal grin.[31]

The combination of this easy slippage between categories and the child's active gaze underlines the aforementioned adult anxieties surrounding children's spectatorship of horror films. As demonstrated, for example, by the British tabloid media blaming *Child's Play 3* (Bender, 1991) for inspiring the murder of toddler James Bulger by two ten-year-olds, a reactionary contingent of adult society fears that a once-innocent child will become irreversibly traumatized and/or depraved just from watching horror films. Such fears are simplified, unevidenced and use the horror genre as a convenient scapegoat to reaffirm conservative ideas of childhood innocence and passivity. In fact, a wealth of evidence shows that many children – depending on their age, level of maturity and other individual traits – find viewing horror to be a pleasurable and cathartic experience that can offer a variety of social and personal benefits, and such children use sophisticated viewing strategies to manage their levels of fear.[32] Despite this,

---

[29]Robin Wood, *Hollywood from Vietnam to Reagan . . . and Beyond* (New York: Columbia University Press, 2003), 67.
[30]Dominic Lennard, *Bad Seeds and Holy Terrors: The Child Villains of Horror Film* (Albany: State University of New York Press, 2014), 52.
[31]This easy slippage is demonstrated by a surprisingly creepy black-and-white publicity still of Shirley Temple holding a rabbit, taken by Otto Dyer in 1934.
[32]See David Buckingham, *Moving Images: Understanding Children's Emotional Responses to Television* (Manchester: Manchester University Press, 1996) and Sarah J. Smith, *Children, Cinema and Censorship: From Dracula to the Dead End Kids* (London: I. B. Tauris, 2005), 105–40.

horror, children and the relationship between them continue to be defined in simplified and harmful terms that elide nuance. This mirrors the way that *Watership Down* has been treated in the media discourse outlined at the beginning of this chapter and in the way that rabbits are treated in reality and in film.

However, there is a space within contemporary horror cinema that refuses these reductive binaries: the children's horror film, a category that disrupts and redefines the boundaries and expectations of horror and childhood.[33] Children's horror films are addressed towards a child audience, where the traditionally 'adult' content expected of the horror genre, like extreme violence, sex and moral ambiguity, is excluded or mitigated to achieve age ratings that signify suitability for children.[34] Most importantly in the context of this chapter, children's horror films depart from the traditional representation of children (and certain child-like animals, as I will get to) as either victims or perpetrators of violence. Instead, Megan Troutman argues that children's horror films like *Monster House* (Kenan, 2006), *Coraline* (Selick, 2009) and *ParaNorman* (Butler and Fell, 2012) 'rewrite mainstream depictions of children as passive and vulnerable' by having their child protagonists '[engage] in violent behavior that seems to challenge the notion of childhood innocence'.[35] In my own work, I have argued that these subversive on-screen children imply an equally subversive child viewer of address who is invited to take pleasure, catharsis and identification from these representations.[36]

Children's horror films therefore provide an alternative to the restrictive adult gaze so often applied to child characters within horror, and they destabilize traditional notions of child spectators of horror as passive and impressionable. Children's horror films are particularly subversive because they take Lennard's concept of the villainous 'looking child' of adult horror and redefine this as a child protagonist with whose agentic and empathetic perspective the audience is aligned. Such children are 'looking children' in that they bear witness to all manner of horrific events and have access to restricted, 'adult' knowledge. In *The Monster Squad* (Dekker, 1987), for example, the child heroes see and fight monsters that their parents dismiss as figments of their imaginations, covertly spy on their neighbours undressing

---

[33]Filipa Antunes, *Children Beware! Childhood, Horror and the PG-13 Rating* (Jefferson: McFarland, 2020).
[34]Catherine Lester, 'The Children's Horror Film: Characterizing an "impossible" subgenre', *The Velvet Light Trap*, 78 (2016): 22–37.
[35]Megan Troutman, 'It's Alive . . . AGAIN. Redefining Children's Film Through Animated Horror', in *The Palgrave Handbook of Children's Film and Television*, ed. Casie Hermansson and Janet Zepernick (Basingstoke: Palgrave Macmillan, 2019), 149–50.
[36]Catherine Lester, *Horror Films for Children: Fear and Pleasure in American Cinema* (London: Bloomsbury, 2021), 13.

and watch slasher movies at the drive-in. All the while, the children's active looks are formally reinforced by an empathetic camera that remains at their eye level and mise en scène that emphasizes their status as marginalized beings in a large, frightening world that does not take them seriously. These formal and representational methods construct an ideal spectator who is themselves a 'looking child' who watches and enjoys the 'taboo' contents of the horror genre.

Watership Down follows the conventions of children's horror by representing its rabbits in nuanced, multifaceted and horrific ways that defy simplistic representations of rabbits and children as victims or villains in adult-addressed horror. By extension, the film's inclusion of violence transgresses normative expectations of children's media and how children are assumed to receive and interact with it. To approach *Watership Down* as children's horror therefore allows it to be read as a sophisticated text that grants its rabbits, and by extension child audience, the agency and variation they are usually denied.

Watership Down as children's horror

Watership Down is not strictly a children's film nor a horror film. Director and producer Martin Rosen insists that he 'did not make this picture for kids at all', but in the UK at least, the child-friendly connotations of the film's U certificate, its animated form and rabbit subjects indicate otherwise.[37] With regard to its status as horror, *Watership Down* is labelled by *The Guardian* as one of the ten 'best scary films that aren't horror movies', and it could easily be described as a number of other genres, including drama, war film and fantasy.[38] However, there are compelling arguments that *Watership Down* is a horror film, such as Leanne Weston's contribution to this volume.[39] For the purposes of this chapter, I consider *Watership Down* to be a 'children's horror film' in that it is a film that is regularly viewed by children, contains the gore and violence expected of the horror genre and evokes the horror genre's intended emotional responses of fear and revulsion.

---

[37] 'Martin Rosen quoted in Power, 'A Piercing Screen'.'
[38] Andrew Pulver, 'The Fear Within: 10 of the Best Scary Films That Aren't Horror Movies', *The Guardian*, 30 October 2020. https://www.theguardian.com/film/2020/oct/30/the-fear-within-10-of-the-best-scary-films-that-arent-horror-movies (accessed 5 October 2021).
[39] See also Brandon Grafius, '"And Whenever They Catch You, They Will Kill You": Martin Rosen's *Watership Down* (1978) as Horror', in *Critical Conversations in Youth Horror Film and Television*, ed. Ethan Robles and Kyle Brett (Bethlehem, PA: Lehigh University Press, forthcoming).

Most importantly, *Watership Down* is children's horror due to its varied representations of rabbits as child substitutes who take part in, and bear witness to, horror and violence. However, not *all* of the rabbit characters in *Watership Down* sustain readings as children; this would be just as simplistic as reading all of the human characters as the same age in any other children's horror film. Indeed, what makes *Watership Down* interesting as a film about rabbits is that it departs from the dichotomy of cute victim/monstrous villain I have outlined earlier. It does this by representing *multiple* rabbits in the same text and allowing each of them to have distinct personalities, moral alignments and narrative roles. The film presents a hierarchy in which some rabbits hold positions of authority, making them analogues of the unsympathetic, evil or ignorant adults in children's horror. The Chief Rabbit of Sandleford Warren who does not believe Fiver's vision of the warren's impending destruction shares more in common with the myopic parents and teachers in children's horror films like *The Monster Squad* than with actual children. He is further coded as an 'adult' by his grey fur, white whiskers, eyebrows and eyelashes, and his gravelly voice. Similarly, the totalitarian General Woundwort takes up the role of the children's horror antagonist normally occupied by a monstrous adult figure with a deep hatred of children, like the witches in *Hocus Pocus* (Ortega, 1993) or *The Monster Squad*'s Count Dracula. Woundwort and the Chief Rabbit's status as intimidating, authoritative figures is formally communicated by low-angle shots that '[make] them appear even more fearsome and overpowering than they already are'.[40]

In *Watership Down*, therefore, reading the rabbits as child substitutes applies primarily to the group of refugee rabbits whose perspectives we follow for most of the film. Like the human child protagonists of children's horror, their status as vulnerable beings in a big, bad world is emphasized by high-angle shots and long shots that dwarf the rabbits by their surroundings.[41] However, even reading these rabbits as children risks oversimplification by not acknowledging the ways that children vary wildly in age, maturity and other characteristics. *Watership Down* differentiates the core group of rabbits without falling prey to the 'cutifying' human gaze applied to most other animated rabbits. This is neatly demonstrated by model sheets (see Figures 2.2 and 2.3 in Chapter 2) used in the production of the film, where each of the core rabbits is given distinguishing physical features in order to best reflect their unique personality traits; for example, 'runty' and 'awkward' Fiver is physically small and animated with a sense

---

[40] Tom Jordan, 'Breaking Away from the Warren', in *Children's Novels and the Movies*, ed. Douglas Street (New York: F. Ungar Publishing Company, 1983), 233.
[41] Grafius, '"And Whenever They Catch You, They Will Kill You"'; Jordan, 'Breaking Away from the Warren', 233.

of near-constant quivering moment, while 'big-hearted', 'strong' Bigwig is physically large and sturdy. While *Watership Down* does not entirely escape the anthropomorphizing tendencies of mainstream animation, it stands apart as a film that resists these as much as possible in the pursuit of a diverse but relatively realistic group of rabbit characters. It is also possible to read the rabbits as differing ages, where Fiver and Pipkin are figured as younger, more vulnerable children to the older and more confident Hazel, Bigwig and others. An instructive point of comparison is children's horror film *ParaNorman*, in which a group of adolescents is tasked with saving their town from zombies and ghosts. The youth characters range in age from pre-teens to late-teens. Protagonist Norman, a medium, is analogous to *Watership Down*'s Fiver, as they are both the youngest of their respective groups and align with the 'looking child' figure of the children's horror film. Fiver and Norman have clairvoyant abilities that allow them access to information that other characters do not have, but to which the audience is privileged by the film showing us what Fiver and Norman can see, constructing us in turn as 'looking children' rooted within their subjective experiences. Thanks to their abilities, Fiver and Norman have disturbing visions of impending doom that they are motivated to avert or avoid with the help of sympathetic allies in the form of other rabbits or children. These representations of agentic children or child substitutes whose exposure to images of horror *benefits* their wider communities are a stark contrast to moral panics that treat children's contact with the horror genre as a societal calamity.

What *Watership Down* also shares with *ParaNorman* and other children's horror films is its levity (provided mainly by the seagull sidekick Kehaar), a tone of hope and optimism, and a happy ending in which good triumphs over evil. However, these more characteristically 'child-friendly' elements of the film are frequently overlooked or ignored. While the extreme level of graphic, bloody gore displayed in the film is where *Watership Down* departs from most other children's horror films, it is, as Sam Summers points out in Chapter 11, drawn along moral and empathetic lines. For example, Bigwig's near-death experience in the snare showcases the rabbits' ingenuity and solidarity as they hurry to free him, in contrast to the morally inferior rabbits of Cowslip's Warren who stand by and allow Bigwig to perish. While rabbits of all moral alignments engage in violent behaviour in the film, the most shocking instances are committed by Woundwort, the humans who gas Sandleford Warren, and a morally neutral dog who Hazel goads into driving Woundwort's army away, securing victory for the rabbit protagonists. *Watership Down*'s use of violence, along with its anti-fascist and ecological themes, therefore has clear narrative and moral purpose that is in keeping with dominant, adult-defined expectations of children's media. Defending violent content in children's films only in terms of its pedagogical or moral value risks being just as reductive as arguments against it, but it seems strange that this aspect is often overlooked in mainstream discussions of the film.

Conclusion

Or maybe this cultural overlooking of the text's 'beneficial' aspects is not that strange at all. There are exceptions: in one of the more nuanced takes on the film, Phil Hoad constructs himself as akin to Fiver, or other 'looking children', by writing that the experience of seeing the film as child was a 'vision of fear that first hooked [him] on the power of cinema'.[42] However, the negative responses that the film attracts are the most prominent. Filipa Antunes explains that should a children's text be too scary, or a horror film too child-like, 'the culture quickly excises it' for transgressing accepted boundaries of these categories.[43] *Watership Down* provides a unique case where this excision happens repeatedly and publicly; the film is dragged out to rehearse tired debates about suitability in children's media and to serve as a cautionary tale for parents, regulatory bodies and film producers alike about the 'dangers' of inflicting too much horror on children, regardless of the text's positive aspects. But as I have argued elsewhere,

> The problem is not that *Watership Down* is horrific . . . but rather that we lump children into a homogenised group that responds to all media in the same way, regardless of age, emotional maturity or taste. . . . *Watership Down* is not for all children – but those children who are ready and willing to engage with it may find much more to like than just violent delights.[44]

The flattening of nuance with regard to the film's violence and its supposed effects on the child audience is mirrored by the way that the film's remarkably varied representations of rabbits are routinely ignored by a public discourse that instead attempts to force rabbits and children into the more familiar, easily digestible victim/villain dichotomy.

---

[42] Phil Hoad, 'Watership Down: The Film That Frightened me the Most', *The Guardian*, 30 October 2014. https://www.theguardian.com/film/filmblog/2014/oct/30/watership-down-the-film-that-frightened-me-the-most (accessed 5 October 2021).
[43] Antunes, *Children Beware!*, 1.
[44] Catherine Lester, 'Watership Down: Family-friendly BBC Version Risks Losing the Power of Epic Original', *The Conversation*, 13 December 2018. https://theconversation.com/watership-down-family-friendly-bbc-version-risks-losing-the-power-of-epic-original-108699 (accessed 5 October 2021).

The U rating that *Watership Down* carried in the UK until 2022, when it was re-classified as PG, may have inadvertently helped to reinforce such reductive thinking. At the time of the film's classification in 1978 fewer ratings were available than today, meaning that the BBFC examiners assigned to *Watership Down* had to choose between the permissive U ('Universal') and the more restrictive A ('Adult') that indicated that a film's content 'may be unsuitable for young children', without clarifying what is meant by 'young'.[45] Antunes, writing on the similarly limited North American ratings system of the early 1980s, argues that this provided 'no way to signal suitability for different kinds of children'.[46] In effect, then, the narrow rating options in 1978 may have helped to reinforce a view of all children as having the same levels of maturity and tolerance for horror.

However, it is likely that *Watership Down*'s U rating, and the outrage this has generated over the years, is partially responsible for the film's continued cultural legacy by keeping it in the British public consciousness. By way of concluding, then, I want to return to the user-generated memes discussed in the introduction of this chapter and perform a more nuanced and generous reading of them, in the same way I have done for the film's rabbits. Reading these and similar responses as expressions of fear, trauma or 'anti-fandom'[47] forgets that they may also function as expressions of sincere fandom and/or 'working through' of lingering trauma by reaching out to other affected viewers.[48] Indeed, the 'therapist' meme was posted to Reddit where it attracted comments including agreement with the meme's sentiment, praise for the film, quotations of memorable lines or simply the question, 'Which movie is this?'[49] These comments allude to two further, interrelated functions of these memes. They can be read as paratexts that warn potential viewers about *Watership Down*'s upsetting imagery and emotional effects in a similar way to film ratings or content warnings. I suggest that they can therefore flag additional caution about the film's content that is not adequately signalled by its age certificate, its

---

[45]'History of the Age Rating Symbols', *British Board of Film Classification*. https://www.bbfc.co.uk/education/university-students/bbfc-history/history-of-the-age-ratings-symbols (accessed 11 May 2022). See the Introduction of this volume for detail on the BBFC's classification history of *Watership Down*.

[46]Antunes, *Children Beware!*, 49.

[47]Jonathan Gray defines anti-fans as 'those who strongly dislike a given text or genre, considering it inane, stupid, morally bankrupt and/or aesthetic drivel'. Jonathan Gray, 'New Audiences, New Textualities: Anti-Fans and Non-Fans', *International Journal of Cultural Studies* 6, no. 1 (2003): 70.

[48]My use of 'working through' draws from John Ellis's discussion of this concept in relation to traditional broadcast television allowing audiences to collectively and simultaneously 'work through' cultural anxieties. John Ellis, *Seeing Things: Television in an Age of Uncertainty* (London: I. B. Tauris, 2000), 74.

[49]'watership down, It even has scenes where rabbits are gassed', *Reddit*.

status as an animated talking animal film, or other paratextual information. Simultaneously, these fan paratexts promote *Watership Down* to those who feel that they, or their children, are ready and eager to engage with it. The emotional pleasures that it offers – including joy, sadness, humour, suspense and, yes, fear – are just as diverse as *Watership Down*'s rabbit characters and its child audience.

CHAPTER 14

Mourning Hazel-rah

Catherine Sadler

Love the Animals. God has given them the rudiments of thought and joy untroubled. Don't trouble it, don't harass them, don't deprive them of their happiness, don't work against God's intent.[1]

In *Mourning Animals* Margo DeMello claims that the 'deaths of animals, companion, farmed or other, is one of the defining features of human's relationship with them'.[2] This chapter brings together ideas of death and mourning with the depiction of Hazel-rah's death in the film version of *Watership Down* (Rosen, 1978). It attempts to unpick why we might grieve for Hazel and how this grief might connect to ideas of childhood and our relationship to other species. It also considers the other animals that we might mourn – pets or companion animals – and those that are not mourned, and the idea of what Judith Butler terms a 'grievable' life, and how rabbit as wild animal, companion animal and farmed animal is in possession of both a grievable and an ungrievable life. In doing so it looks at work by women artists, writers and activists and explores the idea that mourning Hazel, and other animals, is a necessary and important act.

---

[1] Fyodor Dostoevsky, *The Brothers Karamazov* (1879) quoted in Richard Adams, *Watership Down* (London: Oneworld Modern Classics, [1972] 2018), 162.
[2] Margo DeMello, ed. *Mourning Animals: Rituals and Practices Surrounding Animal Death* (Michigan: Michigan State University Press, 2016), vii.

Modern and contemporary theories of mourning point to the idea that there are a myriad of things that can be mourned. Freud writes of mourning as 'the reaction to the loss of a beloved person or an abstraction taking the place of that person, such as fatherland, freedom, an ideal and so on'.³ Written in 1917, this could still seem to be quite a radical statement in terms of conventional understandings and behaviours of mourning, expressions of which are more likely to be acceptable when they are about the death of a person or persons. For Judith Butler, loss also has wider reverberations and implications and constitutes 'social, political and aesthetic relations'.⁴ James Stanescu argues that 'Mourning is always a political act',⁵ and the idea of grief and mourning being a powerful state or condition is increasingly evident in contemporary discourse and activism around animal rights and the climate emergency. Extinction Rebellion's protest in October 2019 stated: 'In the midst of Rebellion, we will express our profound grief for Extinction', and that 'Grief is subversive. Grief is not a negotiation with Death; it is a Courageous Love letter to Life.'⁶ Similarly utilizing grief and mourning as protest is 'Remembrance Day for Lost Species', which takes place on 30 November each year and describes itself as a chance to explore the stories of 'extinct and critically endangered species, cultures, lifeways, and ecological communities', and notably embeds notions of intersectional thinking into conversations about these losses, emphasizing that they are 'rooted in violent and discriminatory governing practices'.⁷ Grief and mourning are also evident in academic thinking and debate around human and non-human animal relations, and more widely our relationship to the natural world. The relationships humans have with other animals are explored in Susan E. Davis and Margo DeMello's extraordinary book *Stories Rabbits Tell: A Natural and Cultural History of a Misunderstood Creature*, which focuses on the rabbit and the unusually complex role(s) it occupies in human culture. In its foreword Jeffrey Moussaieff Masson writes that 'the limited and often contradictory notions about rabbits' have deemed them 'an animal unworthy of either respect or research', something the

---

³Sigmund Freud, *On Murder, Mourning and Melancholia* (London: Penguin, [1917] 2005), 203.
⁴Judith Butler, 'After Loss, What Then?', in *Loss: The Politics of Mourning*, ed. David Kazanjian, David L. Eng, and Judith Butler (Berkeley: University of California Press, 2003), 467.
⁵James Stanescu, 'Species Trouble: Judith Butler, Mourning, and the Precarious Lives of Animals', *Hypatia* 27, no. 3 (2012): 568.
⁶'London Rebellion Extinction March: There is Strength in Grief', *Extinction Rebellion*, 2019. https://rebellion.earth/event/london-rebellion-extinction-march-there-is-strength-in-grief/ (accessed 6 October 2021).
⁷'Remembrance Day for Lost Species', *Lost Species Day*. http://www.lostspeciesday.org (accessed 6 October 2021).

book avowedly attempts to challenge.⁸ That rabbits are worthy of respect is something *Stories Rabbits Tell* has very much in common with both Richard Adams's novel and Martin Rosen's film *Watership Down*.

'I haven't been the same since': Watching *Watership Down*

I first saw *Watership Down* in the year of its release, 1978, when I was aged nine. My dad took me and my younger brother to watch it at the Embassy cinema in Fareham, Hampshire – a cinema that was demolished in 1984 to make way for a new building that, dismally, ironically, in terms of thinking about animal death, houses a McDonalds.⁹ When I recently spoke to my dad about us watching the film, he joked that I 'haven't been the same since'. This joke, of course, has truth in it, and the lasting emotional impact on those who saw *Watership Down* as children is characteristic of discourse around the film, as is the decision at the time by the BBFC to classify the film as a U certificate. This certification is discussed often and elsewhere (including in other chapters in this book), but it is fair to say that the attendant judging criteria that it 'may move children emotionally during the film's duration, [but that] it could not seriously trouble them once the spell of the story was broken'¹⁰ might have been a little optimistic. In 2016 the head of the BBFC said that *Watership Down* would be rated a PG if it were to be released now¹¹ and indeed, that reclassification by the BBFC from U to PG has now happened in 2022 with the release of the film in a new format.¹² Gerard Jones argues that death is an 'emotional, visual and philosophical presence in the story from the start',¹³ and in remembering that first experience of the film it is the instances that highlight this presence

---

⁸Jeffrey Moussaieff Masson, 'Foreword', in *Stories Rabbits Tell: A Natural and Cultural History of a Misunderstood Creature*, ed. Susan E. Davis and Margo DeMello (New York: Lantern Books, 2003), xiii.
⁹Ken Roe, 'The Embassy', *Cinema Treasures*, 2017. http://cinematreasures.org/theaters/37989 (accessed 6 October 2021).
¹⁰'Watership Down', *British Board of Film Classification*, 15 February 1978. https://darkroom.bbfc.co.uk/original/1b0cb7188e02ac62c6cdcce5f2d1b928:2199e5760ab7c37b5b037fdee3a35735/watership-down-report.pdf (accessed 25 October 2021).
¹¹'Watership Down "would be rated PG today" says BBFC head', *BBC News*, 30 March 2016. https://www.bbc.co.uk/news/entertainment-arts-35924936 (accessed 6 October 2021).
¹²'Watership Down', *British Board of Film Classification*. https://www.bbfc.co.uk/release/watership-down-q29sbgvjdglvbjpwwc0yotyxnjm (accessed 27 August 2022).
¹³Gerard Jones, '*Watership Down*: "Take Me with You, Stream, on Your Dark Journey"', *The Criterion Collection*, 26 February 2015. https://www.criterion.com/current/posts/3475-watership-down-take-me-with-you-stream-on-your-dark-journey (accessed 25 October 2021).

of death that I recall most clearly: the gruesome scenes in the Sandleford Warren when the rabbits are being poisoned, General Woundwort's bloody, frothing mouth when he is fighting Bigwig, and the scene where Hazel has been shot and the Black Rabbit of Inlé makes an appearance (as does the song 'Bright Eyes'). These recollections are underpinned by a feeling of being unsettled by seeing rabbits depicted in a way that was more realistic than I had seen before – these rabbits were not like Bugs Bunny or Peter Rabbit, or those in other books read as a child. DeMello claims that *Watership Down* is unique in this aspect, and that unlike other rabbit stories, Hazel and the rest of the characters are not used symbolically; that is, they are depicted as themselves, as rabbits (albeit those that speak human language).[14] To view this more realistic representation of rabbits as autonomous creatures with lives of their own, and to see that in a children's film, is/was in itself both a radical gesture and in hindsight, highly likely a radical experience, and one which was/is arguably an important one to have at that age (and why I view the decision by the BBFC to rate it a PG with some regret). My most clear memory, however, is of the scene towards the end of the film, in which Hazel dies. Hazel is the most elevated of the (living) rabbits – given/adopting the '-rah' suffix, which indeed denotes someone great in the lore of *Watership Down*. He is the hero of the story, and his death, which Jones describes as 'joyous as it is poignant' is depicted as tranquil, painless, peaceful.[15] It is the kind of death we might wish for ourselves and those we love. We could argue that in this story of *Watership Down* he has earned such a death. But it was/is also upsetting and a little frightening, that encounter with death. The 'joyous' refrain of 'All the world will be your enemy, Prince with a Thousand Enemies' (which does not happen in the book) infuses the scene with drama and emotion, and a sense of, or desire for, being connected to something bigger than ourselves. It is also a device that shifts us from any feelings of fear and upset to feelings of consolation and thrill at the prospect of a rabbit afterlife and a 'continuation' of Hazel-rah. The moment of death, that transition and transformation from being alive to being dead, is depicted by the movement of Hazel's body as we see it/him breathing in and out, followed by the stilling of the breath and the slump of the ears as we watch Hazel's 'spirit' rise from the unmoving body he leaves behind to join the Owsla of El-ahrairah (Figure 14.1).

It might have been the first time that I had seen anything approximating a realistic death, and even now, over forty years later, that stilling of the body and the fall of the ears is the moment at which everything shifts emotionally in the scene. This transition and stilling of breath will be familiar to anyone who has had to have their pet or companion animal euthanized, and I am

---

[14]Davis and DeMello, *Stories Rabbits Tell*, 194.
[15]Jones, '*Watership Down*: "Take Me with You, Stream, on Your Dark Journey"'.

FIGURE 14.1 *Hazel's death scene.*

not alone in being affected by this scene. This is borne out by the previously mentioned general discourse around *Watership Down*, and by selected comments underneath a YouTube post of a clip of Hazel's death, presented here verbatim, which indicate the depth of feeling it evokes about our relationship to him and to other animals:

1. i cried try watching without impposible
2. Try not to cry challenge TBH
3. that's it! I'm in bits now. this part always gets to me (and I'm 40 fer christ sakes.)
4. first time i saw watership down it REALLY scared me its genuinly a scary film for me! but when hazzel died i vowed never to watch it again. i never thought about it for like 5 years untill yesterday when i found the song 'bright eyes' on my phone! lol (this made me cry again!)
5. First seen this movie when I was about 8 years old and it made me cry then it still does now and even just the song 'Bright Eyes' makes me cry. I always think of my own little bunny pals when I watch this, Patch, Pogo and Danni never forget you and hope you are all running around somewhere and happy. Love you all so much and will never forget you.
6. only saw at my nans, up to the song Bright Eyes. I demanded my nan to take it off I hate it but love the film at the same time. I love my guinea-pig so much. He died on 21 April, one morning. I cried so much I miss him alot :'(Love you Pancakesss?!:)

7   I also have to cry everytime I see it. Maybe I cry because I lost 2 rabbits and that video remembers me in them . . .[16]

The last few comments also clearly point to the relationship between feelings for Hazel and feelings for animals the writers have been in close proximity to or had close relationships with – pets or 'companion' animals, or 'bunny pals'. Particularly lovely is the syntax of the last comment, that the video 'remembers me in them', which sums up some of the complex identifications and affiliations between human and non-human animals, and also to some extent the idea of the ongoing nature of the relationship between the dead and the living that occurs in some theories of mourning. It is also worth noting that while 'Bright Eyes' does not accompany Hazel's death in the film, it feels so closely intermingled with the scene that is largely a performance of mourning for him – 'How can the light that burned so brightly, suddenly turn so pale?' asks the lyric. How can something alive (we loved or cared about or identified with or were rooting for – our 'bunny pals') now be dead? Pretty big questions to be asking in a children's film. Gary Budden notes that 'there is radicalism [even] . . . in the melancholy "Bright Eyes" . . . accompanying a rabbit's death',[17] which points to how *Watership Down* remains so significant a film, and how mourning animals, even fictional, animated, wild rabbits, is generally considered to be unusual. The heartfelt comments from the clip of Hazel's death, however, and on a clip of 'Bright Eyes' demonstrate its lasting emotional impact and meaning to those in mourning.[18] What they also seem to indicate is that the mourning of Hazel – and grief at the loss of companion animals – displays or reveals or evokes something about a relationship with animals that may occur at an early age.

Kinship imaginary

In his exploration of fairy tales, *The Uses of Enchantment*, Bruno Bettelheim writes that 'the line between humans and animals is much less sharply drawn for children than for adults, so the idea that animals can be children or turn into humans . . . seems quite possible'.[19] This idea of being interchangeable

---

[16]Sadly, these heartfelt comments disappeared when this clip was deleted from YouTube sometime between 2018 and the time of writing and has been unable to be traced.
[17]Gary Budden, 'The Warren Is Empty: Watership Down At 40', *The Quietus*, 8 October 2018. https://thequietus.com/articles/25442-watership-down-film-anniversary-review (accessed 6 October 2021).
[18]'Art Garfunkel – Bright Eyes', *YouTube*, 26 September 2013. https://www.youtube.com/watch?v=cGyQmH9NZcw (accessed 6 October 2021).
[19]Bruno Bettelheim quoted in Davis and DeMello, *Stories Rabbits Tell*, 183.

is not only one of empathy or identifying with a character but raises the possibility of an imaginative and diffuse co-identity and intermingling between human child and rabbit. It is possible then that Hazel's death may evoke such strong feelings because it not only reminds us of our connection to other living things, but that there is a sense that we might have been tangled up in not just identifying with him, but also *as* him, in the narrative journey of *Watership Down*. Butler notes that Freud 'reminded us that when we lose someone, we do not always know what it is *in* that person that has been lost'.[20] When we think about this in relation to mourning Hazel and the notion of a mixing up of the identity of human/child/rabbit, it seems entirely possible that part of our sadness at his death, part of the feeling of loss, is also about finding out that we have lost something of ourselves.

Joshua Russell highlights this idea of affiliation in Lees Fawcett's work on the importance of the relationship between children and animals – both real and fictional – that 'children's experiences with and narratives of nonhuman animals form the basis for what she [Fawcett] calls a "kinship imaginary", an interspecies ethics built up of the kinds of curiosities that emerge from shared experiences'.[21] It may be that this inter-species ethics that is key to the 'kinship imaginary' is not only a possible co-identification but also a felt solidarity between those with a similar approximate amount of perceived power. This power and affiliation are put to use in a famous scene from another film, *Giant* (Stevens, 1956), in which the children in the film ask if the turkey on the table for Thanksgiving dinner is the turkey they have become attached to and cared for (loved), asking 'is that Pedro?' and bursting into tears when it is confirmed that it is. It is easy to view this scene as humorous, and depicting the naivety of children in not understanding how the world is, but there is also something going on in which the very notion of a kinship imaginary or an inter-species ethics and affiliation is being denied, or has been put aside by the adults involved. This, ultimately, reflects poorly on them, in not taking into account the tender feelings the children have for Pedro and allowing him to live. DeMello argues that, like animals, 'children know all too well the deep pain of being undervalued or misunderstood, and they know too well the very immediate transformation that can occur with simple kindness and love'.[22] She does sound a cautionary note, however, about an over-romanticizing of the idea of an innate connection between children and animals, advising that in Victorian times a kind of kinship imaginary was constructed/encouraged between children and animals (pets),

---

[20]Judith Butler, *Precarious Life: The Powers of Mourning and Violence* (London: Verso, 2004), 21.
[21]Joshua Russell, 'I Remember Everything: Children, Companion Animals, and a Relational Pedagogy of Remembrance', in *Mourning Animals*, ed. Margo DeMello (Michigan: Michigan State University Press, 2016), 83.
[22]Davis and DeMello, *Stories Rabbits Tell*, 180.

in order to engender 'middle-class virtues, like kindness and self-control, in young people', and particularly in boys, who it was hoped would have what she describes as their tendencies to be violent, diminished.[23] Nevertheless, the perception of an affiliation and alignment between the two is common one. Russell argues that animals and children in domestic spaces have also come to define a sense (or ideal) of domestic life, and that they both serve as 'central figures in discourse around vulnerability, innocence, maturity and development'.[24]

Mourning animals

Stanescu argues that mourning is another way of establishing kinship, in 'recognising the vulnerability ... of the other'.[25] This is not only a felt kinship with others who mourn animals but also a kinship with the animals being mourned. These ideas of kinship (imaginary), affiliation and/or an interspecies ethics also seem to have a parallel with the idea of the incorporation of the dead into the lives of the living in that it depicts another example of interconnectedness – a kinship with the dead. Jacques Derrida proposes that, unlike models of mourning that are based on the idea of having to 'relinquish' the dead, that is, to have 'gotten over it' or to have reached 'closure', mourning is actually an opportunity for an ongoing relationship between the dead and the living.[26] Joan Kirkby argues that this proposal of Derrida's offers new possibilities for how we consider mourning, that it creates the 'possibility of an ongoing creative encounter', which 'upholds the idea of community and reminds us of our interconnectedness with our dead'.[27] This idea of community and interconnectedness feels both apt to the narrative of *Watership Down* and in the context of mourning Hazel, as particularly useful, as it allows us to think about how we might use Hazel's death to explore the potential of mourning to affect us and effect change. The creative or productive potential of loss is also something that is present in Butler's work on mourning, which is used frequently in discussions around mourning animals, notably her ideas around the possession of a 'grievable' life. Like Derrida, Butler argues that loss is not something that is 'overcome' but is 'condition and necessity' for something that she identifies

---

[23]Davis and DeMello, *Stories Rabbits Tell*, 68.
[24]Russell, 'I Remember Everything', 83.
[25]Stanescu, 'Species Trouble', 569.
[26]Joan Kirkby, '"Remembrance of the Future:" Derrida on Mourning', *Social Semiotics* 16, no. 3 (2006), 461–72.
[27]Kirkby, 'Remembrance of the Future', 469.

as 'oddly fecund, paradoxically productive'.[28] Loss is not something that can be undone, in the sense that despite the fact that we may feel that we are, as she writes, 'undergoing something temporary, that mourning will be over and some restoration of prior order will be achieved'[29] that there is actually no possibility of that; we are irrevocably changed by loss – that is, I 'haven't been the same since'. For Butler, in a state of loss we exist in this 'new place', which, she argues, may offer opportunities to configure new communities.[30] This idea of a 'new place' and the configuring of new communities again neatly echoes the narrative arc in *Watership Down*.

Linda Monahan argues that while most non-human animals are outside of acceptable human mourning, those that are more likely to be are pets or companion animals, who are 'increasingly mourned in ways that are traditionally reserved for humans'.[31] Pet cemeteries, monuments and memorials, and the proliferation of online memorial sites run by organizations such as PDSA and the Blue Cross in the UK, are testament to this. However, despite this increase in perceived acceptability, the complex processes, behaviours and rituals around human death, grief and mourning are still more complex when it comes to (non-human) animals. There may be even more of an imperative to 'get over it' than if it were a person being mourned, and a discrepancy in terms of value attached to the life that has been lost, and the legitimacy or acceptability of the depth of feelings at the death of a pet or companion animal. Stanescu discusses the problems encountered by those mourning animals (in this case, not just companion animals) and the idea of what he calls 'social unintelligibility', which he defines as a denial of those feelings, a 'failure of recognition by others, a failure to code as reality what you know reality to be'.[32] The consequences of this are essentially an erasure or disappearance, of both the one being mourned and of the person mourning. This is also known as 'disenfranchised grief'.[33]

The majority of animals that are mourned more publicly in online memorial sites are dogs and cats, but a discussion of mourning Hazel must look at examples of the mourning of rabbits. Davis and DeMello claim that before rabbits were bred as pets in the nineteenth century there is evidence that they were 'cherished as personal companions' by women, and that in Renaissance times, there are reports of women creating tombs and 'funerary

---

[28] Butler, 'After Loss, What Then?', 468.
[29] Butler, *Precarious Life*, 22.
[30] Butler, 'After Loss, What Then?', 468.
[31] Linda Monahan, 'Mourning the Mundane: Memorializing Road-Killed Animals in North America', in *Mourning Animals*, ed. Margo DeMello (Michigan: Michigan State University Press, 2016), 151.
[32] Stanescu, 'Species Trouble', 579.
[33] DeMello, *Mourning Animals*, xii.

FIGURE 14.2 Claire: Last Kiss (after Beuys) 7 May 2011. *(From the series 'Claire: Last Days', 2011.)* Julia Schlosser.

odes' for their dead rabbits.³⁴ *Animal Graves and Memorials* by Jan Toms includes a gravestone at the pet cemetery in Newport on the Isle of Wight that has the inscription 'Goldie. God Bless Our Bunny',³⁵ and an endearing photograph of a little black-and-white rabbit named Keogh Dicken (2016–18) features in the PDSA's 'National Collection of Pet Memories', accompanied by a tribute 'A special little boy with a beautiful soul'.³⁶ The mourning of a rabbit can also be seen in the work of artist Julia Schlosser, although she is working in a more forensic, contemporary art mode. Her practice is described as examining the 'multilayered relationships between people and their pets',³⁷ and her 2011 work *Claire: Last Days* is a project of mourning that documents the body, belongings and artefacts of the life and death of her companion rabbit. *Claire: Last Kiss (after Beuys)* depicts Schlosser holding the body of Claire in her arms, her hair obscuring her face as she is bent over the rabbit's body in this kiss (Figure 14.2). This is a familiar pose, of both demonstrating and hiding grief, and a composition that is seen often in depictions of mourning in art. Schlosser is dressed in

---

³⁴Davis and DeMello, *Stories Rabbits Tell*, 65.
³⁵Jan Toms, *Animal Graves and Memorials* (Princes Risborough: Shire Publications, 2006), 8.
³⁶'Donate in Memory: Keogh Dicken', *PDSA*. https://www.pdsa.org.uk/donate/donate-in-memory/view-tribute/45957_Keogh-Dicken (accessed 6 October 2021).
³⁷Ciara Ennis, 'The Lives of Others: The Work of Julia Schlosser', *Exposure: The Journal of The Society for Photographic Education* 45, no. 2 (2021): 10.

black and her arms hold Claire's body, whose front paws are visible under Schlosser's hair. Claire's head points towards the direction of the sunlight coming in through the window in the right of the image, as if proffering an idea of a rabbit transcendence – something that is key to Hazel's death in *Watership Down* (and recalls the motif of light in 'Bright Eyes': 'how can the light that burned so brightly suddenly turn so pale?'). It also perhaps illustrates a contrast between the light and the dark aspects of loss, of the possibility of concurrent celebration and grief in mourning. Schlosser also references Joseph Beuys's seminal 1965 performance, *How to Explain Pictures to a Dead Hare*, in which he carried the body of a dead hare around an exhibition of his work – touching its paws to the artwork and whispering explanations of the work to the hare, cradling her/him in his arms.[38]

Claire's body, 7/15/2011, 1.58pm, is a scan of the body of the rabbit being held by Schlosser after her death, the rabbit's eyes open slightly and the position of Schlosser's hands making its ears appear more upright, as if alive. By scanning Claire's body Schlosser affirms the physical connection and contact between them both and alludes to and perhaps echoes a medical scan procedure that Claire may have undergone during treatment for her illness. Like the moment in Hazel's death scene when his ears slump, both *Claire's body* and *Claire: Last Kiss* appear to inhabit that time close to the moment of death, in which everything is transformed, cannot be undone and perhaps depict a way of Schlosser continuing to be with Claire and care for her and begin to make the physical and emotional adjustment to her being not-alive. Alongside the images of Claire, and the evidence of her actions when alive, such as *Basket (Claire chewed the bottom out of this basket)*, are medical paraphernalia used for the treatment of her illness – a pharmacy bag, food and equipment to administer fluids. This gathering in and documentation of all that is left also not only depicts Schlosser's love and care for Claire and functions as a way of remembering and mourning her, and celebrating her life, but can also be seen as a means of constituting or approximating her in her absence – the next best thing to her being alive.

The mourning of companion animals and an 'ongoing creative encounter' with the dead are found in work by other contemporary artists and writers. Sophie Calle's response to the death of her cat Souris includes a touching photograph of the dead Souris lying in a cat-sized coffin[39] and the creation of an album of songs – *Souris Calle* – having asked artists and musicians including Bono, Pharrell Williams, Michael Stipe, Laurie Anderson, The

---

[38]RoseLee Goldberg, *Performance Art: From Futurism to the Present* (London: Thames & Hudson, 1988), 149.
[39]Sean O'Hagan, 'The Cat in the Coffin Almost Steals the Show . . . The Deutsche Börse Photography Prize', *The Guardian*, 1 March 2017. https://www.theguardian.com/artanddesign/2017/mar/01/the-cat-in-the-coffin-almost-steals-the-show-the-deutsche-borse-photography-prize (accessed 6 October 2021).

National, Jarvis Cocker and Jean-Michel Jarre to contribute songs and music to commemorate her cat.[40] Laurie Anderson's film *Heart of a Dog*, which in the opening scenes includes Anderson's saying, 'Hello, little bonehead, I'll love you forever', is a moving exploration of her relationship with/to, and the death of, her dog Lolabelle alongside a parallel narrative about the death of her mother, and husband Lou Reed.[41] Poet Eileen Myles's *Afterglow (a dog memoir)* is a similarly imaginative, loving and lyrical account of her and her dog Rosie's life together and, ultimately, Rosie's death. Myles, like Schlosser, photographed Rosie's belongings in order to use them as starting points for new pieces of work, and *Afterglow* itself seems to pay homage to another book about a dog – Virginia Woolf's *Flush: A Biography*, written about and from the perspective of Elizabeth Barrett Browning's spaniel.[42] This selection of mournings can be categorized as animals/rabbits with a grievable life, being known and loved as individuals with whom one has shared a life. For the animal/rabbit that does not possess such a life, it is a very different story, and in looking further at ideas of mourning in relation to Hazel and to try and understand some more about an inter-species ethics that permits a mourning of him – a rabbit with a grievable life – it seems necessary/useful to look at the lives of others. Rabbits are the fourth most farmed animal in the world with over 1.2 billion farmed and slaughtered each year.[43] It is not surprising that the majority of these rabbits are farmed intensively, kept in cages and not able to display species-specific behaviour. The existing discourse around 'ungrievable' lives Butler describes as 'a silent and melancholic one in which there have been no lives, and no losses' and the violence against these rabbits is permitted because they are effectively invisible and innumerous.[44] For Derrida the use of the term 'animal' itself to describe the huge variety of species is problematic – 'to say "animal" and put them all into one category . . . is a very violent gesture'.[45] He argues that this language creates an environment in which violence against other species is permissible. Photographer and activist Jo-Anne McArthur attempts to resist this silence, violence and invisibility; her projects including 'Hidden' and 'We Animals' document, expose and bear witness to the treatment and exploitation of other species by humans. Her work is often very difficult to look at in its depiction of the abject, the dead, the traumatic and traumatized in a variety of contexts – including zoos, farms and abattoirs. A series of

---

[40]Sophie Calle, *Souris Calle*, art exhibition (Paris: Perrotin, 2018).
[41]Laurie Anderson, *Heart of a Dog*, DVD (London: Dogwoof, 2015).
[42]Eileen Myles, *Afterglow (a dog memoir)* (London: Grove Press, 2017).
[43]'Farm Animals: Rabbits', *Compassion in World Farming*. https://www.ciwf.org.uk/farm-animals/rabbits (accessed 6 October 2021).
[44]Butler, *Precarious Life*, 36.
[45]'Derrida on Animals', *YouTube*, 5 December 2007. https://www.youtube.com/watch?v=Neu4kI_Yi0A (accessed 6 October 2021).

touching photographs by McArthur depict (farmed) animals in sanctuaries, being mourned at their death. McArthur says, 'We're not accustomed to seeing a human grieve animals reserved solely for eating and exploitation', but these photographs depict humans doing precisely that.[46] *Shmuel and Patty* (2013) shows a sick piglet that had been rescued by animal rights activists who after dying was cradled and wept over and mourned by the women at an animal sanctuary. *Shmuel Being Bathed* (2013) shows the washing of the piglet's body after his death, something that is often done in human practices or rituals of mourning. Common to both Schlosser's and McArthur's work is the image(s) of women holding or cradling the bodies of these dead and mourned animals. Some would characterize these mournings as acts of (over)sentimentalism or anthropomorphism, or the manifestation of some mental health issues (the 'social unintelligibility' or 'disenfranchised grief') or social and cultural privilege, but they also demonstrate an idea of kinship and solidarity – that is, we are all animals, we can all be mourned when we die. The criticism of such mourning behaviours also has a political tone – Stanescu suggests that because of the radical potential of mourning it has often been 'feminized and regulated to the private sphere', and that this is due to the 'politics of sexism – a politics that isolates women and isolates feelings of grief'.[47] 'Love is a political act', says Nicole R. Pallotta[48] and, as Alison Hennegan claimed in her lecture on Woolf's *Flush*, 'sentimentality is [also] a matter of perspective'.[49]

There is a scene in the director's cut of *Donnie Darko* (Kelly, 2001) where the characters are discussing *Watership Down* in class. Donnie asks, 'Why should I mourn for a rabbit like it was human?' to which the teacher replies, 'Are you saying that the death of one species is less tragic than another?' Donnie answers 'of course' and goes on to list why – '[rabbits] have no history books, no photographs, no knowledge of sorrow or regret'; that is, they are not human. His list echoes Dostoevsky's entreat to 'Love the animals' in terms of ascribing rudiments of thought to other species, but he goes on to say, 'I just don't see the point in crying over a dead rabbit . . . who never even feared death to begin with.' His classmate reproaches him 'You're wrong . . . these rabbits can talk, they're the product of the author's imagination, and he cares for them, so we care for them, otherwise we've just missed the point.' The point being perhaps both the importance of storytelling in cultivating a relationship or affiliation (or kinship imaginary)

---

[46]Jo-Anne McArthur, 'Who Is It Acceptable to Grieve?', in *Mourning Animals*, ed. Margo DeMello (Michigan: Michigan State University Press, 2016), 201.
[47]Stanescu, 'Species Trouble', 578.
[48]Nicole R. Pallotta, 'You're My Sanctuary: Grief, Vulnerability, and Unexpected Secondary Losses for Animal Advocates Mourning a Companion Animal', in *Mourning Animals*, ed. Margo DeMello (Michigan: Michigan State University Press, 2016), 184.
[49]Alison Hennegan, 'Flush: A Biography', unpublished online presentation, Virginia Woolf Season, Literature Cambridge, 10 April 2021.

between author, rabbit, reader/viewer and what it reveals to us about the 'real' lives or narratives of them/us all. Of course that rabbits or any animals should be allowed to live their lives only on condition of their being incorporated into a human narrative is in itself problematic, but it could be argued that there is a usefulness in storytelling, in this case the story of *Watership Down*, in that it reminds us of our interconnectedness, and our imaginative and emotional capabilities. This emphasis on storytelling and narrative also points again to the narrative gap, the narrative absence, the silent and melancholic discourse that Butler describes, which allows for the 'ungrievability' of billions of animal lives.

Love the animals

Watership Down allows us and impels us to think differently about rabbits, and Hazel's death allows us to (re)consider the importance of our relationships to and with other species. Gary Budden describes the film as depicting 'bravery . . . trust, love, morality and integrity'.[50] Perhaps then, when Hazel dies, we feel that not only have we lost someone great, someone who embodies these qualities, but that we may also be reminded of our own feelings or need for them and, indeed, our capacity for them. Stanescu reminds us that

> vulnerability is the basis of sociality, the basis of community . . . It is our very ability to be wounded, our very dependency that brings us together. Mourning . . . can bring us together in monuments, in rituals, in shared stories and memories, and sometimes in collective action.[51]

Vulnerability, community, dependency, shared stories and memories, collective action – these things are all present in *Watership Down* in abundance. Derrida writes that 'the dead look at us with a look that is not ours to do with what we will, but a look that is a call to responsibility'.[52] Hazel – that most responsible of rabbits – before he dies, looks over to the younger rabbits playing, and El-ahrairah says, 'Don't worry about them, they'll be alright.' But this 'being alright' is not something that can be said of the majority of the lives of real rabbits and why questions about grievable and ungrievable lives in a mourning of Hazel are important. 'Men will never rest till they've spoiled the earth and destroyed the animals,' says Holly

---

[50]Budden, 'The Warren Is Empty'.
[51]Stanescu, 'Species Trouble', 578.
[52]Derrida paraphrased by Kirkby, 'Remembrance of the Future', 461.

in Adams's novel,[53] and it seems that a mourning of Hazel that considers kinship (imaginary), responsibility, an ongoing relationship with the dead and the creative and transformative potential of loss is essential to forging new narratives, behaviours and actions around rabbit/animal lives and deaths in order to arrest that destruction.

Butler speculates that 'Perhaps mourning has to do with agreeing to undergo a transformation (perhaps one should say *submitting* to a transformation) the full result of which one cannot know in advance'.[54] This relationship between mourning and transformation in relation to *Watership Down* is seen in the idea mentioned earlier in the chapter – 'I haven't been the same since' – and is also wonderfully articulated by an eleven-year-old reviewer on the Into Film website: 'What an amazing film half way through [possibly the "Bright Eyes" sequence] i think my Heart went for a little walk and came back again as different form [*sic*].'[55] It is hard to imagine a better review than that. It is perhaps also hard to agree to or submit to the transformation that mourning engenders when that transformation might risk the possibility of exposing ourselves to trauma, and to feelings of powerlessness or grief, to 'social unintelligibility', and knowledge of acts and systems of unbearable violence and cruelty. But perhaps like Hazel and the rest of *Watership Down*'s rabbits, who undergo their own trauma and danger to get to their titular home, we can hope that where this transformation, this mourning of Hazel might lead us – the 'new' place of loss, a reconfigured heart – is worth it.

---

[53] Adams, *Watership Down*, 163.
[54] Butler, *Precarious Life*, 21; emphasis in original.
[55] 'Review by Robyn, 11', *Into Film*, 26 May 2012. https://www.intofilm.org/films/reviews/424974 (accessed 2 November 2021).

GUIDE TO FURTHER RESEARCH

This non-comprehensive guide provides an overview of primary and secondary sources relevant to *Watership Down* and its critical contexts. In addition to the following, the British Film Institute's National Archive in London holds primary sources on the film including a post-production script and pressbook. This guide does not include sources relating directly to Richard Adams's novel or adaptations of this source to other media.

Production, form and legacy

Adams, Richard. *The Watership Down Film Picture Book* (Harmondsworth: Penguin Books, 1978).
   A collector's item that tells the story of the film through hundreds of high-quality stills with accompanying text by Richard Adams, a preface by Adams and a foreword by Martin Rosen.

Bell, Richard. 'Warren Street', *Wild Yorkshire*, 5 November 2002. http://www.wildyorkshire.co.uk/naturediary/docs/2002/11/5.html
   Bell offers a brief reflection on his work as a background artist on *Watership Down*, including some of his own sketches of the interior of Cowslip's Warren and further insight into John Hubley's vision for the film.

British Board of Film Classification. 'Watership Down', https://www.bbfc.co.uk/education/case-studies/watership-down
   The BBFC's original 1978 classification report for *Watership Down* and a brief overview of the film's ongoing classification history. The official BBFC podcast also includes a number of episodes relevant to *Watership Down*, the U rating and classifying horror in children's films.

Eberts, Jake and Terry Ilott. *My Indecision Is Final: The Rise and Fall of Goldcrest Films* (London: Faber and Faber, 1990).
   Eberts was a Canadian film producer known for co-founding Goldcrest Films, but before this his very first project was to executive produce *Watership Down*.

This personal history of Goldcrest, co-written with Ilott, includes a detailed recollection of the financial difficulties in bringing the film to the screen.

Jones, Gerard. 'Watership Down: "Take Me with You, Stream, on Your Dark Journey"', *The Criterion Collection*, 26 February 2015. https://www.criterion.com/current/posts/3475-watership-down-take-me-with-you-stream-on-your-dark-journey

Jones's essay, also included with the Criterion Collection DVD and Blu-ray of *Watership Down*, is a wide-ranging retrospective of the film that considers in particular the film's value for young audiences.

Jordan, Tom. 'Breaking Away from the Warren', in *Children's Novels and the Movies*, ed. Douglas Street (New York: F. Ungar Publishing Company, 1983), 227–35; also reproduced online at *Scraps from the Loft*, 15 March 2019. https://scrapsfromtheloft.com/movies/childrennovels-and-the-movies-watership-down-1972/

Jordan approaches *Watership Down* as a work of adaptation, focussing on its use of colour and form.

Morley, Angela. 'How the Music Score for the 1978 Feature Film *Watership Down* Came Together', *Angela Morley*. http://www.angelamorley.com/site/watercues.htm

Morley reflects on her musical score for *Watership Down*, including scans of the original music cue sheet.

Scovell, Adam. 'More Handmaid's Tale Than Peter Rabbit – Why Watership Down Remains a Terrifying Vision of the Land', *British Film Institute*, 12 March 2018. https://www2.bfi.org.uk/news-opinion/news-bfi/features/watership-down-martin-rosen-richard-adams

Scovell locates a part of *Watership Down*'s cultural legacy in its realistic representation of the rural landscapes, which he argues broke new ground for deromanticizing the British countryside on film.

Waddell, Calum. *Taboo Breakers: 18 Independent Films That Courted Controversy and Created a Legend from BLOOD FEAST to HOSTEL* (Tolworth: Telos Publishing, 2008).

Chapter 14 focusses on *The Plague Dogs* (1982), Rosen's follow-up to *Watership Down*. The chapter features an interview with Rosen in which he reflects on the production and reception of *Watership Down*.

Genre

Antunes, Filipa. *Children Beware! Childhood, Horror and the PG-13 Rating* (Jefferson: McFarland, 2020).

Lester, Catherine. *Horror Films for Children: Fear and Pleasure in American Cinema* (London: Bloomsbury, 2021).

Neither of these books addresses *Watership Down* directly, but in discussing the category of horror films for children – and the sociocultural and industrial tensions facing this category – they explore issues of key relevance to *Watership Down*'s reputation as a frightening children's film.

Walters, James. *Fantasy Film: An Introduction* (Oxford: Berg, 2011).
Walters provides a useful critical introduction to the fantasy film genre, with analysis of *Watership Down* in Chapter 6.

British children's cinema and animation

Brown, Noel. *British Children's Cinema: From the Thief of Bagdad to Wallace and Gromit* (London: I. B. Tauris, 2017).

Stewart, Jez. *The Story of British Animation* (London: British Film Institute, 2021).
Brown and Stewart each provide informative overviews of British children's cinema and British animation, respectively, and they contextualize *Watership Down* within these industrial modes.

Animated animals and eco-cinema

Davis, Susan E. and Margo Demello. *Stories Rabbits Tell: A Natural and Cultural History of a Misunderstood Creature* (New York: Lantern Books, 2003).
A history of rabbits throughout society and culture. Chapter 4 provides an overview of fictional representations of rabbits including the novel and film versions of *Watership Down*.

Höing, Anja and Harald Husemann. 'The Vicious Cycle of Disnification and Audience Demands: Representations of the Non/Human in Martin Rosen's *Watership Down* (1978) and *The Plague Dogs* (1982)', in *Screening the Nonhuman: Representations of Animal Others in the Media*, ed. Amber E. George and J. L. Schatz (Lanham: Lexington Books, 2016), 101–16.
Höing and Husemann compare representations of human/non-human relationships in Rosen's adaptations of *Watership Down* and *The Plague Dogs*. While *Watership Down* is the better remembered film for its 'traumatic' legacy, the authors demonstrate that it is rather tame and conventional compared with *The Plague Dogs*, which is even more daring, shocking and confrontational for being a rare example of a 'non-anthropomorphic animated animal picture'.

Pike, Deidre M. *Enviro-Toons: Green Themes in Animated Cinema and Television* (Jefferson: McFarland, 2012).

Stanton, Rebecca Rose. *The Disneyfication of Animals* (Basingstoke: Palgrave Macmillan, 2020).

Wells, Paul. *The Animated Bestiary: Animals, Cartoons, and Culture* (New Brunswick: Rutgers University Press, 2008).
Although these three books by Pike, Stanton and Wells do not address *Watership Down* in detail (or at all, in Pike's case), they will nevertheless be of use to researchers with a general interest in animated representations of animals and the environment.

INDEX

activism   85–6, 92, 107–9, 222–3, 233–4
Adams, Richard   1, 11, 26, 16 n.57, 40, 49, 60, 75, 92, 106, 135, 140, 145–9, 163, 224
Addams Family, The   46
Adorno, Theodor   77, 78, 88
Akira   212
Alice   212
allegory   75–6, 83, 92, 98, 100, 123, 127, 131
'Angel of Death'   159
Animaland   45
Animal Farm   45, 76, 100, 136, 165
Animal Logic studios   131
animal rights   92–3, 107, 223, 234. See also activism
Animals of Farthing Wood, The   18, 105–6, 106 n.8, 112–14, 116
animation
   animated aesthetics   19
   animated fantasy   164, 174
   animated violence   8, 20, 178–9, 188, 190, 193–4, 197–8, 202, 205
   cel animation   5, 16, 193–4, 197–9
   divine affinity   20, 205
   Furniss's continuum of   178, 187–8, 190
   stop-motion animation   5
   3D computer-animation   189
anthropomorphism
   anthropomorphic animals   86, 96, 101, 127, 195, 203–5, 218
   anthropomorphic cutesiness   92
   anthropomorphized spectres   81
   de-anthropomorphize   202

Aristocats, The   50
Arrighi, Luciana   18, 125, 198
Art Brut   71
Arthur Humberstone Animation Archive   16, 41–2
Australia
   Australian Aboriginal Art   18, 125, 172
   Australian animation   18, 118, 123–6
   feral rabbits in   119–20
   Indigenous-Australian aesthetic   118
   Indigenous-styled animation   125
avant-garde   78
Avco Embassy Pictures   39

Bad Seed, The   214
Bakshi, Ralph   3, 130
Bambi   4, 5, 28, 46, 164, 212
Batt, Mike   7, 137, 147, 173
BBFC   6, 9–11, 11 n.41, 13, 14, 19, 60, 100, 114, 153, 181, 220, 224–5
   A rating   60
   child-friendly   114
   PG rating   13, 224–5
   U rating   13–14, 60, 100, 181, 209, 224
Beaster Bunny, The   208
Bedknobs and Broomsticks   50
Belstone Fox, The   17, 89–99, 101
Benjamin, Walter   78, 80, 81
Beowulf   189, 190
BFG, The   47
Bigwig   6, 11–12, 30, 31, 70, 81, 86–7, 111, 113, 115, 139, 154, 157, 168, 171, 173, 176, 182–7, 190, 201, 218, 225

INDEX

Bill and Ted's Bogus Journey 212
Billy and Tilly Bluegum 214
Billy Bear 123
Bimbo's Auto 124
Blackavar 15, 185, 187
Blackberry 30, 36, 141
Black Jack 91
Black Narcissus 170
Black Rabbit of Inlé 21, 83, 88, 140, 172–3, 225
Bloch, Ernst 87–8
Born Free 92–3
Br'er Rabbit 80, 208
'Bright Eyes' 7, 18, 137, 139, 150, 173, 173 n.22, 225–7, 232, 236
British Board of Film Classification. See BBFC
British Film Fund Agency 25
Buffy the Vampire Slayer 208
Bugs Bunny 124, 129, 212, 225

Call of the Wild, The 109
Cameraless Animation 44
Campion 30, 158
Cannes Film Festival 37
CBeebies 12, 13
Celia 208
Censor 19
Central Office of Information (COI) 91
Charlie Brown and Snoopy Show, The 47
Chief Rabbit 30, 48, 49, 87, 217
child audiences 8, 10, 14, 20, 21, 153, 208, 211
childhood. *See also* trauma
   conservative ideas of 214
   horror and childhood 215
   Western childhood 101
Children's Film Foundation, The (CFF) 92
children's horror films 20, 151, 211, 215–18
Child's Play 3 214
Chitty Chitty Bang Bang 91
Cinema International Corporation (CIC) 39
Claire
   Last Days 231
   Last Kiss (after Beuys) 231, 232

Claire's body 232
colour. *See also* landscape
   absence of 165, 172
   animated aesthetic 172
   colouration 183–4
   colour red 169, 170, 173
   as an exotic otherness 168
   expressionistic colour 165
   and violence 182, 199
Command and Conquer Red Alert 2 159
conlangs 61–4, 67–72. *See also* Lapine
Connelly, Dennis 124
Coraline 151, 215
Cowslip 15, 16, 30, 31, 67, 81, 86, 99, 168–9, 174, 218
Croydon, John 28

Dandelion 30–1, 67, 141, 145
Dann, Colin 106, 112
Dastardly and Muttley 180
del Toro, Guillermo 2, 18
Disney
   Disney-esque aesthetic 7, 12, 50, 179
   Disney-Formalism 4, 5
   Disney stereotype 5
   non-Disney 129–30
   sentimentalism 89, 101
   sub-Disney 6
   Walt Disney studios 2–6, 44, 101, 130
Dodo, the Kid from Outer Space 46
Donald Duck 77–8, 84
Donnie Darko 212, 234
Don't Look Now 169
Doonesbury 34
Doonesbury Special, A 34
Dot and the Bunny 126
Dot and the Kangaroo 124–6
Duncan, Phillip 4, 29, 46

Eberts, Jake 2, 26, 28
eco-doom 105–17
Ecology Party, The 107
ecopedagogy 18, 105–17
Efrafa 2, 15, 86, 99, 100, 157, 168, 172, 176, 185, 187

INDEX

El-Ahrairah 21, 34, 67, 69, 79, 164, 172, 177, 204, 225, 235
Elephant Called Slowly, An 92–3
Everybody Rides the Carousel 82
expressionism 77, 83, 98, 112, 165
Extinction Rebellion 223

Fantasia 28
Fantastic Planet 3, 130
fascism 20, 85
  anti-fascist 218
Fatal Attraction 208
Favourite, The 208
Felix the Cat 123
Film'78 8
Fiver 2, 8, 12, 30–2, 36, 62, 68–9, 75, 79, 81–3, 87, 98–9, 110, 114–16, 119, 139–41, 144, 150 n.1, 151, 155, 156, 157, 159, 164–74, 177, 190, 201, 204, 217–19. *See also* Black Rabbit of Inlé
Flipper 109
Frith 15, 21, 34, 79–82, 88
Fritz the Cat 130

Garfunkel, Art 7, 137, 139, 150, 173
Garrett, Robert 26, 28, 29
gaze
  adult gaze 212, 215
  Apollonian gaze 82
  child's active gaze 214
  gazed upon 166–7
  human gaze 20, 212–13, 217
  of rabbits 214
G. B. (Gaumont British) Animation 44
gender 14–15, 86
genre. *See also* horror films
  children's film 100
  genre classification 152–3
  genre conventions 68
  horror genre 213–18
  representations of rabbits in 213
  subgenre 90, 151
Giant 228
gore 87, 114–15, 153–4, 159, 177, 182, 184–5, 187–90, 216, 218. *See also* violence

Green Party UK 107–9
grief 21, 113, 157, 169, 173, 222–3, 227, 230, 232, 234, 236
  disenfranchised grief 230
Gross, Yoram 124–6
Guy, Tony 16

Halas & Batchelor 45–6, 50, 100, 136, 165
Halas, John 45–6
Halloween 214
Hannson, Bo 18
Harvey 208
Hazel 2, 15, 30–1, 36, 47–9, 62–3, 67–8, 70, 75, 81, 83–7, 99, 99 n.6, 116, 139, 155–6, 165, 167, 172–3, 177–9, 184–5, 187–90, 201, 218. *See also* Black Rabbit
  Hazel's death 21, 87–8, 139–41, 222, 227–36
Hazel-rah. *See* Hazel
Heart of A Dog 233
Hedgerow 63, 165, 174
Hell March 159
Hill, James 92
Hocus Pocus 217
Holly, Captain 30, 99, 110–11, 113, 115, 160, 170–2, 174, 235
homeland 87
horror films 19–20, 104–5, 151–3, 169, 189, 208, 211–19. *See also* children's horror films; genre
How to Explain Pictures to a Dead Hare 232
Hrairoo 69. *See* Fiver
hrududu 70, 84, 168. *See also* Lapine
Hubley, Faith 27, 34, 49 n.21
Hubley, John 3, 5, 7, 16, 27–9, 31, 33–5, 39–40, 46, 48, 49 n.50, 69, 84, 125, 198, 198 n.15
  firing of 26, 32–5, 38, 49, 52, 82
Hubley Studios 32–4
Human Centipede, The 200
humanimal 196, 203
Humberstone, Arthur 16, 41–59
Hyzenthlay 30, 157

INDEX

identity
    animal identity   196
    cultural identity   14
    language as an   67
    national identity   146, 166
    rabbit identity theft   64, 228
    representation of   15

Jackson 5ive, The   46

Kehaar   2, 7, 13, 30–1, 52, 63, 84, 85, 100, 130, 141, 184–5, 218
Kes   91
kinship imaginary   227–8, 234
Klingon   61, 72
Kumiko, the Treasure Hunter   208

Lapine   17, 60–72, 80, 85
Last Unicorn, The   3
Lion, the Witch and the Wardrobe, The   47
Lion King, The (1994)   4, 164
Lion King, The (2019)   189
looking child   214–16, 218. *See also* gaze
Lord Frith   119. *See* Frith
Lord of the Rings, The   3, 130

McCraith, Jack   120–1
McKenna, Virginia   93–4
'Main Title'   138, 143–5
Marxism   78–9, 83, 85
    Marxist optimism   80
    post-Marxists   86
memory
    autobiographical memory   42–4
    British cultural memory   7, 149
    collective folk memory   100
    memory of death   195
Mickey Mouse   3, 86, 124
Mij   93–4
Monster House   215
Monster Squad, The   215, 217
Monty Python and the Holy Grail   208
Moor Hall   45, 50
Morley, Angela   18, 129, 135–41, 145, 147–8, 150, 150 n.1, 153–4, 156–7, 161

Mostel, Zero   30–1, 63, 100, 141
Musical Paintbox   45
Music Inspired by Watership Down   18
mythology. *See also* Australia
    creation myth   118, 125, 164, 172–3, 205
    Lapine myth   67, 69
    mythical power   19, 190
    mythical world   80, 88
    myth-inflected dystopianism   87
    myth narrative   81, 123
    place myth   166–7, 174
    political myth   75
    rabbit mythology   140
    Western mythology   123
myxomatosis   40, 121–2
myxoma virus. *See* myxomatosis

National Film Finance Corporation   91
National Velvet   90
naturalism   78–81, 83, 85, 87, 92, 113–14, 116, 174, 177–8
    aesthetic naturalism   88
    narrative naturalism   86
    naturalistic rabbit's eye   84
Nepenthe Productions   2, 29, 32–3, 37, 39, 60
Night of the Hunter, The   208
Night of the Lepus   208
Noddy Goes To Toyland   46, 53–4
nostalgia   18, 89, 138, 167
Nuthanger farm   63, 131

Ofcom   210
Old Yeller   90
Oliver!   91
Omen, The   214
Osmonds, The   46
Other
    cartographic otherness   85
    children as others   213
    exotic otherness   168
    experience of the Other   71
    humanity as Other   98
Outsider Art   71–2
Over the Moon   212
Owsla   158, 225

ParaNorman 215, 218
pastoral music 135, 137–8, 142–3, 147
PEOPLE party 107
Peter Rabbit 18, 131–2
Pinocchio 4, 151
Pipkin 30, 99, 218
Plague Dogs, The 3, 47, 165
Potter, Beatrix 28
Psycho 152, 156
puppetry 5, 109

Quenya 72
Quest 139–40, 145

Rabbit Haemorrhagic Disease Virus.
    See RHDV
rabbit-ness 76, 80, 83, 86
Rabbit Stew 18, 124
realism 17, 19, 80, 163–6, 179, 180,
    182, 187–9, 193, 197, 200–1
    brutal realism 90
    hyperrealism 179, 181, 184
Règle du Jeu, La 194, 196, 197,
    208 n.6
Remembrance Day for Lost
    Species 223
remix videos 149, 150, 153, 158–62
Requiem for a Dream 159
RHDV 122
Ring of Bright Water 17, 89, 91–3,
    95, 98
Robin Hood 50
Rooty Toot Toot 34, 35
Rosen, Martin 1–6, 8–14, 16, 25–41,
    46–50, 69, 70, 79–83, 86, 89,
    100–1, 104, 106, 109–10, 112,
    128–9, 131, 136–7, 140, 142,
    145–6, 148, 198, 216, 224
Run Wild, Run Free 90

Sand Castle, The 129
Sandleford Warren 2, 36, 70, 76, 98,
    110, 113–14, 139, 217–18, 225
Schlosser, Julia 231–3
Scooby Doo 180
sentimentality 90, 160, 234. See also
    Disney
sexuality 15, 101, 212

Sexy Beast 212
Shmuel and Patty 234
Shmuel Being Bathed 234
Silver 30, 49
Sixth Sense, The 214
Snowman, The 165
Snow White and Seven Dwarfs 11,
    28, 178–9
Soames, Richard 35–8
sound effects 18, 146
soundscape 18, 146, 150 n.1, 157
soundtrack 40, 111, 130, 139, 141–7,
    150 n.1, 154, 156, 158–9, 187
Souris Calle 232
Stalk 212
storyboards 29, 32–8, 46, 82, 194,
    197–201
    diegetic storyboard 198
Subtitles 8, 17, 19, 69, 150, 157–8,
    160, 162
SuperTed 47
Survivors 91
Sweet Dreams 160
symbolic child 91, 96, 97

Tag 95–6
Tales from Watership Down 62
Tarka the Otter 17, 89, 91–8, 101
tharn 70. See also Lapine
Thumper 4, 50, 208, 211–12
trauma
    childhood trauma 7, 8, 89, 104,
        114, 116, 126, 150–1, 161, 193,
        206–8, 210–11, 214
    trauma narratives 105
    traumatic legacy 14–15
Travers, Bill 93, 96

Us 212
utopia
    extra-terrestrial utopias 86
    insufficiency of utopia 17
    new utopia 81
    utopian dreamworld 88
    utopianism 85, 88
    utopian literature 85
    utopian praxis 86
    utopian voyages 85

Venturing Forth   139
Village of the Damned   214
violence
    authentic violence   180
    comic violence   181
    environmental violence   105–6
    graphic violence   130, 150, 178, 189, 193–4, 197, 199
    human sadism   79
    mythical power   19, 190
    rabbit massacre   159, 200
Violet   15, 140, 154, 158, 171
'Violet's Gone'   140–1
visual symbolism   70
vivisection   4

Wallace And Gromit: The Curse of the Were-Rabbit   130–1, 208
Waste Not Want Not   123

watercolour. *See also* colour
    impressionist watercolours   165
    watercolour background   5, 142–3, 177
    watercolour imagery   144
Watership Productions   36, 39
Western animation   4, 6
When the Wind Blows   3
Williamson, Malcom   18, 128–9, 136, 138, 147, 150 n.1
Wizard of Oz, The   11, 151
Woundwort, General   2, 30–1, 127, 129, 139, 141, 156–7, 168, 176, 185, 187, 190, 207, 210, 217–18

Yellow Submarine   46, 91, 130

Zootropolis   164

www.ingramcontent.com/pod-product-compliance
Lightning Source LLC
Chambersburg PA
CBHW062133300426
44115CB00012BA/1903